Anarchism, Marxism,
and the Future of the Left

Anarchism, Marxism, and the Future of the Left

Interviews and Essays, 1993–1998

Murray Bookchin

A.K. Press
Edinburgh and San Francisco

1999

Anarchism, Marxism, and the Future of the Left

ISBN 1 873176 35 X

AK Press   AK Press
PO Box 40682   PO Box 12766
San Francisco CA Edinburgh, Scotland
94140-0682 USA   EH8 9YE

A catalogue record for this title is available from the Library of Congress

Cover and book design:
fran sendbuehler
mouton-noir — Montréal
fran@mouton-noir.org

For Janet, again ...

Contents

Part III: The Future of the Left

Preface

The interviews and essays that appear in this volume were conducted and composed between 1993 and 1998 and reflect my thinking about the events and experiences of those years. This contemporaneity, however, is somewhat deceptive. In many respects, these interviews and essays also constitute an assessment of my experiences in the 1930s, the immediate postwar period, the 1960s, and the long period of capitalist stabilization that prevails as the century draws to its close.

They reflect the views of one who has been a leftist and a revolutionary all his life and remains one today, when neither the designation nor the ideas enjoy popularity. I have never measured the truth of an idea by its standing in opinion polls, neither as a young man during the Depression decade nor in my late seventies, in a decade unmatched in my lifetime for its mediocrity, mean-spiritedness, and triviality.

For the most part, the interviews and essays speak for themselves. The historical interviews were conducted by a friend born after the Second World War who was eager to learn about specific events in radical twentieth-century history, some of them legendary to young leftists today. Hence it was unavoidable that I should talk about events that I either witnessed personally or observed from afar. I can only hope I conveyed even a modicum of the excitement that prevailed during those periods.

The largest essay in this book – "Whither Anarchism?" – expresses real concerns I have about the future of the anarchist scene in the United States and elsewhere. A breed of self-styled anarchists – generally influenced by the individualism of Max Stirner, Situationism, and the present-day cult of self-centeredness – has emerged that may well mark the end of anarchism as a social ideal if it prevails in the years ahead. I criticized this tendency in my 1995 pamphlet *Social Anarchism or Lifestyle Anarchism,* and now in "Whither Anarchism?" I examine the responses that it has received. The chic, personalistic, and often asocial attitudes of many of my lifestyle anarchist critics is reflected not only in the ad hominem nature of their attacks but in their willingness to surrender the best ideals of the anarchist tradition in favor of primitivism, mysticism, biocentrism, egotism, and other regressions.

In the months since "Whither Anarchism?" was completed, several more works critical of my views have been published. My replies will appear on the website <http://www.tao.ca/~ise/library/index.html>.

On the whole, this book tries to preserve the revolutionary tradition, to learn from it, and to create a left-libertarian synthesis of its various tendencies, a synthesis that addresses the new developments of capitalism and advances the potentialities of a rational society. It is guided by the conviction that the capitalist system is inherently self-destructive, and by the knowledge that it will not give way to a free socialist or communist alternative peacefully. Unless there is a "final conflict" (as the "Internationale" puts it), society as such will decompose to an appalling yet unforeseeable extent.

Whether future generations will face capitalist barbarism or create a libertarian communist society will vitally depend upon the extent to which left-libertarian theory can correctly appraise today's developments and establish a serious movement to influence and even catalyze a social revolution. I hope that this book will offer perspectives both on producing such a conflict and on contributing to the formation of a movement that can undertake the basic social changes so direly needed in the years ahead.

This book would not have been produced without the aid of Janet Biehl, my companion and colleague, who assembled it from a small mountain of rambling transcripts, knitted them together into a readable sequence, edited them with her usual care and insight, and finally structured the book into a unified whole. She has my particular thanks for her research assistance on "Whither Anarchism?"

Anarchism, Marxism, and the Future of the Left

I am deeply grateful to Doug Morris, who conducted the bulk of the interviews that appear in this book. Not only did he organize and carry out the videotaping of the interviews, he did the painstaking work of transcribing each one – then generously made the transcripts available for the book.

My thanks to my longtime colleagues at the Institute for Social Ecology – especially Dan Chodorkoff, Chaia Heller, and Paula Emery – for their help in reconstructing the events of 1992-93. Thanks as well to my friends Tom Athanasiou and Chaz Bufe for their valuable and timely advice.

Finally, I am grateful to Ramsey Kanaan of A.K. Press, who has been unwavering in his support for this and earlier projects that his press has handled, and whose friendship has been a source of deep gratification for me during recent ideological disputes.

Readers who want to know more about my ideas should consult my other books, particularly *Post-Scarcity Anarchism,* the revised edition of *The Philosophy of Social Ecology, Remaking Society,* and *From Urbanization to Cities.* Those who are interested in the revolutionary tradition may find my three-volume history of popular movements during the revolutionary era, *The Third Revolution,* to be of interest, as well as *The Spanish Anarchists.* (For more information on these works, see the listing at the end of this book.)

They may also write to the Institute for Social Ecology for information about its summer program in social ecology, at the e-mail address <ise@igc.apc.org>. For information about the newsletter I coedit, *Left Green Perspectives,* please write P.O. Box 111, Burlington, Vermont 05402.

Part I

From Marxism to Anarchism:
A Life on the Left

A Marxist Revolutionary Youth

Interviewer: Janet Biehl

You have been involved with the Left all your life, initially as a Marxist and later as an anarchist. How did it come about that, from your earliest years, you were a revolutionary and became part of revolutionary movements?

In my family a strong commitment to revolutionary ideas and traditions dates back to Russia before the Bolshevik Revolution, in fact well before the 1905 Revolution. I can't say how long my family had been living in southern Russia before then, perhaps for centuries, but my maternal grandmother, Zeitel Carlat (later Kaluskaya) was born around 1860 in what was called Bessarabia in her day but is now called Moldova. At that time, from the 1860s to the 1890s, the principal revolutionary movement in Russia was the Narodniki, or "Populists." Most Narodniki were populistic socialists, tilting toward anarchism. Probably the most famous Narodnik group was the one that assassinated Tsar Alexander II in 1881 – they were called Narodnaya Volya, "the People's Will."

My grandmother lived very far away from Moscow and St. Petersburg, the important political centers of Russia, but she belonged to the Narodniki too. She and my grandfather (Moshe Kalusky, whom I never knew) were populist socialists of this kind. Both of them also belonged to the movement of Jews to emancipate themselves from archaic Jewish traditions and religious orthodoxy: the Jewish "Enlightenment," or the Haskelah. Their outlook was not very Jewish; in fact, they were consciously secular. According to one family story, my grandfather's father had been a rabbi (actually, almost every Jewish family seems to claim to have a rabbi among its ancestors). But when my grandfather finally cut his hair, dressed in secular clothing, and adopted secular ways, his religious father – my great-grandfather – disowned him and even said the Kaddish, or prayers for the dead, in his "memory." Even though they lived in the same town, my great-grandfather refused to recognize his own son when they passed on the street.

Moshe Kalusky was a writer for the Russian progressive and Yiddish press – to the extent that such periodicals were permitted to exist under tsarism. His wife Zeitel, my grandmother, was a bookkeeper in a workers' cooperative. The area in Bessarabia where they lived was close to the border of Romania, and both Moshe and Zeitel were involved in a lot of activity, helping people who wanted to escape tsarist oppression in Russia – mainly politicals who were fleeing the Okhrana, the tsar's secret political police – by guiding them across the frontier into Romania. And of course they would help revolutionaries from the West go back to Russia to engage in political activity there. They also smuggled literature into Russia. My uncle – my mother's brother – later told me that when he was a boy, on the eve of the 1905 Revolution, they were also involved in smuggling weapons into Russia from Romania.

After Moshe died in 1906 or 1907, Zeitel and her daughter Rachel – my mother – and her son Daniel and some of her brothers and sisters immigrated to the United States, where they lived on the Lower East Side. There they became involved in the labor movement among the immigrants. It wasn't an American-style labor movement that they joined; they joined the labor movement among the Russian immigrant community in the Lower East Side, one that retained its Russian traditions and political ideals. In a sense, they remained a part of the Russian workers' movement, even after they came to the United States. They belonged to workers' clubs, choruses, and educational societies that were culturally Russian.

The labor movement at that time was rooted in a very rich community life, which unfortunately we no longer have today. Most people didn't have telephones then, and of course they didn't have typewriters or radios or television sets, so they continually mingled with each other in neighborhood spaces and communicated with each other directly, on a face-to-face basis. There was an incredibly rich street life and a very rich radical political life, with lectures, meetings, and choral groups. Emma Goldman lived in the neighborhood and spoke frequently in meeting halls. Eugene V. Debs, Bill Haywood of the IWW, and less luminous figures came around when they were in New York. Everyone lived on a rich diet of public lectures and meetings.

In 1917, when the Bolsheviks, under Lenin and Trotsky, took power in Russia, almost everyone in the radical movements, it seemed, all over the world, became a Bolshevik. It made very little difference whether you had been a Marxist or an anarchist or a social democrat. In 1917 you enthusiastically greeted the overthrow of the tsar, and you waved the red flag and sang the "Internationale," which became the official anthem of Bolshevik Russia. You simply became a Bolshevik as a matter of course, especially if you were Russian. You didn't have to have read much about what was happening to understand which side you were on.

I was born in January 1921, after my family had moved to the Bronx. The Revolution was still going on to some extent even then, and as a boy I was completely suffused in this buoyant atmosphere of revolutionary dreams and visions. I continually heard stories about the Russian Revolution, which made it a very tangible reality to me, not a distant event in newspapers and books. People talked enthusiastically about how the world was changing, because it seemed as if the world was going to transform itself completely. The heroes and heroines whose pictures hung on the walls of my home included Rosa Luxemburg and Karl Liebknecht from the German Revolution, as well as heroic figures from the Russian Revolution of October 1917 and Russia's revolutionary past.

The ambience in my family's home derived not only from the Russian Revolution but even more basically from the revolts of agrarian people struggling against precapitalist despotisms. My grandmother's and mother's populistic-anarchistic socialism was a struggle not only against capitalism but also against feudalism. It was actually very anti-hierarchical. So before I ever heard about Robin Hood, I knew about Stenka Razin, the Don Cossack from the 1600s who rose up and led great masses of Russian peasants and Cossacks against tsarism, and about

Emilian Pugachev, who, about a century later, led still another great uprising of Cossacks, peasants, and even Asian mountaineers, against Catherine the Great. I had a better knowledge of revolutions in Russia than of events in the history of the United States.

That revolutionary sensibility remained with me throughout the 1920s and 1930s. In fact the first language I spoke was Russian, although I've since forgotten it. I was never given a Jewish education, or taught Hebrew or even Yiddish, or exposed to Jewish rituals. Basically, my family educated me in revolution. My mother took me to various Communist events of one kind or another, even though she wasn't a member of the Communist Party. She took me to Communist picnics and once to Yankee Stadium, if I remember correctly, to celebrate the flight of two Soviet aviators over the North Pole in the late 1920s.

The neighborhoods I lived in were passionately radical in one way or another, not only the Russian Jewish neighborhoods but the nearby Irish and Italian ones. New York at that time, I should explain, was made up of a thousand villages, with variegated immigrant populations and cultures, living in a very intense neighborhood life. The families were still old-style and patriarchal, although women really played a decisive role in the home. In most families you had three generations living together – at least, that was my experience. My own family was relatively unstable by comparison with others, but even in my family my grandmother lived with my mother and me, and other families certainly had more aunts and uncles and siblings all living together or near each other. I didn't have any brothers and sisters, but I did have an extended family, consisting of my grandmother's brothers and sisters and their children, and relatives on my father's side, who lived in different parts of the city. They had all been born in the nineteenth century and were really nineteenth-century people, from a village or small-town society that had not yet been deeply affected by a market economy. Their roots were still in an old agrarian world, not an urban industrial one. We would all get together every week for family meals in which the radicals would debate with the relatives who were upwardly mobile about the merits of socialism over capitalism; or the various communists and socialists in the family would argue the merits of their doctrine over that of the others.

Anarchism, Marxism, and the Future of the Left

You've often said that the 1930s were not fully capitalist. Could you explain what you mean?

When they came to New York, both of my parents of necessity became proletarians, in the strict sense of the word. They worked in the garment district, at appallingly long hours for little pay. This was at the time when trade unions were still being established, and they joined the Industrial Workers of the World when it was still in its glory days. But in the 1920s and 1930s capitalism was very different from what it is today. It was certainly a dominant economy – in the factories, in the transportation system, in mining, and even to a growing extent in agriculture. But in the ordinary small shops of the garment district in New York, where my parents worked, we still had an early, almost artisanal form of capitalism, one in which people could still relate to each other personally as well as economically. Capitalism was above all still an economy and only an economy, however; it was largely confined to the economic sphere and hadn't yet penetrated into society as a whole. It hadn't become a form of everyday life. It was limited mainly to the part of life where one earned a livelihood.

Within the neighborhoods and towns and villages, on the other hand, there was a largely noncapitalist world. Each night, when my parents came home from their shops, they would enter a very different world from the one in which they worked. They would pass out of the highly industrialized capitalist world and go back into the precapitalist world where they really lived as people rather than proletarians. This world was much like the precapitalist world that had existed before the Industrial Revolution. Here everyone seemed to know everyone else intimately. There were still many craftsmen all around. Even the stores were "mom and pop stores," where the owners lived in the back of the store – where they had their apartments. We didn't have the huge supermarkets and retail outlets that are ubiquitous today. You would get fruit and vegetables at one shop; then you went to another, the butcher shop, where you could buy only meat, or to the fish store, where you bought only fish. Then you went to the bakery for bread and cake, usually made on the premises, and so on. Cigar makers sat in store windows rolling cigars from tobacco leaves, exposed to passersby – they enchanted me as a kid.

They used to play games with my friends and I as we watched, trying to show how deft and skillful they were, and they chortled at each other as we looked incredulously at them. You could go into a tailor shop and buy a suit, and it would usually be tailor made. The tailor would buy the cloth he needed, then measure you, and prepare a handcrafted suit. Many other articles of clothing were bought precisely that way. There were hat stores, and shoe stores, where a cobbler might also make your shoes for you. It was an intense, vibrant neighborhood world that, in many respects, could have existed centuries ago, before capitalism emerged.

Nor did you have to go very far from the city to get to a farm area. All you had to do was cross the George Washington Bridge or, before the bridge was built, take the ferry across the Hudson, and you could walk directly into open crop fields. I used to walk a great deal in those days in areas around the city, going from my apartment to the river, then across the bridge and along the Palisades into open areas of Englewood Cliffs and other places that are now dense suburbs.

So the neighborhood was very much intact as a community, even in New York City, with all the sentiments, sounds, and even the smells of the Old World. And people in these neighborhoods were intensely class conscious, so much so that even those highly skilled workers who were relatively well off knew they were exploited. Everyone knew who was a boss and who was a worker. One knew that a marked social distinction existed between the two classes, which appeared not only in behavioral patterns but in the clothing they wore. Workers wore snap caps – you've seen them in movies like *The Sting* – usually pulled down jauntily on one side – and leather jackets, with sheepskin linings, which in those days were fairly inexpensive. In short, working people had a visibly different way of walking, of dressing, and they were very plainly not members of the wealthy classes.

People who were political radicals didn't think in terms of Marxist concepts such as surplus value and a labor theory of value. They thought quite simply in terms of the rich and the poor. They saw themselves as workers, and they saw their bosses as capitalists, but the word *capitalist* was interchangeable with *rich,* and the word *worker* was interchangeable with *poor. Toilers* was another very commonly used word for workers. Workers weren't just poor and exploited, they were toilers. My own family infused the language of "scientific socialism" – of "proletarian" and "wage labor" – with a more populist rhetoric of "rich" and "poor," of "bosses" and "workers."

Above all these working-class communities had an intense sense of solidarity. Most of the people in a neighborhood came from the same European country and spoke the same language, different not only from English but from the languages of immigrants from other countries. We had a "Little Israel," if it can properly be called that at the time, and a "Little Italy," and a "Little Ireland," and even Anglo-Saxon areas where "poor whites" lived. What I remember most, however, was the intense sense of class solidarity that they all shared.

When Sacco and Vanzetti were electrocuted – it was 1927 – I was six years old. But it was an event that I will never forget. There are some things that always stick in your mind, no matter how many years have passed. For a while it was uncertain whether Sacco and Vanzetti were going to be electrocuted, but when it happened, newspaper boys ran around through the streets with their newspapers, yelling "Extra! Extra! Sacco and Vanzetti electrocuted!" All the lights in my neighborhood came on, and everyone came out, some in their nightclothes, to get a paper. The sense of solidarity was intense! After all, I lived in a Jewish neighborhood, and the victims were two Italian anarchists, but people were literally weeping. I was awakened, and my grandmother, with tears running down her cheeks, waved a copy of the newspaper in front of me, with sketches, I think, of both men in electric chairs. Not only was her face drenched in tears, but so was my mother's. My grandmother said to me: "This is what the bosses do to ordinary workers. Never forget it!"

So looking back, I believe that these people were not really integrated into a capitalistic, commodified, and marketized way of looking at the world. They had not been colonized by the competitive market the way people are today. They had a very strong moral sense and were profound-ly idealistic, guided by the values of a traditional society. They cherished the agrarian and village values of their independent economic world and mutualistic support systems. It was very easy for such people to develop a political culture that was inherently anticapitalistic – and I regard it as the greatest privilege that I knew them intimately and was raised by them.

Thus we had two worlds in powerful tension with each other: an old-world, a preindustrial, and at the same time an intensely class-conscious world, and an industrial capitalist world that, while part of one's life, was never one's whole life. Two distinct worlds were separated from each other, cautiously "eyeing" each other, as it were, reconnoitering the places where one could break into the other. Unbeknownst to most of the Marxists at the time, a conflict was going on that was even more basic than that between wage labor and capital: the conflict between traditional society and the industrial capitalist economy that was beginning to invade it.

In those days capitalism had a very distinct face, to an extent that it doesn't today. It was still highly personified. J. P. Morgan was still alive; the original old Rockefeller was still pontificating on MovieTone News about how he got rich and why children should go to Sunday school. Andrew Mellon and Henry Ford were continual presences, and we identified capitalism with these very real people, not with anonymous corporations or trade names. Being ruled was felt as a personal experience. Evil did not seem to be an impersonal phenomenon, as it does in our corporate world today; it had a recognizable visage, which made it possible for the oppressed to single out and identify "it" clearly as a tangible and recognizable object of opposition.

Of course, in the 1920s much of the United States didn't feel the same way about capitalism that we did in our New York neighborhoods. In fact, many Americans were obsessed with an American dream according to which they would all become capitalists or, at least, "men of substance." There was a feeling of prosperity in some quarters, and many people were making enormous amounts of money on the stock market. The stock market became a craze into which people put their money, if they had any, in the hope of acquiring wealth. Even Western Union boys used to invest in the stock market and, in between delivering telegraph messages, call up their brokers.

Anarchism, Marxism, and the Future of the Left

What impact did the Depression have on you personally?

The crash of 1929 seemed to suddenly stop everything. People lost their savings, banks were wiped out. The New Deal was devised to pull the country out of the Depression, but the programs didn't work, not by a long shot. Millions of unemployed were engaged in projects carried out by the WPA, or Works Progress Administration, such as constructing swimming pools, post offices, and so on. But no one around me seemed to be living in secure or even decent economic conditions.

    Although my family never invested in the stock market, the crash of 1929 divested us of whatever economic stability we had. My father had already abandoned us in 1926, and only a few months after the 1929 crash, my grandmother died of a heart attack. That left me alone in our Bronx apartment with my mother, who herself was very much at loose ends. We had to face the full weight of unemployment and poverty created by the Great Depression. Food was scarce, and my mother would take me to Salvation Army headquarters or to a church, where we would get on a breadline, sometimes blocks long with eight people deep, to get soup and bread. She usually couldn't pay the rent, and quite a few times we were evicted, our possessions heaped in a pile out on the sidewalk. In 1933 and 1934 we lived in a series of boardinghouses, moving from one to another. Once in 1934 we had no place to sleep for three days, and sometimes I didn't eat for a day or two at a time, while my mother went around to her friends trying to borrow money or get food and a place for us to sleep. Finally she underwent what she regarded as the humiliation of going on "relief" or welfare.

How did you become involved in the Communist movement?

One evening in 1930, shortly after my grandmother died, the doorbell rang in our Bronx apartment. When I opened the door, I found a boy, slightly older than me, hawking copies of a magazine called *The New Pioneer*. He asked if I wanted to buy one. "What does it say?" I asked. "It tells young people the truth about what's going on in America," he said. "It shows you that Washington was a drunkard, that Jefferson owned slaves, and that there is no god. Are you interested?" I was thrilled! I invited him inside, and he sat down and told me about his organization, the Young Pioneers, and invited me to attend one of its meetings.

I attended the meeting – it was held only a few blocks away from my house – and thus entered the American Communist movement. At that time, in addition to the Communist Party of the United States, the Communist movement had two sections for young people: the Young Pioneers, for children, and the Young Communist League (YCL), for teenagers fourteen and older. Their purpose was to groom children and youths for future Party membership. I joined the Pioneers at the age of nine, in 1930, and remained in it until 1934, at which time I was coopted into the YCL. I took in everything that both the Pioneers and the YCL had to offer, including a rigorous education and highly disciplined organizational training.

When I was thirteen and fourteen, I also went to the Workers' School, on Thirteenth Street, in the tall national headquarters building of the Communist Party, where I heard exciting lectures on *Capital,* radical history, politics – you name it. We had an intensely vibrant, active theoretical life, which gave a rich meaning to our everyday experiences. In fact, it was the Communist movement that truly raised me, and frankly they were amazingly thorough. They raised me during one of the most insurrectionary periods in the history of the Communist movement: the so-called Third Period.

I should explain that by the early 1930s the Communist International in Moscow divided the history of the revolutionary period from 1917 to 1935 into three periods. The First Period, between 1917 and 1923, was one of revolutionary upsurge, in which Communists were expected to use revolutionary shock tactics wherever possible and tried to sharply distinguish themselves from all other working-class parties by their revolutionary fervor. Socialists, for example, were attacked as "opportunists," or "renegades," or "labor fakers," while Communist labor organizers tried to form parallel, Communist-controlled unions, or "dual unions," in opposition to existing ones. The period from 1923 to 1928 was designated the Second Period, in which the revolutionary tide was seen to have ebbed, and Communists were permitted work with other elements of the labor movement – the same ones who, during the First

Period, they had regarded as opportunistic. Together we were expected to form a "united front" around specific issues, and labor organizers could work in the conventional trade unions. Finally, in 1928, at its Sixth World Congress, the Comintern announced the beginning of the Third Period, in which a new revolutionary wave would sweep us into socialism. Everywhere in the world, including the United States, Communists were called upon to revert to First Period policies: dual unions, and denunciations of other leftist organizations as opportunistic and "social fascists." Demonstrations became extremely commonplace and took on a violent, near-insurrectionary appearance.

Why did you move toward Marxism and not toward anarchism? Was it entirely the result of the circumstances of your birth and upbringing, or was it in any sense a conscious choice?

For one thing, there were hardly any anarchists to be found. My first personal encounter with anarchism came when I was about twelve, after my mother and I moved into a boardinghouse that was run by an anarchist named Tabeck and his wife. Knowing that I was in the Communist movement, Tabeck was very eager to convert me to anarchism. But the only literature he had to offer me in those days was Kropotkin's *Appeal to the Young* and the statutes of the International Working Men's Association. This was not exactly the kind of literature that would have won me away from the Marxist heritage that I associated with the Bolshevik Revolution.

Still, Tabeck's ideas interested me, and when I asked him what anarchists would do if a war broke out, he said, "We would engage in sabotage!" That kind of adventurism had a visceral appeal to me, but even at the age of twelve, having read Marx's *Wage Labor and Capital* and *The Communist Manifesto,* and made some groping studies of volume one of *Capital,* I already knew more about political economy than he did. And the snatches of historical materialism that I had already acquired seemed to beggar his vague, uninformed militancy.

Second, Tabeck left me with the impression that he was an armchair revolutionary. He seemed completely isolated and had very meager social ideas. The anarchist movement, such as it was, was vastly overshadowed by the Communists and even the Socialists, both of whose movements were relatively large. In 1932, during the depths of the Depression, Norman Thomas, the Socialist candidate for president, got almost a million votes, more than Eugene V. Debs did in 1912, which had been previously regarded as the heyday of American socialism. And the Communist candidate got another 160,000 or 170,000 votes. So you see, these were relatively big movements, although not very large by comparison with the Democrats and Republicans.

These numbers seemed to mean that all our dreams as Marxists and as revolutionaries were soon going to be fulfilled. As terrible as the Depression was for so many people in the United States and in other countries, for us it had very promising meaning. Of course, every one of us felt economic deprivation personally – as I said, I saw my mother's furniture carried down into the street every few months because of evictions, a standard routine during the Depression. At times one could see a whole block along which the sidewalk was strewn with the furniture of people who were being evicted from their apartments for nonpayment of rent.

Yet despite this kind of material deprivation, Communists and Socialists and, probably, whatever anarchists were around still felt strangely exhilarated. Overshadowing everything was the magic and romance of the October Revolution, the drama of it, and the fact that one was part of world-historical events. These were not facts that one could easily dismiss. The legend of the Bolshevik Revolution, combined with the territory it had cut out in the Soviet Union, made it very difficult for radicals to leave the Communist movement.

We saw revolution in terms of a class struggle on the part of the working class, the industrial proletariat, which was numerically very large at that time in the United States. In the 1920s the assembly line became the standard mode of mass production, and with it came industrial workers, and unions, and workers' parties. As Communists, we had a very coherent outlook, according to which the working class would take power and establish a proletarian dictatorship, which would be more democratic, in fact, than the American Constitution because the people would finally control the press, not an oligarchy of a few capitalists.

Anarchism, Marxism, and the Future of the Left

And we saw workers in action doing revolutionary things, or so it seemed to us. They were going out on strike, they were very deeply class conscious – an amazing attribute that seems to have been forgotten today, at least in the United States. Workers knew that they were *workers*. It was a period in which two major general strikes occurred in America – a general strike in San Francisco, led by Harry Bridges and the longshoremen, which essentially closed down the entire city, and another in the same year, 1934, led by the Trotskyists, who controlled the Transport Workers Union in Minneapolis.

In Europe, too, the Austrian workers broke out in an armed insurrection in the same year. The Social Democratic workers in Vienna raised red flags and fought against the Dolfuss regime with rifles and machine guns, after which their uprising was suppressed. (You see a glimpse of that insurrection in the movie *Julia,* when Jane Fonda, playing Lillian Hellman, goes to Vienna: you can see workers with their hands on their heads being marched through the street by the Austrian army.) And later in 1934 there was a massive insurrection in Spain. I'm not talking about the Spanish Civil War but the uprising of Asturian coal miners, who held cities like Oviedo for several weeks against the Spanish Foreign Legion, one of the most brutal military forces in the world at that time. We heard accounts of the upheavals going on in Germany, and exiled Italian antifascists told us about the occupation of factories in Italy in 1920.

In the midst of this seemingly revolutionary period, certainly this period of upheaval, the place where I lived, New York City, became an intensely political city – perhaps the most political city in the United States at the time. Like Paris, it was intoxicating to live in New York, and the city attracted people from all over the rest of the country. Life in the streets, in people's homes, in parks – everything was infused with radical politics. Radical politics especially permeated the culture of the immigrant neighborhoods.

All my aspirations, subjective as well as objective, were political and permeated by Communist idealism. In the Pioneers we subordinated personal commitments to our commitment to the revolution in general and to the party and our socialist fatherland in particular. We earnestly believed that if we could eliminate the causes of class conflict and private property, if we socialized production and distributed wealth according to the principle "From each according to ability, to each according to need," we could create the most complete kind of democracy possible – a truly free and vibrant collectivist society, in which individuality would flourish, and in which democracy would be so widely accepted that the very word would disappear from the popular vocabulary. There would no longer be anything to counterpose to it.

Our Marxism, sixty years ago, was not so anti-utopian as Marxism seems nowadays. Lenin's *State and Revolution* had demarcated a democratic and stateless communist utopia rather explicitly. We believed that a communist society would be so accessible, simple, and transparent that any cook, as Lenin put it, would be able to participate in the administration of public affairs. Since the means of communication, propaganda, and education, not to speak of the military forces, would be in the hands of the people, a proletarian dictatorship would actually lead to greater democracy, not less, than existed in the most bourgeois democratic societies.

What was your view of the Soviet Union?

It seemed quite obvious to us at that time that the Soviet Union was the authentic world-historical vanguard of socialism and that as such it had to be defended at all costs. Whenever we were asked why there was so little democracy there, we had a pat answer: the Soviet Union was under siege, beleaguered by the entire capitalist world. That situation actually made it all the more incumbent upon us to make our revolution in America and in industrialized European countries, largely to free the USSR of the burden of authoritarian rule – although we would never have used the word *authoritarian* with respect to the Stalinist regime. "Comrade Stalin," we thought, *wanted* to democratize Russia. Soviet propaganda presented him to us as a plain man who puffed on a pipe and wore a drab uniform, and if he wasn't eloquent, it was because he was a man of the people. This was the image that was cultivated by the Communist parties of that time, and it ill befit "bourgeois democrats" to complain about the lack of democracy in the "glorious Soviet Union." In any case, in the early 1930s, Stalin seemed to be more or less in the background, and we rarely gave him much thought. We would never have regarded ourselves as "Stalinists" but simply as revolutionary Communists.

Despite these illusions, however, what strikes me about the Left of my generation was its intense idealism. We looked back to great figures like Chernyshevsky, the Narodniki, and Lenin for inspiration – and to Rosa Luxemburg and Karl Liebknecht, who gave their lives for their ideals. We were idealistic in the very real sense that we were ready to die for the revolution. Moreover, we worked hard at the small daily tasks of propaganda and routine organizational work, every day, to promote it. We did the sustained work, the utterly boring and tedious work of typing, handing out leaflets, organizing, proselytizing, and changing consciousness, so necessary to building a lasting organization. Our revolutionary patience and steadfastness may not have been exciting, but it was a marvelous school in fostering commitment to ideals, whether we got immediate results or not.

What was your lived experience of being a Communist in those days?

Our lives were intensely political. We gave enormous amounts of our time to discussions, in our branch meetings, at streetcorner meetings, at gatherings at local parks, and at demonstrations. At Pioneer and later YCL meetings we would plan political actions or arrange for support for other actions. But at least half of *every* meeting was devoted to what was called an "educational," where we would formally discuss current events and elucidate aspects of the "party line," or a comrade would make a one- or two-hour presentation analyzing some topic, like events in Europe; or bourgeois culture, explaining how a seemingly innocent movie such as *Tarzan of the Apes* was imperialistic, making fun as it did of African people. We would discuss every aspect of life, including personal life, in rigorous class terms, including sex and school and family relationships. A question-and-answer period would invariably follow, after which we would go to a local cafeteria and carry on our discussion into the early hours of the morning.

We didn't try to avoid meetings – in fact, we avidly looked for them. They were the arena and central focus of our lives. Our plans, our ideas, our practice were all wrapped together, every day, in these meetings – public or organizational. We were committed to fighting for a revolution that some of us never expected to see in our lifetimes – a revolution, in short, that we believed was necessary for human progress in itself, not simply to satisfy our own interests. In short, we were never guided by a desire for immediate gratification, and seldom were we depressed by our failures and defeats.

In New York, which was not a predominantly industrial city like Detroit, workers' action above all meant demonstrations, confrontations with landlords over evictions, head-on encounters with the police, the takeover of welfare centers – in short, crowd actions of one kind or another. Very often, four or five of my close Pioneer or YCL comrades and I would wander around the city looking for picket lines to join. Or we looked for people who had been evicted and carried their furniture back into their apartments. Invariably, we looked for an open-air meeting, where we could get into debates with our opponents. Later we were always on the lookout for fascists, who roamed the streets in gangs, often wearing storm trooper uniforms, similar to those in Germany, and for people selling Father Coughlin's fascistic periodical, *Social Justice,* or anti-Semitic Christian Front literature.

Because it was the Depression, there were also great hunger marches. Thousands of people in the Communist movement would rally in various parts of Manhattan and march toward city hall carrying banners with slogans such as "Bread, not war," or "Butter, not guns." These were great standard slogans of the revolutionary past as well as present. It probably would have been easy for us to communicate with the Parisian workers who fought under red flags on the June barricades of 1848.

But Communists weren't satisfied with bringing out large numbers of people and peacefully voicing grievances. We wanted to engage in revolutionary "gymnastics," so to speak, such as street fighting. In the Pioneers and the YCL, we tried to do this by holding demonstrations that were clearly opposed by the authorities. When the police intervened, we invariably got into street fights with them. I remember one illegal demonstration in which we tried to "seize the streets," to use the language of that time. The demonstration itself was headed by crippled veterans of the First World War in wheelchairs, men dressed in their old army uniforms. They were followed by still other veterans wearing garrison caps, then some fairly husky unemployed men – longshoreman types – and thousands of unemployed adult workers. The demonstration moved up toward city hall, and as Federal Square came into view, the "Cossacks," as the mounted police were called, stretched across an entire street, ready to attack us with their clubs. Once we saw them, we braced ourselves for a charge.

Suddenly, clopping on the cobblestones, the horses descended upon us, but we refused to run away. We wanted to confront them with physical force of our own. So when they began to clobber demonstrators, we tried to fight back with the wooden planks that supported our banners. (To many of us, this was as close as we could get to an insurrection without having actual weapons in our hands.) Sometimes we actually knocked the "Cossacks" off their horses and ganged up on them, after which they would pull out leaded blackjacks, while undercover cops surfaced in our midst. As the fighting intensified, the whole demonstration turned into a wild melee that ended only after Black Marias, or police wagons, drove in and arrested us en masse.

Such demonstrations occurred periodically during the early 1930s. But our greatest legal demonstrations were on May 1. During the Third Period, at that time, a Communist May Day demonstration usually numbered about sixty thousand people. Later I also became active in the trade union movement, which swept across the United States after 1935. I did labor organizing in northern New Jersey. Adult Communist organizers in the CIO (Committee for Industrial Organization, as it was then called) would ask older YCL youths to go out and "man" picket lines (I'm not trying to be gendered in my language, but the fact is that that was the sort of language that was used at the time) and distribute leaflets before factories and mills. Because I looked much older than my years, I did a good deal of that kind of work even when I was going to high school – and certainly afterward.

Murray Bookchin

What kind of propaganda did you do on behalf of the movement?

I was coopted into the YCL before the minimum age of fourteen, since I showed a great deal of promise, at least in the eyes of my "troop" leader. Mine was a YCL "street unit," whose section headquarters, shared with the Communist Party, was located on Tremont Avenue in the Bronx. At first I was given a Pioneer troop to lead; later I became the educational director for my YCL unit, which meant de facto that I was the political leader of the branch, since it was I who decided on the content of the all-important educationals for our regular weekly meetings. And because I was the educational director for my branch, I was also expected to be its principal theorist.

In 1934 I became what was called a "Red Builder." What this meant was that every evening at twilight I and other comrades went to an appointed place – in my case, the Simpson Street IRT subway station – where we picked up bundles of the next day's *Daily Worker* from a delivery truck. All of us wore aprons that said "Read the Daily Worker," and underneath, "Organ of the Communist Party USA" and "Section of the Communist International." After picking up about a hundred newspapers, I would trek up Simpson Street itself, a major Bronx thoroughfare, toward Crotona Park, hawking the *Daily Worker* along the way.

That was a time when people would race after me to buy the Communist Party's official organ. In fact, I would normally sell about half of my *Daily Workers* merely by walking toward the park, which in the early evening would be filled with radical adults – hundreds of them – debating in small groups over esoteric points of Marxism as well as current political issues. It was an astonishing sight! Once I got there, every second or third group of people hailed me to buy one or several papers. My route then took me over to the intersection of Tremont and Crotona, where people sauntered around, waiting for open-air meetings to start. I earned about a dollar a day, which was enough to buy myself and my mother food for the next day. The welfare department, of course, knew nothing of my "extracurricular" activities.

It was all my comrades and I could do to wait for the evenings to come. After I finished selling most of my *Daily Workers,* my own YCL open-air meetings would begin, and our speakers would have lively debates with sizable crowds of listeners. During the summertime these public meetings began around eight o'clock, when people went out for an evening walk. In those intoxicating days, before there was television, socializing in the streets was the normal way people spent their leisure hours. Many of my neighbors spent the evening strolling outside or taking in a meeting. Around seven-thirty in the summertime, it would still be daylight, and people would begin milling around the Indian Lake in Crotona Park, where they formed into the numerous discussion groups I described.

In this lightly wooded area, hundreds of men – and I'm sorry to say they were almost all men, very few women were involved in these debates – would be discussing and arguing in groups of three or four about economic questions, theories of revolution, and political issues. They were mainly Communists. But there were also some Socialists, Trotskyists, and Lovestoneites around who argued with us – the "Stalinists," as Trotskyists and Lovestoneites called members of the YCL and the Communist Party. We had furious arguments about Trotsky's alleged underestimation of the role of the peasantry, his theory of permanent revolution, and Stalin's belief in the possibility of socialism in one country. There were arguments about the nature and significance of German fascism. Would Hitler be able to stay in power, or would the German Communists soon be able to replace him? Were "social fascists" (the Communist name for Socialists) really responsible for the ascent of the Nazis to power? Was the Socialist policy of supporting German president Hindenberg – the lesser evil – correct, or were the Communists right in pursuing an unrelenting revolutionary line?

Apart from these theoretical questions, there were earnest discussions about the development of the trade union movement, about blacks, the nature of imperialism, and the likelihood of war. It is almost impossible for me today to recapture the excitement of those discussions, their extraordinarily high level, and their intensity. Angry men, immigrants from southern and eastern Europe, as well as their sons, went at each other with fury and passion. They argued in a blend of languages, mixing Yiddish or Italian with English, or occasionally they spoke in a colorful Irish brogue. Excitement moved like a tremor through these small groups that, collectively, sometimes totaled a thousand people or more.

As I said, Pioneer and YCL groups held their own streetcorner meetings. During our regular meetings we would generally prepare a list of speakers who we believed were able to address the crowds, and then we would set up a speaker's stand – a platform with a railing that the speaker could grip, and room on its front for the insignia of the organization. A few steps led up to the platform. Every radical group, I suspect, owned one of these streetcorner stands – during those days you could actually buy them at local hardware stores.

I must admit that for thirteen-, fourteen-, and fifteen-year-olds, it was immensely challenging to address perfect strangers, mostly adult workers, at streetcorner meetings or more informally in Crotona Park. I would face my expectant, sometimes hostile audience sternly and begin talking at the top of my lungs so that I could be heard over the voices of the other speakers across the street. "Comrades and fellow workers," we normally began, "I herewith open this meeting of the Young Communist League!" Our voices had to be loud and forceful, and our gestures – generally raising our arms and clenching our fists – had to be very dramatic. We had to reach the eyes as well as the minds of the adults in the audience if we expected to be taken seriously. There was no way one could fudge around with these often stern working people. I would then introduce my subject: "I would like to talk to you about the deepening crisis of capitalism and the danger that fascism poses for us today" – and off I would go, without any notes to guide me.

We deliberately used sensational phrasing: "Imperialism and war are on the horizon! We face today the possibility of a second world war that will wipe out Western civilization!" Gesturing, clenching my fist, sweeping the air with my hands and crying out dramatically, I would usually collect a large crowd or increase the size of an existing one, and people would usually hear me out to the end of my speech. It was a living school for learning how to speak forcefully and effectively. I was speaking not to students but to *workers,* and not to my fellow young people but to serious *adults* – a challenge that young radicals today seldom have occasion to face. We were all orators in those days – a phenomenon I miss terribly in the faceless 1990s.

During the question-and-answer period that followed, questions would range from the enthusiastically sympathetic to the savagely hostile. Most of the questions, given my radical neighborhood, came from Socialists, or occasionally a Trotskyist or Lovestoneite, and they were usually about the finer points of Marxist theory. You had to be prepared, in those days, to answer very difficult questions as fully as possible, or you would simply be laughed off the platform by ruthless audiences as theoretically incompetent. If you didn't make it, it was really thumbs down for you – there were no ifs, buts, or maybes from the more knowledgeable workers in the audience. (Very few people in the audience were liberals – the majority were garment workers, with a number of young intellectuals from City College, the center of radical higher education in the city, or even from the splendid high schools that New York had in that era.) I would be asked questions such as "Do you believe Lenin was right in suppressing the Kronstadt sailors in 1921?" Of course, I had to give the party-line answer, namely that the sailors by 1921 were mainly peasants and therefore petty bourgeois in background, or worse, that they were counterrevolutionaries financed by imperialist powers, and other such nonsense. I would then be challenged to provide documentation and sources, and my challengers and I would trade what hard facts we had with each other. Often other members of the audience would get into the argument, sometimes almost trading blows over particularly incendiary issues.

A dissident Communist might ask a question such as, "Is it correct today to call the Socialists 'social fascists'?" and later, during the Popular Front era after 1935, "Is it revolutionary to form coalitions with middle class or capitalist parties?" I might be asked about the lessons of the Paris Commune or any number of the revolutions, insurrections, or events that occurred over the past two centuries, or about the Italian-Ethiopian war of 1935 and other events of the day. Some opponents might accurately recite passages from *Capital* or Lenin's *State and Revolution* by memory, and I had to have quotations of my own available to countervail their arguments. If a Trotskyist asked me, "Did Lenin believe that socialism in one country was possible?" I had to be ready to give the exact quotation I needed, as well as the page number of the text in which it appeared.

It was a tremendous, fiery school for propaganda and agitation. Either we were effective orators or we were finished, and the public humiliation would not only be personal, it would reflect on our entire Pioneer or YCL branch. In these duels we were responsible for the integrity and prestige of our organization as well as the political reputations of our individual comrades. As a result, we were magnificently trained in public agitation. We were obliged to master Marxism and Leninism and know a good deal about Trotsky's and Lovestone's ideas, as well as other radical spinoffs. The training we received was remarkable, and the confidence we gained when we succeeded was enormous.

How was it that a movement and party that were seeking to form a democratic utopia could accept so much authoritarian control from above?

We accepted the need for Communist hierarchy and centralization because we believed that the great achievement of the Bolsheviks had been to form a highly institutionalized, hierarchical, well-structured, and centralized organization that could effectively match the capitalist state. We believed that these institutions and methods were preconditions for the seizure of power. In our eyes it would have been impossible to defeat the bourgeoisie in the civil war that we believed would inevitably follow a successful uprising, without creating an organization and leadership comparable to that of our capitalist enemies. We accepted the need for military forces because we were convinced that ultimately Red Guards or a Red Army would have to fight furiously against White Guards or a bourgeois army in a revolutionary situation. In those days this scenario still seemed quite plausible, since, as I said, workers' insurrections were still occurring repeatedly in Europe during the interwar period. It was still an era where arms were comparatively simple, where a revolutionary's gun could be matched against the gun of a soldier, even machine gun against machine gun and artillery piece against artillery piece. Airplanes still seemed rather fragile in the early 1930s and, certainly in cities, secondary to ground warfare.

So the idea of armed citizens overthrowing the capitalist system was not far-fetched. The real question for us was how to organize more effectively than the bourgeoisie, and how to seize power, which seemed quite possible if we organized our forces well. Therefore we easily accepted hierarchical and centralized organizations. In this respect our thinking ran parallel to that of the bourgeoisie at the time, and to the militarism of the capitalist state. We thought we represented the future and they represented the past. We believed we would ultimately win because of the inexorable laws of history. In that period, with that kind of perspective, it was quite easy to be relatively authoritarian. We lived in a revolutionary culture, let me emphasize, one that distinguished revolutionary demands from merely reformist ones, and one that thought in terms of the insurrectionary overthrow of capitalism, not its improvement.

What we did not know was that Stalin was not a revolutionist. We did not realize that his expulsion of Trotsky in 1928 marked the definitive end of the Bolshevik Revolution, even of Leninism, or that he was about to eliminate nearly all of the old Bolsheviks who had led the October Revolution. The Third Period policy really served to mask Stalin's policies inside the Soviet Union. He had embarked on a seemingly "radical" domestic policy, notably the "Five Year Plan," to collectivize the Russian peasantry as well as industrialize the country. This policy ultimately claimed millions of lives in rural areas. The Third Period policy, in effect, led us to believe that what was happening in Russia was a move to the left instead of an attempt to destroy the Russian peasantry as an independent class, exploit it ruthlessly, and introduce a totalitarian regime. (When the Hearst press published pictures of starving Russian peasants dying in rural roads, we denounced them as fascist propaganda and claimed they were really pictures from a famine in the early 1920s. We were completely wrong, of course.)

But during the Third Period, Communist parties outside of Russia all had to veer sharply to the left – in fact, toward an insane ultraleftism. In the United States this policy was merely absurd, but in Germany it had very tragic results: it abetted Hitler's rise to power by dividing the German Left. Stalin, in effect, was using the Communist parties in other countries not to foster revolution abroad but to camouflage a vicious policy of his own at home.

I have to emphasize that the American Communist movement, both during the Third Period and during the next one, the Popular Front period, did not articulate an indigenous American radicalism. American Communists merely formed a section of the Communist International, or Comintern, and they were obliged to follow its line to the very letter. We focused massively on the Soviet Union, almost to the point of nationalism; in fact, we gave our allegiance to the Socialist Fatherland over any other cause as well as country. Communist parties throughout the world actually functioned as though they were part of the Russian Commissariat of Foreign Affairs. Vivian Gornick was wrong to call her book *The Romance of American Communism* – it should have been called "the romance of Russian chauvinism." We were so inspired by the Soviet example, by its traditions, language, its ways of thinking and functioning, that we were in many respects an exile movement. Here I think some of the "new social historians" who have been writing about the American Communist movement gravely misread the overall attitude of the responsible and reliable American cadres. We thought in terms of obedience to Russia, and our allegiances, almost on a patriotic level, were to Russia and its survival. Even those who had no roots in Russian culture saw the Soviet Union as the "fatherland of the world proletariat" in every sense.

When did you become disillusioned with Communist policies and practices?

In 1935, when the Communist International announced the end of the Third Period and initiated the Popular Front, clearly in the interests of Soviet foreign policy. Quite suddenly, rather than work for a world revolution, Communists around the world were called upon to support their own home-grown middle-class liberal and social democratic parties, including the Democratic Party in the United States, to create a broad supraclass "front" against fascism. Instead of furiously attacking them, we were now expected to work hand in glove with liberals and social democrats. In the 1936 presidential election, Franklin D. Roosevelt – the same Franklin D. Roosevelt whom the party had denounced as a fascist during the Third Period – was now supported, albeit indirectly: the party raised the slogan "Defeat Alfred Landon" (Roosevelt's Republican opponent in 1936), which, in effect, meant "Support Roosevelt." In time the Communist Party adopted the ludicrous slogan "Communism is Twentieth-century Americanism," to remake itself into an American movement, albeit with a Russian political idiom.

Thus, Stalin simply offered the services of the Communist parties of the world (with the possible exception of parties in Asia) to their respective capitalist classes, with the caveat that whenever Russia needed them for its own foreign-policy purposes, they could be used for those ends. The Popular Front was once again actually a policy calculated to serve the exclusive interests of the Soviet Union – in this case, its foreign policy interests, since it feared that Nazi Germany would eventually threaten Russia, and Stalin was eager to form nonaggression pacts with the Western countries to protect his regime. Later, of course, he did not hesitate to sign a nonaggression pact with the Nazis and praise Hitler as the idol of the German people – and the party changed the line from a prowar one against fascism to an antiwar line.

How did you view the Popular Front?

From the start I emphatically opposed the Popular Front policy as a form of class collaboration. Whatever its problems, the Third Period line had appealed to my strong revolutionary and class impulses, impulses that I've never lost in all the years since.

Not that I had been entirely happy with the Third Period line. For example, I opposed its automatic condemnation of the Socialists as "social fascists." I wanted to speak in a comradely fashion to the Socialists, to work with them, and to form a "united front" with them on many issues. I especially disliked the Stalinist ban on any factions within the Party, particularly after I read the history of the Bolshevik Revolution and learned about the many factions that the Russian party had tolerated at that time. Even before 1935, I was critical of the Party's antifactionalism and its lack of internal democracy.

But the Popular Front in 1935 bitterly disillusioned me, as it did many other militants who still believed in the Third Period *revolutionary* policy. We regarded it as a betrayal of Marxism-Leninism, of socialism, and of the class struggle. But within the Party dissidents were prevented from forming factions, so we had no choice but to leave it as individuals. I simply drifted away – I stopped attending YCL meetings.

No less startling to me, in 1936 came the Moscow show trials, which made me acutely aware of Stalinism and encouraged me to read Trotsky's writings. But in the summer of 1936, even before I began to break with Stalinism completely, one of the greatest events in revolutionary history exploded onto the international scene: the Spanish Revolution. Between February and July 1936, almost daily, newsreels showed footage of thousands of workers with clenched fists marching in the streets of Barcelona, Madrid, and other Spanish cities. I could see them waving flags, although from the black and white newsreels of the time, I couldn't determine whether they were black, red or black and red. Something marvelous was clearly going on in Spain, but I wasn't sure exactly how the political alignments fell out on the Spanish Left.

What was actually happening, of course, was that a genuine proletarian revolution was occurring in Spain, and it involved the largest anarchosyndicalist movement in the world, the CNT (the National Confederation of Labor). The CNT had an anarchist vanguard (anarchists used the word *vanguard* back then quite freely), the FAI, the Iberian Anarchist Federation, which indirectly influenced about a million out of 24 million Spaniards. This anarchosyndicalist movement was huge, with its black-and-red flag (which was later emulated in Latin America by the Sandinistas and others – the black, of course, stands for anarchy and the red for socialism based on workers' control of factories). Anarchosyndicalist militants and many socialists collectivized a huge portion of the Republican area in northeastern and southern Spain, especially in Catalonia and Aragon, and established workers' control of industry and agriculture – that is, they established workers' committees that took over and managed factories and land. In fact, the greater part of the factories in Catalonia, the northeastern stronghold of the anarchosyndicalists, were taken over by these committees, and the land, especially in the eastern half of Aragon, was collectivized. Private property, to the extent that it was permitted to exist, was very carefully controlled.

Anarchism, Marxism, and the Future of the Left

At the time, how much did you know about the collectivizations and the FAI?

Absolutely nothing. The Spanish Revolution, as opposed to the Spanish Civil War, was kept a calculated secret in the United States. The liberal press and the Stalinist press, which had joined together in that bizarre honeymoon called the Popular Front, made sure the Spanish Revolution remained virtually unknown to the American public. The liberal press printed little or no news about the anarchist collectives or the anarchist militias, to the best of my recollection, still less about an anarchosyndicalist revolution in 1936. The Stalinist press, needless to say, completely concealed the fact that a revolution was occurring in Spain. They called the Spanish Civil War a conflict between democracy and fascism, essentially tying it to the goals of Stalin's foreign policy.

The few writers who were trying to tell the truth about the Spanish Revolution at that time had their books suppressed. It was not until late in the war, first in Britain and much later in the United States, that the truth began to come out. One UPI reporter, Burnett Bolloten, who in no sense of the word could be called an anarchist (if anything, he was sympathetic to the Popular Front regime), was stationed in Madrid as a correspondent in 1936. When a revolution clearly broke out, he was shocked to see how nearly all American news organization suppressed the news about the revolution, a phenomenon he later described in a book called *The Grand Camouflage*. Bolloten was a deeply honest man. In the 1960s, when I was doing research for my book on Spain, he provocatively told me, in the course of a long telephone conversation, that the Spanish Revolution had been in many respects much more profound than the Bolshevik Revolution, and that a conspiracy of silence had concealed its full scope from the general public.

It took some effort on my part to find out what was going on in Spain, but I went to libraries and found a number of informative books on the Spanish labor movement. That was when I learned that the movement was largely syndicalistic in character. These disparate impressions gave me a visceral feeling that Spain was indeed undergoing a proletarian revolution, which I fervently supported and which the Stalinists were trying to repress. Spain suddenly became a focal point for all the convictions I had nourished over most of my young life. Although I drifted back again into the YCL, it was entirely to "help Spain," not to support the Stalinists' Popular Front policy, which I detested.

This is not the place to tell the story of the Spanish revolution. Suffice it to say that after 1937 the revolution went downhill, and the conflict ceased to be a revolution. It became merely a military conflict, in which Franco's forces eventually prevailed.

How did you get involved in the labor movement?

Even in my late high school years, adult Communist union organizers repeatedly recruited many YCL comrades and myself to go into northern New Jersey's industrial towns to distribute leaflets and provide backup in the CIO's drives to unionize workers. This work was often very precarious: we had to watch out for company goons, who collected at the railroad stations to prevent us from entering town or to beat us up if we distributed union leaflets. These goons meant business in their attempts to obstruct our work and were very brutal when they caught us.

After I graduated from high school, I had to go to work on a full-time basis. I was hired in Queens as an apprentice electrician and later as a foundryman in New Jersey, where I became a union shop steward and my local union's secretary. In those days we were not burdened by any union bureaucracies; I had to work nearly all the time as a molder and pourer, which meant that the union paid me only my regular hourly wage (72 cents), when I had to engage in grievance work in the plant.

After a stint in the military, I got a job in a General Motors installation, where I became active in the United Auto Workers. In all, apart from my time in the army, I spent about ten years as an industrial worker and union activist. The proletariat that I knew – mainly black foundrymen and Ukrainian machine shop workers – was a deeply class-conscious and union-oriented one.

I took some adult education classes in Spanish and French, but in general I was spared the virus of academic cretinism that is so widespread among campus radicals today. Much later, under the G.I. Bill, I took technical courses – but by then my thinking and character had been formed by real-life experiences, not by a cloistered college world.

Anarchism, Marxism, and the Future of the Left

Looking back at the 1930s, what I would like to emphasize is that it was an era of social transition, one that was neither fully capitalist nor fully precapitalist. Class conflicts between workers and the bourgeoisie were still intense and overt and, in fact, were exacerbated by the Great Depression, which seemed to throw the country back to the late nineteenth century, when farmers with a measure of support from the urban proletariat combined to form the militant populist movement. The very large immigrant population – mainly oppressed Irish, Eastern Europeans, Jews, and Italians – gave this movement a socialistic coloring. Capitalism had yet to come into its own, to commodify vast areas of life, to coopt the trade union movement. Hence the United States and much of Western Europe lived in the tension between a precapitalist and a capitalist world. The Second World War, in my opinion, profoundly changed this situation, leading to the ascendancy of capital in the West and its globalization on an unprecedented scale elsewhere in the world.

The Postwar Period

Interviewer: Doug Morris

How did the Second World War affect your activities as a revolutionary?

By 1937 I was entirely fed up with the class collaborationist policies of the Stalinist movement and was shocked by the Moscow trials. Even before the Stalin-Hitler pact in September 1939, I began to read Trotskyist literature and attend Trotskyist forums. Thus, during the war I was actively involved in the Trotskyist movement. Trotsky had many faults, not least of which was the destruction of the Kronstadt Commune and the repression he visited on almost every one of the oppositional socialist and anarchist movements in 1918 and 1919. But in the late 1930s he stood up against Stalin – the counterrevolutionist par excellence of the era – and he did so almost entirely alone. All the liberals at the time supported the Stalinists: not just *The Daily Worker* but *The New York Times,* which promoted Stalinist propaganda through Walter Duranty, its chief correspondent in Russia. In fact, besides Trotsky, the only people who seemed to oppose the Stalinists were the Hearst Press, and the reactionary right-wing press generally. Trotsky stood almost alone on the Left and courageously, with only a few thousand supporters, remained a bitter opponent of Stalin from a Bolshevik point of view. If only for his heroic stance as an anti-Stalinist revolutionary, Trotsky won my deep admiration and my ideological support.

Anarchism, Marxism, and the Future of the Left

When the war came, we expected that it would be like the First World War – another imperialist war. We thought it would end as the First World War had ended, in workers' insurrections and a vast, Europe-wide proletarian revolution. Only this time, as Trotsky concluded and which I believed, it would mean the end of capitalism and the creation of a Socialist United States of Europe, perhaps even a socialist America. This hope seemed quite realistic at that time. After all, we were steeped in revolutionary ideas that were more advanced than those that had existed before the First World War. Hopefully most Marxists were no longer reformistic Social Democrats, as so many had been in 1914, and they were committed to one or another form of revolutionary Bolshevism – in my case Trotskyism. As Trotskyists we were convinced that the Second World War would not last as long as the First, that it would end quickly, in fact, and probably in a German Revolution, one that would be more advanced than the revolution of November 1918.

But as the war progressed, no revolutionary movement appeared on the horizon. We had to ask ourselves a decisive question: How would capitalism unfold if the Second World War did *not* end in revolution? After the rise of fascism, the upsurge of the worker's movement in the 1930s in the United States, the Civil War in Spain (which was really the most liberatory revolution by the most advanced working class that history ever produced), and finally the cataclysmic war that was in the offing: What if, despite that tremendous upheaval, the proletariat did not rise up and take power? What if capitalism came out of the war intact? Was it even *conceivable* that it could? And if it did, what would it mean for our Marxist perspectives? These were heart-wrenching problems that placed our most cherished ideals in the balance, and indeed, as it turned out, the rest of the twentieth century.

It's interesting to recall what Trotsky himself had to say about the prospects opened by the outbreak of the war. He was, after all, not only Lenin's closest collaborator but, for us, the most far-seeing revolutionary of the 1930s. And I still believe he was a remarkable man, however much I may disagree with him today, a man who showed a great deal of insight into the events that were occurring around him by the early 1930s and who tried to formulate programs that could uproot capitalism and replace it with what he conceived to be a socialist and ultimately a communist society. Remember, too, that Trotsky's ideas became increasingly democratic toward the end of his life, and his vision was more expansive than it had been in 1917 and throughout the 1920s.

What Trotsky said was that if capitalism came out of the war intact, if the war did not end in proletarian revolution, then we would essentially have to reevaluate all our theories. That is to say, we would have to go back and reevaluate most of our basic Marxist principles.

Unfortunately, Trotsky never lived to see the end of the war. He was assassinated in 1940. But those of us who lived on saw that capitalism not only survived the war intact but, as I felt, came out of it stronger than it had ever been before. During the 1950s and afterward, capitalism was far more intact than it had been in the 1930s or earlier. It was far more stable, and certainly the American working class was far more bourgeoisified than it had ever been in its entire history. Despite strikes and demonstrations, the workers were relatively quiescent, even in Europe, where the greater part of sixty million people were lost in a war far bloodier than the war from which emerged the Russian Revolution of 1917. We saw few, if any, signs that the proletariat – certainly in the United States – was about to rise up against the capitalist class and establish socialism.

Germany, in fact, was like a graveyard. During the war the German workers, once very militant with a huge Communist Party, didn't even conduct a strike against the Nazis. They fought right up to Hitler's bunker, it seemed, defending the Nazi regime to the last rather than rising up against it. Nor were they quite anti-Nazi after the war. As to the German middle class, it was in many respects still pro-Nazi. The resistance to Nazism in other parts of Europe had taken the form mainly of *national* struggles rather than internationalist *class* struggles.

What could be said about the Italian workers? To be sure, Italy had a huge Communist Party, as did France. In fact, Italian and French workers were almost completely absorbed into those parties. But these parties were quite reformist – in fact, they continued to do everything they could to prevent a real social revolution from occurring, despite their revolutionary rhetoric. In Britain the Labor Party came to power, but it was not, so far as I could see, functioning as a revolutionary movement. It was really *modifying* capitalism, not *replacing* it.

Anarchism, Marxism, and the Future of the Left

The war, moreover, revealed that the Russian Revolution had completely degenerated. Appallingly, Russia had become a land of smug elites: its field marshals and generals were hardly distinguishable from the Nazi generals themselves, while the Russian army was as patriotic as any bourgeois army. Stalin was manically purging countless people in a fit of paranoia that can only be regarded as pathological. Before he died, he was on the point of initiating a mass displacement of Jews to Siberia. Above all, the Russian working class was completely inert. It showed no signs of resisting Stalin, let alone overthrowing his regime. What had happened to the very memory of the Revolution? In the United States the veterans were lavished with goodies. We were given the "52-20 Club," as it was called, the leisure to find a place in civilian life for fifty-two weeks on twenty dollars a week; free or low-tuition college education, depending on how much time we had served in the military; low-interest mortgages; and so on. America's participation in rebuilding Europe's cities and industrial infrastructure kept domestic factories humming well into the 1950s, and that all-important need for material security, which we so completely lacked in the 1930s, was more or less satisfied. At the same time, the needs of the military led to a massive industrial revolution based on electronics, nucleonics, and chemistry (including antibiotics), producing a period of incredible economic growth.

The economy was burgeoning. By 1948 we began to see the fatal decline of the Old Left. After the establishment in that year of the Progressive Party, largely by the Stalinists, and Henry Wallace's presidential campaign, the American Communist movement slowly shriveled to sectlike proportions. It also lost the sizable trade union base that it had acquired in the 1930s, especially as a result of the 1947 Taft-Hartley Law, and the successful effort of Philip Murray of the CIO to drive out the Communist unions. The class consciousness of the 1930s visibly waned, and soon everyone began to adapt to a resurgent and more stable capitalist system. In 1946 there was a huge strike at General Motors, at a time when I happened to be a GM autoworker. With the end of the strike, the autoworkers returned to their jobs after gaining civil service-type benefits, safety nets, and so forth, that greatly vitiated their traditional militancy.

Even trade union democracy in the United Automobile Workers, for which the UAW had been famous, was beginning to wane. When Walter Reuther took over the UAW, he all but eliminated the shop steward system, and soon "professionals" – that is, full-time union grievance men, paid by the company! – began going around in electric carts to settle grievances. Even presidents of some UAW locals were paid by the company rather than by the union.

Soon the old class antagonisms became entirely muddled. It was no longer clear that capitalism, as Marx had predicted, would destroy itself by reducing workers to an intolerable state of poverty. Instead, labor and capital began to join together in a "happy union," such that capital was able to use many unions in order to remove labor militants. The radical workers of yesterday stopped wearing their union buttons and moved to the suburbs. Detroit changed completely. In the 1930s it had been a real community, with trolley cars filled with lively working-class patrons; by the late 1940s and early 1950s, the trolleys disappeared and buses replaced them. In fact the workers who moved to the suburbs began to own private cars. Earlier, they had been stridently class conscious; now they became superpatriotic – the McCarthy period guaranteed that – and incredibly, they began to think less and less in class terms and more and more in middle-class terms, infused with middle-class values. They began to work entirely within the system, negotiating contracts that gave them better wages, longer vacations, and perhaps better working conditions, but leaving the prevailing social order unquestioned.

Although I didn't live or work in Detroit, I recall seeing one strike leader in the 1950s on a TV interview refer to "us middle-class workers." Frankly, that staggered me. I had never heard workers in the 1930s call themselves middle class. They had often taken pride in the fact that they were members of the *working* class, that they were the muscles of the economy, not its parasitic paper-pushers. During demonstrations they had not sung hymns like "We Shall Overcome" – they had often gone militantly for the police with wooden planks and stones, and the police had answered in turn with tear gas and sometimes even by firing shots into a crowd. In 1937 during the Memorial Day Massacre in Chicago, for example, the police actually fired into a crowd of strikers and killed about a half-dozen or more workers and wounded another thirty. But in the

1950s this militant sentiment began to fade away, and strikes were giving way to formal, businesslike labor negotiations.

What conclusions did you draw from these postwar changes?

In the light of these developments, my comrades and I realized that we had to pay closer attention to what Trotsky had said in 1939 and review all our basic theories about the working class and capitalism. We had to reconsider our ideas and rework them very carefully. We had to decide what was valid and what was not valid in Marxism, to which I had adhered up to 1945 and even later.

How should I respond to these changes? I asked myself. Should I move toward social democracy? But it would have been unthinkable for me to become a social democrat – nothing could possibly make me do that. Or maybe I should drift further to the right and join the *National Review,* as the former Trotskyist James Burnham did, and sit cheek-to-jowl with reactionaries like William F. Buckley. Or maybe I should work for the Right, like Jay Lovestone. Lovestone had been the general secretary of the U.S. Communist Party in the late 1920s, but after the war he became what amounted to little more than a CIA agent, working with George Meany of the AFL-CIO to build antiradical unions in Europe. This was precisely what many former revolutionaries I knew were actually doing. But the fact that the labor movement was not going to play a hegemonic revolutionary role didn't mean I was going to work against the labor movement. Of course, I could become "practical" and pursue a financially rewarding bourgeois career, learn to live within the system, try to reform it, and in the process improve my own standard of living. As a veteran, I could easily have enrolled in a university on the G.I. Bill and become a professional. But what would have been the point? If society was irrational, why should I debase myself by becoming irrational as well? If I was going to be political, I wanted to be political as a revolutionary.

My experiences in the Pioneers and the YCL in the 1930s; the idea that we weren't going to have the kind of revolution that followed the First World War, or even the kind of crisis or Depression we had in the

1930s; my experiences with the highly centralized Communists, and even with the Trotskyists, who retained the centralistic tradition of the old Bolsheviks; the need to go beyond a class analysis (although *not* to discard one) and try to rework old ideas in new ways that made sense in the postwar world – all of these imperatives led me to try to form a coherent point of view that could lead to fundamental social change without producing bureaucracies, such as the Russian Revolution had done, and without relying on the industrial working class alone, which was dwindling numerically anyway.

By this time I was also thinking a great deal about *how* capitalism was changing *other* aspects of life. It was beginning to drastically alter the entire environment, the natural world in which we live. Eisenhower initiated a huge superhighway program. For the first time we saw highways that had so many lanes, we could count them only with chilling difficulty before we arrived at figure-eight interchanges and the like. In Los Angeles the trolleys were replaced by automotive freeways, and with them came the appalling air pollution that still marks Los Angeles today. In New York Robert Moses cut wantonly through city parks that I had played in as a youngster, bringing in monstrous superhighways. The "mom and pop stores" began to disappear, and huge shopping centers appeared in areas in New Jersey that had once been completely agricultural. Their parking lots were larger than the shopping centers themselves, with huge roads feeding into them.

Additionally chemicals were being used to solve every kind of problem. In 1949 to 1951 the country was insanely captivated by the idea that technology was going to bring us unimaginable wonders without any risks.

Consider the story of nuclear power. Everyone on the Left was horrified by the dropping of nuclear bombs on Hiroshima and Nagasaki. Then immediately the Atomic Energy Commission (which is now known more soothingly as the Nuclear Regulatory Commission, in one of those lovely name changes, such as the change from "Department of War" to "Department of Defense") began to spread the message that nuclear power plants would bring us unlimited power.

First of all, I really opposed the use of nuclear energy, mainly because of the dangers produced by nuclear wastes. The problems became somewhat evident in 1954, when the United States exploded an H-bomb in the Pacific. At that time I belonged to a group that was named after the magazine it published, called *Contemporary Issues*. Our people could no longer ignore the fact that new social conditions existed that were different from those that had prevailed in the 1930s; indeed, most of them had been Trotskyists but, like myself, decided that we had to make a total reappraisal of capitalism after the war. I was working with this group, helping it produce *Contemporary Issues* after 1948. And in 1954, when the hydrogen bomb was tested somewhere out on the Bikini atoll, it produced worldwide concern, in part because two Japanese fishermen who were dusted by the fallout died, and others became ill. I wrote a fiery leaflet called "Stop the Bomb," and our group gave out about 20,000 copies in New York. We also sent copies to Japan, where the largest Japanese daily, with a circulation of nine million readers, translated the leaflet and published it on page three. Perhaps nine million people in Japan read it! Suddenly we were flooded with hundreds of letters by Japanese who could write in English, solidarizing with our efforts and even sending us pictures of themselves.

Was there a peace movement at the time, or any organized opposition to nuclear power as well as nuclear weapons?

At that time, the peace movement was mainly criticizing the *military* use of atomic power, its killing power as a weapon; in fact, many peace activists supported the "peaceful" uses of the atom, namely nuclear power. The peaceniks, as we called them, believed that nuclear weapons were dangerous, but they gave surprisingly little attention, if any at all, to radioactive fallout, even counterposing the "peaceful atom" to the "warlike atom." At that time to attack fallout was, by implication, to attack nucleonics generally, even nuclear power. Happily, my leaflet really produced a profound effect on many of the peace activists that I knew.

I remember that the late A. J. Muste, who was regarded as the father of the peace movement in America, told me personally that the "Stop the Bomb" leaflet completely changed his thinking on nuclear energy. As he put it, the leaflet showed that "it wasn't the bomb alone that we have to worry about. We have to worry about atomic power as well." The *Contemporary Issues* group, I should note, was warning about the dangers of nuclear power throughout the late 1950s. In 1956 a major accident occurred at Windscale, England, as a result of which radioiodine spread over much of Western Europe, and the British *Contemporary Issues* group, as well as my own group in the United States, made the hazards of the accident a major issue.

Thus very early on it became clear to me that capitalism was producing *new* issues. It was not only producing economic problems, important as these always are; it was also producing environmental problems, or more broadly, ecological problems. That awareness, which came to me partly on my own and partly as a member of our group, impelled me to write about environmental pollution and its consequences.

I wrote a number of my early works in *Contemporary Issues* under the pseudonym Lewis Herber. One of them, *The Problem of Chemicals in Food,* was published in *Contemporary Issues* in 1952.[1] In that article I explored the dangers of pesticides and the abuse of antibiotics, among many other related issues. In those days antibiotics were being so widely used that they were even being put in ice to preserve fish, so that giant fishing vessels, with their enormous nets, could remain at sea more or less indefinitely. Also, hormones were being injected into poultry and into cattle to fatten them – hormones that we now know are carcinogenic. Food colorings were being used on a lavish scale – basically coal tar dyes, which were known to be derived from cancer-causing substances. So I wrote a long article, which was also published as a book in 1954 in Germany under my pen name. I said that these technologies, and specifically chemicals, were being used lavishly in agriculture, depositing residues in soil; in prepared foods; and in synthetic materials, primarily because of profit and an ideology of dominating the natural world.

What induced you to develop your ideas on social ecology?

Marx clearly argued that capitalism must either grow or die, that capitalist enterprises must either expand and devour their rivals or else themselves be devoured. In order to be able to grow, a capitalist enterprise in agribusiness must therefore continually turn soil into sand, or a capitalist enterprise, to build shopping centers and expand highways, must turn land into concrete, or to make paper must turn forests into newsprint. I said that these drives in capitalism were pitting capitalist society inexorably against the integrity of the natural environment, that they were forever turning the organic into the inorganic, to the detriment of the natural world. I said capitalism was *simplifying* the planet as well as poisoning it. I stressed the issue of simplification as emphatically as I could.

Around 1958 a disaster occurred in the United States: only a week or so before Thanksgiving, the cranberry crop was poisoned by a herbicide or pesticide, I can no longer remember which one it was. This act of pollution caused a veritable panic. People ran around desperately looking for unpolluted cranberries to make cranberry sauce for their family turkey dinners on Thanksgiving. And I thought, here is a lesson that people will not forget. So I wrote a book that I called *Our Synthetic Environment*.[2] I explored various diseases for which doctors had no diagnosis. I went into the whole question of simplifying the planet. I surveyed agriculture and demanded that we turn toward organic forms of agriculture.

Now you should know that hardly anyone was talking about organic agriculture in those days. And I take great pride in that fact that I was advancing fairly innovative ideas, although they were not exclusively my own. I wrote about how we were raising not only crops but poultry, beef, animals in general, using dangerous chemicals, and I discussed the stresses people were suffering in modern urban life, as well as the problems being created by nuclear reactors and radiation. In short, I ran the whole gamut of what was wrong with our society from an ecological viewpoint, and I related it essentially to the capitalist imperative to grow or die.

Finally I concluded my book with a chapter called "Decentralization," in which I advocated the use of renewable forms of energy – solar energy, wind power, water power, thermal energy – as an alternative to fossil fuels and nuclear fuels. I called for an entirely new dispensation, a new decentralized society in which we could live in harmony with the natural world, using these alternative techniques. Alternative energy was almost unknown at that time. In fact, MIT had explored the possibilities for using solar energy for some years but had finally dismissed its feasibility with the conclusion that it was too costly to compete with fossil fuels. As for wind power, an attempt had been made in Vermont, at Grandpa's Knob, during the Second World War, to test its possibilities, but the effort had been abandoned. It was simply written off. I can say that it was at least somewhat innovative that I argued for an alternative technology, or what I called an "eco-technology," and made a blanket condemnation of the whole relationship of capitalism to the environment.

The book was published in 1962 by Alfred A. Knopf, one of the most outstanding publishers in the United States – a "publisher's publisher," as it was called. Six months later Rachel Carson came out with *Silent Spring* and swamped whatever readership I might have gained. My book sold reasonably well, mainly within the scientific community I may say, but less so among the public. But nobody could compete with Rachel's stylistic magic and her great following as an established nature writer. She did a wonderful job with *Silent Spring,* and it had at least five million readers. But she didn't make, by any means, the wide-ranging critique that I did.

She alerted people primarily to the dangers of pesticides, and her main focus was on birds. The attention she gave to human beings seems only secondary. But even if human beings were a secondary consideration in Carson's book, they were concerned about the kinds of sprays they were using. During those years people were using pesticides and eagerly extolling the "miracles" of chemistry everywhere. One major chemical corporation popularized the slogan "Better things for better living through chemistry." (Years later, they dropped the words "through chemistry" if I'm not mistaken. By then, *chemistry* had become something of a dirty word.) The nature of my critique was recognized very clearly by René Dubos, who became an outstanding environmentalist in later years, and by others who praised the book as more comprehensive than Carson's.

In short, I tried to raise broader issues that had immense cultural implications about the human spirit, about an ethical society, recognizing that both ecology and a very emancipatory vision of society required decentralization. I realized that the views I was advancing came more from an anarchist tradition than from a Marxist one.

Anarchism, Marxism, and the Future of the Left

I was calling for social changes that were more comprehensive than the abolition of classes and exploitation. I was calling for the abolition of *hierarchies* as well, of states, not of economic power alone. Hierarchy was a kind of psycho-institutional power based on social status – in other words, *rule and domination,* not only exploitation for material gain. A classless society, a nonexploitative society, it seemed to me, could still have bureaucracies and states – namely, hierarchies – and even if elites in hierarchies had no material privileges, they had psycho-social privileges – a sense of superiority – that came from dominating people. In Plato's *Republic,* in fact, the guardians deny themselves the good material things of life; they rid themselves of fleshpots, live austerely, on sparse diets, indeed they are very Spartan, but they enjoy enormous authority – they *rule* – and that's what is important to them.

Here let me interject an important point on hierarchy, to counter some of the distortions of my views on the subject. A hierarchy is an *institutionalized* system of domination, by which clearly definable and well-organized strata of people accrue distinct material, cultural, and moral privileges – not merely, as in classes, by the ownership or control of property and the exploitation of labor. Please let me emphasize that every word in this definition is important. Such strata appeared before classes and might well exist after their abolition – notably patriarchy, racial degradation, bureaucratism, nationalism, and so on. One Marxist critic of mine, Joel Kovel, has recently written that some hierarchies can be classified as good.[3] As an example of a "good hierarchy," he cites parental care: parents feed their babies rather than cast a milk bottle into a crib and compel them to feed themselves. Kovel wrongly attributes to me the notion that parental care is a "good hierarchy," but in fact I deny that it is a hierarchical relationship at all. Hierarchy is a *social* term, referring to structures of institutional domination; parental relationships are quasi-biological as well as social. To call a relationship of dependency a hierarchical relationship is to dissolve the meaning of hierarchy as a designation of the structures of domination. Following his logic, one might claim that a sow lying on its side to feed its piglets is evidence of a "good hierarchy," while a frog casting its eggs in a pool where insemination takes place at random exemplifies a "bad hierarch." People who can accept this silly argument deserve Professor Kovel's Zen spin on Marxism.

In any case, as important as it was to abolish classes and exploitation, a classless society, I contended, would not necessarily be a good society. It would also be necessary to abolish domination and the hierarchical structures that yield domination. This approach made me decide very assuredly that I wanted to fight for an ethical socialism, or communism, free of domination, based on confederation, based on an ethics of complementarity, in which people supplement each other with their various abilities instead of ruling each other.

In effect, I developed a form of ecological anarchism, which Victor Ferkiss, referring to my work, later called *eco-anarchism*.[4] The name I gave it, though, was *social ecology*. I started writing about it earnestly in the 1960s. I wrote a series of works, the first of which was an essay, even a manifesto, called "Ecology and Revolutionary Thought."[5] It declared that we are living in the age of ecology. In the days of Galileo and the Renaissance, mechanics had informed the prevailing social outlook, and in the Victorian era Darwinian biology and evolutionary theory had constituted the ideology, at least in the natural sciences. Now, I argued, we are entering the age of ecology. I've since seen this "age of ecology" designation recycled all over the place as though I never said it in 1964.

In this manifesto-essay I pointed out that the ecological crisis that was being produced by capitalism and by hierarchical society with its message of dominating nature, stemmed really from the domination of people. That is, the *ideology* of dominating nature stems from the *real* domination of human by human. Until we abolish the domination of human by human, not only exploitation but also domination, and not only classes but also hierarchies, we would always have an ideology of dominating the natural world. If capitalism continued to exist, with that ideology and with its irrational technological advances, and to grow mindlessly, then we were obliged to eliminate hierarchy, domination, classes, and exploitation before we could hope to achieve an ecological society.

As I've mentioned, I called this eco-anarchist vision social ecology, because ecology is a discipline rooted in the biological sciences, and *how* people deal with the natural world, with "first nature" or biological evolution, depends upon the kind of society in which they live. A society based on a grow-or-die market economy *must* destroy the biosphere because of the very imperatives – growth and capital accumulation – that drive it along this anti-ecological path irrespective of any other factors.

Almost immediately after finishing "Ecology and Revolutionary Thought," I wrote "Towards a Liberatory Technology,"[6] in which I called for the use of solar power and wind power, hydroelectric power, or geothermal energy, indeed all the different renewable forms of energy that could be used in a more ecological social order. Needless to say, in 1964, I was really feeling my way in the dark, because none of these alternatives were being explored as far as I know. It was E. F. Schumacher who made them very popular in *Small Is Beautiful,* but as his references show, he was familiar with my work when he did so. The ecology movement now takes alternative, renewable energy for granted, as though the idea came from the heavens. But that movement didn't really come into existence to any noticeable extent until the 1970s, following the first Earth Day. But that's another story.

What influence did anarchist thinkers – especially Kropotkin – have on the development of your social ecological ideas?

Regrettably, in the late 1950s and early 1960s, very little. I knew from my readings into the history of socialism that my views belonged in the anarchist-communist tradition, and in "Ecology and Revolutionary Thought" I cited Herbert Read, one of the few anarchists whose writings I could find. I read him eagerly. I also found some of Proudhon's writings, although I felt that he was not a collectivist and was not attracted to his ideas. But my basic ideas on an ecological society really came from my decades-long studies of the Athenian polis, Hegel, and even Marx. Specifically, my thinking on ecology was instigated not by the works of any anarchist thinker but by Marx and Engels's remarks on the need to reconcile town and country.

Kropotkin, with whose ideas my work has the strongest affinities, was a well-known name, but his writings were also very scarce years ago. I don't think they were even in print in the United States in the 1950s and

1960s – I know I didn't see them in the bookstores I frequented, apart from his *Appeal to Youth* and *History of the French Revolution*. In retrospect I discovered that there are strong affinities between many of his ideas and my own – oddly enough, more in communalism than on ecology. But I did not come across the relevant parts of his work – like *Fields, Factories, and Workshops* – until long after I had worked out my own ideas. He certainly anticipated my work far more than any other anarchist thinker, least of all Elisée Reclus, who some lifestyle anarchists are proposing today as a precursor of social ecology. I regard Kropotkin as the real pioneer in the eco-anarchist tradition, as well as anarchist communism.

Notes

1. Lewis Herber (pseud.), "The Problem of Chemicals in Food," *Contemporary Issues,* vol. 3, no. 12 (Jun.-Aug. 1952); republished in German translation as *Lebensgefährliche Lebensmittel: Sind Unsere Nahrungsmittel noch Lebensmittel?* (Krailling bei München: Hanns Georg Müller Verlag, 1953).

2. Lewis Herber (pseud.), *Our Synthetic Environment* (New York: Alfred A. Knopf, 1962); reprinted as Murray Bookchin, *Our Synthetic Environment* (New York: Harper Colophon, 1974).

3. Joel Kovel, "Negating Bookchin," *Capitalism, Nature, Socialism,* vol. 8, no. 1 (March 1997), p. 23.

4. Victor Ferkiss, *The Future of Technological Civilization* (New York: George Braziller, 1974), p. 75.

5. "Ecology and Revolutionary Thought" was originally published in *Comment* (1964); reprinted in *Anarchy* [U.K.], 69, vol. 6 (1966). A revised version was published in *Post-Scarcity Anarchism* (San Francisco: Ramparts Books, 1971), which is currently available from Black Rose Books in Montreal.

6. "Towards a Liberatory Technology," originally published in *Comment* (1965); republished in *Anarchy* 78, vol. 7 (1967); and in *Post-Scarcity Anarchism.*

The 1960s: Myth and Reality

Interviewer: Doug Morris

What was the framework out of which the Port Huron Statement grew, and what were some of the successes and failures of the New Left?

The New Left was an extremely complex and often stormy phenomenon, so it might be interesting to step back from the 1960s and give a sense of the years that immediately preceded its emergence. During the Eisenhower era of the 1950s, as many people have written, a sizable portion of the American population began to enjoy a considerable degree of material affluence – indeed, the United States was described during the decade as an "affluent society." Elvis Presley was king, golf was becoming a favorite sport, and suburban values dominated life. Middle-class people were doing well economically, and they expected their lives to be more comfortable with each passing year. A literature began to appear, especially later in the decade, that celebrated such phenomena as automation, proclaiming that the new self-guiding machines would reduce working hours, that people would therefore have more leisure time – as though capitalism would not use the new technology to exploit workers more intensively – and machines would provide Americans with material abundance. A mood of rising expectations swept throughout the country.

I may say that these expectations existed not only among whites but also among people of color. In fact, an impelling factor in the emergence of the civil rights movement was the sense felt by American blacks that they were not getting their fair share of the enormous material wealth that the 1960s economy was generating. Oppressed people felt that they too should have access to the "goodies" that were being produced so abundantly by the "affluent" consumer society, and that they too should be able to enjoy the leisure time to which automation would supposedly give rise.

From a social and political point of view, the 1950s were a very strange period. It seemed that the United States was becoming smug, that the revolutionary era in which I had lived was over, and that the Left had no future – in fact, that it really belonged to the past, to the Depression era, with its years of intense social unrest. My *Contemporary Issues* group thought they were actually the last revolutionaries, and that each generation after us would fulfill George Orwell's prediction, in *1984*, that the system would gradually coopt all dissent and opposition and thereby would become ever more stable. Capitalism would pervade all aspects of life, until society would eventually become totally homogenized. The result would be a gray mediocre culture of self-satisfied people under the complete control of the bourgeoisie and the State. Orwell presented this image of adaptation in *1984*, but Aldous Huxley presented an equally chilling dystopia in *Brave New World* years earlier. We thought American affluence and American suburbanization were gradually leading to these kinds of societies.

But then came an event that shattered this image: the Hungarian Revolution of 1956. Young people who had grown up entirely under a Stalinist regime and had never known other social dispensations – people who, according to the dystopias, should have been completely absorbed by totalitarianism – were suddenly breaking out into open revolt. They took up arms in a mass insurrection, and for roughly a week or so, it seemed that Hungary was going to free itself from Russian control – the occupying Russian army was quite demoralized – and establish a socialistic society that would also be democratic. Councils – or soviets, as Russians call them – were being formed all over the country, councils that did not have the totalitarian character that the "soviets" had acquired under the Stalinist regime. Rather, they were democratic, as they had been in 1917. That was what made the Hungarian Revolution such an exciting event.

When a newly reconstituted Russian army returned to Hungary, the young revolutionaries began to implore the West to send them weapons, which they desperately needed in order to resist the Russian invaders. They naively thought the West, which was supposed to be the sentinel for democracy everywhere, would support them, at least by giving them military aid. Their tormented and pleading radio broadcasts were being transmitted to the United States: "Send us bazookas, send us weapons, that's all we want. We don't want your soldiers – " Then suddenly a broadcast would be cut off because the radio station was being attacked by Russian tanks. Even after all these years, I remember very clearly the anguish our group felt. I wrote a leaflet, "Arms to Hungary," that called on the U.S. government to air-drop weapons to the insurgents. But the Russian army bloodily suppressed the revolution. We felt very bitter about their defeat and about the lost potentiality for a democratic type of socialism.

But one of the intellectual consequences of Hungary was that it made us doubt that the United States – or any other country – could *really* be entirely homogenized, as the Orwellian scenario had it, that a people could completely accept an authoritarian social order. If the young Hungarians, who had known no other society but one controlled by the Russian army and the Stalinist state, had risen up, then maybe we had reason to hope that revolutionaries could emerge closer to home as well.

The cold war was still very intense after Hungary, and many people still thought a "hot" war was unavoidable. In 1959 the movie *On the Beach*, with Ava Gardner, Gregory Peck, and Fred Astaire appeared and had a dramatic effect upon movie audiences around the country. Today many people might regard it as maudlin, but in the late 1950s the movie and others like it were very influential. *On the Beach* depicted the end of the world as a result of the radioactive nuclear fallout that would follow a Third World War, until the last humans perished in Australia. It renewed discussions about the effects of fallout – I've already told you about my "Stop the Bomb" leaflet, written after the first hydrogen bomb was exploded in 1954.

Especially after Stanley Kramer's movie, the ferment against nuclear weapons intensified, and public groups were formed, such as SANE in the United States and the Campaign for Nuclear Disarmament in Britain, to protest nuclear testing and to call for nuclear disarmament. In 1958 the U.S., the USSR, and Britain agreed to a voluntary moratorium on nuclear bomb testing. But when testing was resumed in 1961, women in all parts of the United States united by the thousands to form what they called Women's Strike for Peace. On one day, on November 1, they declared a "women's strike" – many walking out of their homes and offices in protest against the possibility of extinction by nuclear weapons.

Women's Strike for Peace (WSP) developed from a one-day strike effort into a national peace organization that not only spoke in favor of nuclear disarmament but advocated complete international demilitarization to prevent a seemingly oncoming Third World War. Most of the women I knew were very active in this group. My own function in the WSP was to offer suggestions – men were not included in the organization itself – but many women I knew would consult me partly because of my long experience in the labor and Communist movements.

At one point in the late 1950s thousands of women rallied from all over New York City to demand an end to nuclear testing and nuclear bomb manufacturing, and calling for more diplomatic initiatives on behalf of peace. As far as I can recall, WSP's demonstration in New York City was the first to be held there since the 1930s. By the 1950s people had simply forgotten what a mass demonstration was like. So, too, had the police. They simply went crazy, many never having seen a demonstration before. As a result they wildly attacked these very well-dressed women, many of whom were pushing baby carriages. It was a horrendous affair, and everyone was outraged.

Thanks in part to fears of a Third World War and a nuclear holocaust, other peace groups were also formed in the late 1950s and early 1960s. The Student Peace Union (SPU), a strictly pacifist movement, was established in 1959 and soon developed a sizable following on many college campuses. This was very significant: many students were still highly conservative, and Ayn Rand and right-wing libertarianism (or what I would call proprietarianism) were very much in fashion. In fact, the prevailing mood on the campuses made William F. Buckley a cultural hero.

Anarchism, Marxism, and the Future of the Left

Now, however, new, more left-wing and pacifist groups were emerging, such as the Student Peace Union.

Still another organization that emerged in the 1950s, the Committee for Nonviolent Action (CNVA), was a pacifist group that was attached very closely to the War Resisters League (which actually dates back to the 1920s). CNVA members were the first hippies I ever saw. In fact, they created the characteristic dress and decor that many hippies were to adopt in the mid-1960s, letting their hair grow long, even into ponytails, and growing beards. They wore canvas sandals, often dressed in jeans, were vegetarians, and smoked pot. You should realize how uncommon this dress and demeanor were in the 1950s. It wasn't even visible in the beatnik-bohemian scene. Moreover, the CNVA pacifists engaged in direct action: they would swim out to nuclear submarines and climb up on top of them, sitting there so that the submarines couldn't submerge. Naval patrol boats had to go out and forcibly drag them off the crafts, but their actions were given very wide press coverage.

Sometimes "civil defense" air drills would be held. During these "civil defense" drills people were required by law to enter bomb shelters in nearby buildings. A siren would go off, buses and other vehicles had to stop dead in the streets, and the citizenry were obliged to take refuge in clearly marked shelter areas. I need hardly tell you that these drills were quite ridiculous. Well, when the sirens would go off some of us, led by Dorothy Day of *Catholic Worker*, would refuse to take shelter. Instead we would collect openly at the Battery, in lower Manhattan, and militantly remain in the streets. It was during these drills that I came to know and admire Dorothy, a well-known pacifist activist. In any case, since we hadn't taken shelter, we would get a summons or be hauled off to jail, which would make considerable news. In time, more and more people came down to the Battery to join us, until finally the public generally began to recognize the absurdity of the drills and bomb shelters.

In the meantime African-Americans had been stirring in the South for some time already. As early as 1947 blacks and whites went down south in unsegregated buses to segregated areas, where the two "races" were supposed to use separate public facilities and sit in separate public areas. (When people did the same thing in 1961, they were called Freedom Riders.) In 1954 the Supreme Court's decision in *Brown v. Board of Education* declared that segregation in schools was unconstitutional. This was followed in 1957 by the Montgomery bus boycott, which Rosa Parks sparked when she refused to give up her bus seat in a "white" section. In 1960 several black students sat down at the "white" section of a Woolworth's lunch counter in Greensboro, North Carolina. When they were ordered to go into the so-called "colored" section, they refused; moreover, they came back the next day and continued their "sit-in" in the "white" section, triggering an eruption of national proportions. Their action was a spark that lit the kindling, which by now was piled very high. Elsewhere more and more sparks fell on the accumulating kindling – incident by incident – until a broad civil rights movement had emerged, in which blacks demanded their equal place with whites in American society.

Was it about this time that CORE began to organize?

Yes. In my neighborhood CORE – the Congress of Racial Equality – had opened up a store between Avenue A and B on 13th Street, where it sold its literature and held public meetings. When I moved to the Lower East Side, I became involved with the local CORE chapter, or East Side CORE.

The development of CORE was the first big move on behalf of black civil rights in the North. CORE soon began to compete with the legalistic NAACP, the National Association for the Advancement of Colored People; it was the direct action arm of the movement and more militant. It had already gained fame as a civil rights group, partly because of the 1961 Freedom Rides, and it formed picket lines around various Woolworth stores in solidarity with the Greensboro sit-in. Significantly, CORE was a highly integrated civil rights group, often containing many more whites than blacks in the white neighborhoods of New York.

I should emphasize that as the civil rights movement developed, it had a very humanistic form. In 1964 it demanded integration, not segregation or racial separation. When we sang "We Shall Overcome," the second verse was "black and white together," not "black and white apart." Although I disagreed with Martin Luther King, Jr., on many things, especially his pacifist tactics, he nonetheless declared that, "We will see the day when black and white, and Jew and Gentile" – he could have added Muslim – "and men and women will all be together" in sisterhood and brotherhood. He is well remembered for such a formulation in his famous speech before the Lincoln Memorial during the March on Washington. I applauded the civil rights movement for this universalistic approach. When King said he wanted *all* of humanity to enjoy the benefits of freedom, his universalism appealed to the internationalism I had inherited from Marxism.

My CORE chapter had also sent some young people, both black and white students, to the South to participate in the "Mississippi Summer" campaign of 1964 to register black voters. As it turned out, this involved some very dangerous activities and selfless commitment. One of my CORE chapter members was Mickey Schwerner, a young civil rights worker who was killed in Mississippi together with his coworkers, James Chaney and Michael Goodman. They were all shot, and their bodies, which were buried in a dam, weren't found until a couple of weeks later. The three of them – two white, one black – are now legendary figures in the history of the civil rights movement.

Meanwhile, people in my CORE group were getting arrested in one direct action after another. We would go to various parts of the city, picket or demonstrate or sit in, and were often rounded up by the police. In 1964 we and other groups actually succeeded in closing down the World's Fair in New York City for a whole day – I was arrested in front of the Florida pavilion and spent about a week confined in what had been a World War II prisoner of war camp. Like many others, I spent much of the year going in and out of courts in Queens County, while our lawyers tried to negotiate our cases with the prosecutors. That same year a black uprising took place in Harlem. It was the *first* real black uprising of the 1960s – a year before the Watts uprising, before the Newark one, before the Detroit one. My CORE chapter was very deeply involved in it, although the head of my chapter asked me not to go to Harlem because I was white.

Throughout most of the agrarian South, particularly in Mississippi, many blacks were still tenant farmers who lived in small communities on a near-subsistence level. Numerous black students in southern universities joined SNCC, the Student Non-Violent Coordinating Committee (or "Snick," as it was pronounced), and tried to enfranchise them. Often southern sheriffs would train their guns on them for no reason whatever – this wasn't play! – while grinning FBI agents, instead of helping them, would simply stand by, even taking down the students' names. There was also a Northern Students' Movement that paralleled SNCC. It tried to organize black students in northern universities, just as SNCC did in the South, but it never quite got off the ground. I would say that SNCC was on the cutting edge of political activity for black youth in the South, although it had very little impact on blacks in the North. SNCC, too, I should add, was highly integrated; many of its members were whites.

Could you give some account of the formation of the student New Left?

Most of the northern students coming back from the Mississippi Summer, even privileged middle-class and upper-class white students, were deeply moved by their experience, and were highly radicalized by the time they arrived home. Having come up against intense racism in the South, they felt that things had to change not only in the South but throughout the entire United States. The disparities between wealth and poverty, between the material condition of middle-class affluent whites and that of deprived and oppressed black people – all of these disparities were felt very keenly and produced an intense ferment on northern campuses. When a New Left movement began to emerge, it was nourished primarily by this ferment, imparting a broadly populist form to its political and social message.

In the meantime a theoretical ferment had already been going on for several years, laying the groundwork for the creation of a new Left. During the late 1950s C. Wright Mills, a charismatic American sociology professor, began to have an ideological impact on many American students, especially because of his writings on the U.S. class structure. Since 1959 a periodical inspired by his writings, called *Studies on the Left*, had been appearing, together with a British counterpart, *The New Left Review*. Essentially many intellectuals asserted in these pages that the Old Left was dead and that it was necessary to form a new one to deal with the new conditions that had emerged since the 1930s. These periodicals were more of a forum than anything else, and I recall that their perspectives were quite mixed.

The Old Left had really been European in inspiration; except for brief periods when it was relatively ecumenical in its outlook, ranging in its membership from populists and syndicalists to Marxists, even anarchists. It was a European form of movement that had been partly transplanted to the United States. In the 1930s we had essentially been speaking in an idiom that was alien to most Americans and that often estranged them from us. The New Left would try to speak in an American idiom, presenting ideas that Americans could understand and calling for rights to which Americans had historically been committed, despite all the failings that marked American radicalism and American republicanism, since the days of the Revolution.

When Students for a Democratic Society (SDS) was formed in 1962, it was, in effect, a broadly populist movement. Its most famous ideas were presented in the Port Huron statement of that year, which, despite its liberal and even statist quality, was magnificent as an expression of popular alienation. It seemed to argue that capitalism had deprived the American people of all meaning in life apart from craven materialism, and it expressed a felt need to search for broader moral and social goals. These well-written aspirations made it a tremendously powerful ethical statement – Tom Hayden wrote either part or all of it – and SDS used it as a very effective mobilizing document.

As a populist document, it opened up a new perspective for social change: the need to create a movement that would seek not only economic justice but participatory democracy. By *participatory*, SDS meant all-inclusive, a movement that embraced everyone, people of all different races and nationalities. The *democracy* it called for was essentially identical with republicanism, but portions of the movement also advanced ideas of a direct, face-to-face democracy. SDS gave the New Left an institutional form: it gave it a distinct organizational structure and a publication, simply named *New Left Notes*.

Despite the liberalism in its official statements, the SDS membership was potentially libertarian or anarchic in character. Its membership cut across class lines, and people from different classes essentially overlapped with each other. Its populism was radical, not unlike that of the old populist movement in Russia back in the nineteenth century. Its goal was to "go to the people," as young Russian students had done in 1873-74. SDS developed a program called ERAP, or Economic Research and Action Project, in which students were expected to go into the poor urban areas and try to help the people there, as they had done in the South, and call attention to the plight of the poor in a so-called affluent society.

But mainly the New Left sought to reach the enormous student body that had emerged in the United States. Prior to the Second World War, going to college had been a rather upper-class or middle-class privilege, one that was available to only a very small proportion of young people. The most that working-class youth could usually hope to obtain was a high school diploma (which was then very highly respected). But after the war, with the postwar affluence and especially the G.I. bill of rights for veterans, millions of people went to college. Having a college diploma, at least an undergraduate diploma, became an absolute necessity for getting into the better-paying American mainstream. By the early 1960s there were several million university students – about seven million, I think – in the United States. That was a not a small segment of the population or one limited to a small social group; it was a sizable population in its own right, including children of workers as well as bourgeois. And the community colleges, which were somewhat below the official college level, may have had millions more. So the student population was very large, and student issues were not only very important but tended to be charged by the new social issues of the time.

In fact, students came to see the university as a microcosm of society as a whole. They thought they should be able to make, on campus, the kinds of decisions that voting adults were entitled to make in the larger society. They demanded what they called "student power." They claimed that students should be permitted to contribute to decision-making on curricular issues and to engage en masse in college policy-making, including the hiring of faculty members.

The best and the brightest American college students became increasingly committed to radical views such as those of SDS, which were continuous with the best in American radical traditions. They shared the American idea, for which Europeans have always criticized

Americans – that *anything* can be achieved if people resolutely combine to achieve it. This sense of possibility, of hope, of endless experimentation in a so-called New World, is a basically utopian American conception that contributed greatly to the spirit of the times.

Perhaps the most important single act that brought the New Left to wide public attention, however, was a demonstration called by SDS in 1965: 25,000 people marched in Washington in opposition to the Vietnam war. During the early 1960s most Americans were hardly even aware that their troops were fighting in Vietnam. The war began to seriously affect the lives of ordinary Americans only after conscription was stepped up and Lyndon Johnson threw hundreds of thousands of troops into the conflict in Southeast Asia.

After the 1965 march SDS became an increasingly important antiwar movement. The organization established a far-reaching network across most of the country – on college campuses – but it did not try to address the working class. Radical students not only ceased to regard working people as socially hegemonic, but in many respects viewed them as coopted and chauvinistic. The workers reciprocated this distrust in kind; in fact, very frequently. On the East Coast, workers would attack peace activists and behave violently toward countercultural youth. At one point during a demonstration that was being held in front of the Treasury Building on Wall Street, construction workers violently attacked the student protesters. The hard hats that construction workers wore became symbols of reaction, comparable to German Nazi helmets in the Second World War.

How did the counterculture emerge? What were its goals?

The conventional opinion is that the counterculture originated in California – but this is only partly true. To begin with, SDS was not strong in California. The Californians were politically very active and intensely occupied with social issues, but they really stood apart from many radical organizations elsewhere. After the Free Speech Movement in 1964 in Berkeley, they fed into the emerging counterculture, which, I should emphasize, appeared simultaneously in New York's Lower East

Side and then slowly spread to the rest of the country. Initially the counterculture was hardly influenced at all by the New Left. It tried instead to experiment with new ways of life, ostensibly "counter" to the suburban world from which many of its young people came. The children of the 1950s had been raised by highly indulgent parents who lived very cloistered suburban existences, marked, according to the stereotypes we saw in movies, by barbecues and backyard cocktail parties. As suburban children grew older, they were repelled by the whole culture of their parents and sharply reacted against it. Many of them became vegetarians instead of grilled steak eaters, and in reaction to the tidy clothing worn by their parents, they gravitated toward very informal clothing, emphasizing an appreciation of the body, greater sensuality, and explicit sexuality in language and behavior.

The "permissiveness" associated with Dr. Spock's ideas on childrearing was reinterpreted to mean sheer spontaneity – "let the child's spontaneity express itself" – and they embraced quasi-libertarian values across a wide spectrum of behavior: from sexual liberation to dietary liberation. The idea of liberation through sexual expressiveness and artistic creativity became a major theme of the counterculture.

Still another important countercultural theme was communal living. The suburbs were atomized, with lawns that actually functioned as green walls between one suburban house and another. Accordingly the children of suburbia, emigrating from the suburbs to the cities, settled in poor areas like the Lower East Side, or San Francisco's Haight-Ashbury district, looking for a new and inexpensive way of life. There they established communal living arrangements and adopted utopian ideas of a communal society based on sharing, caring, and forming new extended families. It was a very unigenerational family, to be sure: most of the kids were roughly between 15 and 25. But although they formed communes primarily with those to whom they felt closest, these alienated young people generally still considered their entire generation to be one big extended family.

Tompkins Square Park, the largest park in the Lower East Side, had a distinct quadrant in which only radicals and hippies would loll about. Many hippie women came to the park – very innocent-looking kids, many of them from California. They had long sensuous hair and often walked in bare feet on the city streets, which always amazed me, carrying their children like papooses over their shoulders. They must have seemed fairly bizarre to the neighborhood's Puerto Ricans, who formed the dominant population there.

Communal living, alternative diets, sexual liberation all congealed into a distinct countercultural outlook, but one that was far more mystical than political. The counterculture was challenging the values of the system – perhaps even more than was the case with the civil rights movement and SDS – but they were challenging its conventional values, not its social arrangements or political structures. I strongly felt it was very important to try to bring the two together – the counterculture and the New Left, hippies and blacks and antiwar activists, to infuse the counterculture with political radicalism and, in turn, to infuse the New Left with the counterculture's utopianism. In my eyes, a tremendous potential existed for creating a rich cross-cultural, visionary, utopian, even communistic movement, one with a radical anarchistic political ideology and countercultural lifeways marked by unconstrained relations and emancipatory visions.

And in fact, around 1965 and 1966 these movements – the New Left, civil rights, and antiwar movements, and the counterculture – very nearly did draw together. They repeatedly encountered each other in various parts of the country, interacting especially at antiwar demonstrations, and seeming to share radical commonalities. But this was a very limited development. In time, after 1968, the various trends that seemed to characterize the 1960s "movement" began to drift apart. The 1960s, far from expressing one common impulse, was actually an ecumenical expression of different tendencies that, first coming together, soon began to separate and in the end went in very different directions.

In your book of essays from the late 1960s, Post-Scarcity Anarchism, *you discussed, among many other things, affluence in the United States. How important was that affluence to the New Left movement and its ability to organize?*

It was immensely important. The one reality that made these movements *possible* was the compelling fact that the affluence and the feeling of economic security were such that many people could live off the fat of the economy. For all the derogatory remarks that the counterculture made about consumerism, the reality of affluence provided the material basis for the freedom and visions it held in those apparently idyllic years. Despite Johnson's atrocious Vietnam policy, his Great Society gave more social benefits – far more – to many ordinary Americans than any administration since Franklin D. Roosevelt's. LBJ introduced Medicare for elderly people and all kinds of youth, health, antipoverty, urban and conservation programs. Money was flowing out of Washington in torrents, paying not only for the war but for social welfare and improvement programs as well.

It was the "fat" of 1960s America that gave the counterculture the feeling that people did not have to work so hard, that they could live lives of "voluntary simplicity," that they could get down to "essentials" precisely because enough goods were available to provide people with the means of life and the technology to produce material abundance. It was believed that all we had to do was learn how to live cooperatively. These notions fed both movements, the counterculture and the New Left. Had there been an economic crisis in the United States in the 1960s, had poverty affected middle-class suburban youth – I do not believe these kinds of movements would have emerged. The radical and cultural movements of the 1960s were predicated on the ability of the American economy to furnish a wide spectrum of people with the basic means of life, as well as the freedom and the leisure time to engage in political and cultural activity. Technology and the American industrial machine had reached a point where it could make life comfortable and even provide leisure time not only for the middle classes but for workers. Automation could replace a great deal of labor – *potentially* to the benefit of working people and provide the free time to manage society and daily life.

It's important to understand that in the 1960s, the attitude of both the counterculture and the New Left toward technology was basically *very positive*. Expectations of a better life encouraged people to believe that they could create a new world, a participatory democracy, and a new economy. These are anarchic ideas – ideas of post-scarcity, which I very strongly tried to develop and cultivate – with a utopian vision based on the principle of hope, as Ernst Bloch put it. That hope, without which no fundamental social change is possible, was nourished by automation, growing productivity, tremendous economic wealth, an abundance of goods, opportunities for free time, and the ability to live off the fat of society.

The counterculture became possible because you could go down to the Fulton Fish Market, for example, at four o'clock in the morning and find large quantities of relatively fresh fish available for free. My friends on the Lower East Side turned this into a regular practice – in fact, they went to several wholesale centers in the city to get leftover food. It was easy to get bread that was two days old, to pick up full milk bottles, and the like – food was amply available. And on the Lower East Side and in many areas of San Francisco, apartments were extremely cheap, going for only twenty-five or thirty dollars a month. Such rents were very easy to pay even with only one person working, let alone if a whole group moved in and lived communally.

Hippies, following in the wake of the beatniks, also brought spiritualistic ideologies into the counterculture. Young people, who had absorbed radical ideas from reading political works like Albert Camus's *The Rebel*, soon drifted into reading Lao-Tzu, or began to use the *I Ching*, flipping coins to find out what they should do next. Mysticism increasingly encroached upon their revolutionary ideas, but at the time it was still mixed with politics and antiwar activism.

Could you describe your own experiences in the New Left and the counterculture?

My comrades and I formed a study circle called the Lower East Side Anarchists, which soon burgeoned into a minor movement in its own right. I recall that I insisted on using the word *anarchist* when we got started. I also joined the old Libertarian League, which was composed almost entirely of people in their sixties and older, and who were completely puzzled by the views and activities of the Lower East Side Anarchists. We engaged in wide-ranging discussions, and when we obtained discarded printing presses and repaired them, we were able to publish a great deal of literature against the war, racism, and corporations. We were trying to wed the potentially utopistic visions of the counterculture with the socialistic visions of the New Left and with anarchism, basically relying on an ecological perspective to make this marriage. In various demonstrations we were the first to raise black anarchist flags (over which Paul Goodman rhapsodized in *The New York Times*[1]) – and we carried huge banners that read "Ecology, community, revolution." Bystanders knew what "community" and "revolution" meant, but they heckled us about "ecology," whose meaning they did not understand. We would stop when we could and try to explain. I was writing "Ecology and Revolutionary Thought" in 1964, and "Toward a Liberatory Technology" in 1965, which proposed the use of solar energy, wind power, and other renewable sources of energy for an ecological society. To a degree that is now forgotten, the 1960s were not a decade that was enamored of environmental, still less ecological issues.

Our study group also helped to organize the Bowery Poets' Coop, where poets on the Lower East Side – many of whom are now established figures in American poetry – would declaim and expressively inundate audiences with their "feelings." It was after the coop was established that we decided to rename ourselves the East Side Anarchists. In 1965 we opened a bookstore on Ninth Street – the Torch – and issued a magazine called *Good Soup,* which offered a whole series of proclamations, some playful but others very serious. Alas, only one issue of *Good Soup* appeared: as anarchists, our group had decided for libertarian reasons to rotate the editorship around the entire group – with the disastrous result that the preparation of the second issue became the responsibility of someone who was very stoned most of the time, and it never came out.

Nevertheless, it seemed as if the whole world was about to change. We learned of a youth movement in Holland called the Provos. *Provo* meant "provoke," to get people to think, but this group was also very playful: they liked to call themselves the Provotariat. They gallivanted all over Amsterdam, giving out leaflets that called upon people to express themselves and to take their destiny into their own hands, but in a playful way. One time they gave out a leaflet that said, "Write your own leaflet." In contrast to their playfulness, in Japan a very tough student movement called the Zengakuren engaged the police in very serious and ongoing struggles. They would lock arms, put on helmets, gas masks, or big heavy-duty handkerchiefs soaked in water, and even carry bamboo sticks in order to fight with the cops. Oddly, amid all this worldwide ferment, Paris was very quiet. When I went there in 1967, some of my French friends were yearning to go to the United States, which at that time seemed to be the center of all the "action."

What led to the decline of the New Left?

The New Left in the United States reached its high point in 1966, by which I mean the high-water mark of the populist, anarchic tendency in SDS. Yet the roots of the decline of this tendency were present as early as 1964. For one thing, a distinctly antiwhite attitude was emerging in the black movement, even in groups like CORE, which despite its very considerable white membership was shifting noticeably toward a blacks-only outlook. SNCC too was moving toward an antiwhite position. During the Mississippi Summer in 1964, it had eagerly invited white students into the movement, but later people like Stokely Carmichael argued that SNCC was being led by too many whites, and it began to "encourage" them to leave. Abbie Hoffman's fate was a striking case in point. He lamented in *The Village Voice,* I think, that he had been pushed out of SNCC and felt orphaned by the organization.

 For better or worse, black people are only ten or twelve percent of the American population. It was vital for the civil rights movement to reach out to white America if it really wanted to realize its goal of equal opportunity. But once these civil rights organizations excluded whites, they began to shrink – they didn't get substantially larger after Mississippi Summer, and as they moved more and more toward an exclusionary Black Power program, they became ever more isolated from white America.

 Black Power was a form of regressive particularism, and as such it was not calculated to win the sympathy of most Americans. This particularism was exacerbated by Malcolm X in his early days, when he talked about all whites as "devils," even though later on, after he went to Mecca and broke with Elijah Muhammed, he completely changed his mind. The impact of the Black Muslim movement was extremely divisive. Other civil rights organizations, apart from the Southern Christian Leadership Conference, led by Martin Luther King, picked up on this ethnic particularism and added to the isolation.

Where the civil rights movement had once humanistic, Black Power groups began to say that the white man was the enemy. But since when are white men one social category? Many white men and women are impoverished – are they the enemies of black people? Yes, some white males are CEOs who manage major corporations, but others are slowly dying from workplace exposure to toxic chemicals. The category "the white man" neglects to recognize class differences and hierarchical differences among white people, many of whom are also victimized by this system. In my opinion this focus on one oppressed stratum as distinct from the oppressed as a whole was parochial and reactionary. There is no collective "white man" who is the universal enemy of a collective "black man."

A terribly unhealthy, even regressive relationship began to emerge between radical blacks and whites. In the first place, the whites were abjured from playing any leading role in "the movement" (as it was called) and were expected to subordinate themselves to the black militants from SNCC and to a lesser degree CORE, which they stupidly began to do. Advocates of Black Power often felt a great aversion toward the lifestyles of the hippies, whom they called "privileged whites." Many hippies certainly were privileged whites, but they were at least looking for ways to create a new, harmonious society, and increasingly began to drift away from the movement. As for the young white radicals, they began to feel a deep sense of guilt, as though they were collectively responsible for the enslavement of black people, and even worse, a sense of political inferiority, because blacks seemed to be more revolutionary, especially after the outbreaks in Harlem in 1964 and Watts in 1965.

Secondly, the Black Power tendency was very macho and began to call for armed struggle, even at a time when it did not have the support of the majority of African-Americans. The Black Panthers marched into movement meetings, giving orders and telling largely white radical organizations what to do and how to do it. Although the demands of the Black Panthers went well beyond civil rights, many of their leaders had a statist outlook and not accidentally gave ministerial titles to their leaders.

They regarded themselves as a conventional army: when one of their speakers appeared on a podium, he (rarely she) would be guarded by several Panther troopers, wearing Che Guevara-type berets and looking very stern, with their arms folded aggressively together and their feet spread out as though they were ready to engage in combat with any critical questioner in the audience. This combative ambience created a sense of apartness between the Panthers and other movements that they were supposed to be "leading."

These developments were troubling enough. But then a new and even more destructive development occurred in SDS. A new kind of member began to enter the organization, representing a tendency that was alien to its original populism. These new members were motivated mainly by their opposition to the invasion of Vietnam and to the blockade against Cuba. In fact, they were supporters of third world dictators, and their thinking was entirely shaped by the cold war. Once they arrived in SDS, they mounted a concerted and underhanded effort to take over the organization, in a sense giving it a Cold War politics rather than a radical politics.

Naively, many newly radicalized white American radicals were coming to feel that they *were* oppressors, not only of blacks but of many parts of the former colonial world, and they regarded even ordinary American soldiers as low forms of life who were nothing more than tools of imperialism. Correspondingly, new ideologies focusing on the third world – its radical movements, analyses, and ways of organizing against the United States and Europe – filtered into the New Left, which became even less populist and more anti-imperialist in character.

The movie *Battle of Algiers,* which came out in 1965 and depicted the Algerian war of independence in the late 1950s in very heroic terms, captivated these new radicals. Utterly ridiculous parallels were drawn between street demonstrations in New York and Washington and urban guerrilla warfare in Algerian cities. The movie fostered an image that the United States *as such* was the enemy and the third world was made up of revolutionary saints. Given this third world orientation, SDS began to talk to Americans as though the third world constituted the proletariat and all of white America constituted the bourgeoisie.

For a time, even Herbert Marcuse played a very unhappy role in this development. In 1965, I recall very clearly, he gave a lecture at the New York University Law School, in which he said that even though the American proletariat had been coopted by the capitalist system, Marx had been right about the hegemonic role of the proletariat in the class struggle, because viewed on a global basis, the Vietnamese peasants were the real proletariat. This statement shocked me. (It was the first time I had heard it, and astonishingly, I still hear it repeated today by many sincere Marxists.) For one thing, the majority of third world people in the 1960s were mainly peasants and could not by any stretch of the imagination be equated with the industrial proletariat in England and in Western Europe, which Marx had regarded as potentially revolutionary for sound socioeconomic reasons. Perhaps more important, the statement implied that the First World, as the global bourgeoisie, was the common enemy of the third world – an idea that removed the basis for solidarity between the oppressed in both "worlds" and steered young American radicals away from the ways they could be effective, even on behalf of the Vietnamese peasantry.

I doubt that Marcuse retained this idea very long. But it came to be widely held in many parts of the New Left, in some cases as a new theory of the class struggle. Most famously, it became part of Weatherman ideology, with appalling results. White radicals, in effect, began to think in neo-Stalinist terms, picking up on Maoism and the "Red Guards," emulating them in tone, verbal violence, organizational forms, and contempt for populist ideas. By comparison, the Black Panthers seemed almost libertarian.

Another very questionable development in the theoretical outlook of the New Left, both in the United States and in Europe, was the absurd attempt to apply classical Marxism to the *student* movement. In his 1967 book titled *Strategy for Labor,* André Gorz tried to draw a parallel between the working class and the rising student movement. University students, he wrote, far from being a largely middle-class social stratum, were actually a new kind of proletariat. They were proletarians working in a factory called the university. Of course, this dubious analogy jettisoned the concrete distinctions between the proletariat and the middle class, indeed between wage workers and their exploiters.

Anarchism, Marxism, and the Future of the Left

Obviously, university students aren't a proletariat, and any parallels that exist between them are very dubious. Today, when capitalism is very much in the saddle, we can see this with stark clarity. As it happened, the great majority of students in the 1960s never regarded university administrators as their exploiters, comparable to the bourgeois exploiters of industrial labor. And for good reason: they were ultimately going to become professionals themselves, or managers, professors, and even capitalists. The notion that students were proletarians was simply an absurd affectation. By the way, I was later told that just as his book was being translated into English, André Gorz drastically changed his point of view on this question.

These ideas, so far removed from American realities, were brought into SDS largely by Greg Calvert, the organization's national secretary in 1966. He and Carl Davidson, another SDS leader, began to propagate this confused theory in the organization's ranks. They established a committee whose purpose was to educate SDS members into this catchy but very artificial analysis. Before long, SDS and its growing Maoist tendency's literature were cultivating ideas of students as workers and calling for worker/student alliances.

While Calvert and Davidson intended to make students more radical, their student-as-worker ideology actually served to destroy the potentially radical impact that SDS and the student movement could have had on the American people. At a time when most Americans were genuinely puzzled by the upsurge of protest that was sweeping the country, when many older people began to oppose the Vietnam War and tried sympathetically to explore the message of the counterculture – the "movement" was going crazy. Many ordinary Americans were eager to hear, in an idiom they could understand, what the "movement" and the counterculture advocated.

I think millions of Americans could have been persuaded that their society was in need of deep-seated change, if only the "movement's" best ideas could have been made intelligible to them. But instead, the New Left was increasingly speaking in narrow, sectarian terms: first casting the third world as the global proletariat, then casting students as the proletariat, and finally taking recourse to vulgar forms of Marxism.

American Trotskyists and Maoists regarded the unrest in the 1960s as a wonderful opportunity to inject their own sectarian ideas into SDS. By now, in the real world, the political prescriptions of orthodox Marxism had long been out of date. The sharp definitions that distinguished workers from peasants and both from the bourgeoisie were becoming cloudy. Clearly there were capitalists, but the mentality that prevailed among working people was no longer as explicitly class consciousness as it had been in the 1930s. Working people had a largely middle-class mentality – in fact, many thought of themselves not as workers at all but primarily as members of the "working middle class." They very often regarded their unions as machines for gaining benefits, not as vehicles for class conflict, let alone class war.

Still, the various Marxists – Leninists, Maoists, and Trotskyists – all took advantage of the ideological and organizational weaknesses of the New Left. In 1967 a Maoist organization called Progressive Labor, or PL, entered SDS and, with its hard-line Marxist-Leninist-Maoist ideology, attempted to organize caucuses and ultimately take control of the organization. The Trotskyists, for their part, had a "tried, true, and tested" program, which had been fossilized ever since Trotsky was assassinated in 1940; they formed their own student organization to compete with SDS. When young people traveled to Cuba to help harvest the country's sugar crop, they often returned with quasi-Stalinist notions, heavily infused with the mystique of Che Guevara and his neo-Stalinist notions.

It is difficult to describe what a wide variety of pseudo-revolutionaries there were. Some supported even Enver Hoxha, the Stalinist dictator of Albania. These groups not only were opposed to the war in Vietnam, they actively supported the Communist regime in North Vietnam, not to speak of their enthusiasm for Castro in Cuba and Mao in China.

Generally speaking, many SDS "Marxists" didn't give a damn about freedom; they simply supported enemies of the United States – a view that radically divorced them from the majority of Americans. In effect, their politics were being defined by the cold war, not by the real problems – economic, ecological, and cultural – that existed in the United States. Personally I couldn't make sense of a position that, on the one hand, called for self-determination for Cuba and said that the Cuban people had the right to decide their destiny, and yet on the other hand supported

Castro. I refused to support Castro because I opposed all dictatorships. I was a left-wing libertarian, opposed to all kinds of states. I was opposed to the American invasion of Vietnam, and I earnestly wanted the American troops to be withdrawn, but opposing American involvement in Vietnam didn't mean that I supported the North Vietnamese government. North Vietnam was a totalitarian state, and I regarded the support that many SDS leaders exhibited for Ho Chi Minh, Castro, and Mao Tse-Tung as a betrayal of freedom – which by no means meant that I was indifferent to third world struggles. Yet to this day I am still accused by a Zen Marxist like Joel Kovel of being indifferent to third world struggles!

I've seen footage of SDS people, perhaps Weathermen, chanting "Ho Ho Ho Chi Minh, Dare to struggle! Dare to win!" and carrying North Vietnamese flags. I don't imagine this was attractive to most Americans at the time.

Yes, some people in SDS raised North Vietnamese flags, which I objected to vehemently because we were not really part of the National Liberation Front in Vietnam. We were not fighting on the battlefields of Vietnam against American imperialism. Moreover, the most earnest of these flag wavers, the Marxist-Leninists, Maoists, and Trotskyists – were never interested in the aims of SDS as such. They were eager to cannibalize this large organization, to use it, to squeeze it dry. They wanted to recruit members from it to build their own Bolshevik parties – as they construed Bolshevism, in its narrowest, most dogmatic terms. They tried to make the 1960s look like the 1930s. They were digging up corpses and trying to recreate struggles that had long passed into history. Worse, they were not only irrelevant in outlook, they were totalitarian in orientation and shaped by cold war policies.

What did you think anarchists should be doing?

It was very important, I thought, that anarchists should create a strong, well-organized presence in the New Left, one that would be independent of its growing totalitarian orientation, its glorification of third-world neo-Stalinist regimes in the name of anti-imperialism. Only by making changes in the United States, I thought, could we *really* help third world struggles. The main issue, I felt, was to talk to the American people in a language they understood, to voice their hidden aspirations, to bring to the surface their unconscious impulses about the boredom of suburbia, the tediousness of work, the meaninglessness of life, and to give them a sense of hope, to visualize a free utopian future in such a way that they would really believe they could *reconstruct* society. That utopian dimension was very important for me, and I tried to bring it to the anarchists with whom I was working.

I understand that when American delegations went to North Vietnam, the government told them to stop worrying so much about what it was doing, and to stop calling themselves extensions of the National Liberation Front. Go back home, they were told, and win over the American people and change the United States. In this respect the North Vietnamese were absolutely right.

But their American adherents didn't listen to them, and as a result a quasi-authoritarian tone, characteristic of the Stalinist Old Left, crept into SDS, gradually demolishing everything that was new about the New Left. By 1969 the populist idiom of SDS was replaced by the harsh doctrinaire intonations of Leninist-type theses, and the ultraleftist jargon of Bolshevism, as well as by the claptrap about the student as worker, and the need for SDS members to go out and establish an alliance with working-class youth, and with blacks, even as all Americans were being told that they were imperialists – an unbelievable goulash of ideas! SDS members from the early days, or at least the best of them, could no longer deal with these hard-line factions and were even expelled from the very organization that they had founded only a few years earlier.

If the 1960s utopian visions were now declining in SDS, they were being preserved, however feebly, by the counterculture. But as I said, the two never really melded together: the counterculture was never completely politicized, and the New Left was never completely culturalized, if I may use that expression. By 1969, the two movements were divided against each other, one drifting into terroristic adventurism, the other into spiritualistic narcissism.

Anarchism, Marxism, and the Future of the Left

If the Maoist, Trotskyist, and Marxist-Leninist groups played a negative role in "the movement," what was the impact of anarchist groups?

Regrettably, certain anarchist tendencies played a very bad role: specifically, the Up Against the Wall Motherfucker group, which Ben Morea had formed out of an earlier group called Black Mask. Black Mask was a anarchist group that produced a very punchy cultural-political literature in the mid-1960s. Morea was a real genius in this area. Together with a few friends, he would wander around the Lower East Side covering walls with posters that denounced Allen Ginsberg and Timothy Leary as potential sellouts. Black Mask managed to plaster so many posters over Lower Manhattan and send out so many leaflets internationally that people thought his group was a mass youth movement. Actually, apart from some transients, it numbered about five people at most. This supposedly huge mass movement actually never existed – but its impact was remarkable.

Later on, Black Mask became ESSO, an acronym for East Side Service Organization and a play on the old name of what is now the Exxon oil company. Ironically, the money for ESSO came from funds that the city of New York set aside for the purpose of coopting radical youth. In the wake of all the urban unrest at the time, Mayor Lindsay was so eager to calm down the city that he even funded radical groups, hiring the Bread and Puppet Theater to cool things down by presenting street plays during the hot summer nights, when there might be trouble.

Up Against the Wall Motherfucker was the next incarnation of Morea's Black Mask. It acquired a storefront that was also indirectly funded by the city, but in no case were the Motherfuckers coopted by the mayor. They were far too shrewd to be manipulated by anyone, and they emphatically believed in what they were doing.

Basically, the Motherfuckers were cultural radicals. For example, during a New York garbage strike, they dumped garbage in Lincoln Center because they said that cultural garbage was being produced at Lincoln Center and "America turns the world into garbage." They engaged in what you might call "cultural terrorism," using a certain amount of violent rhetoric, but actually doing nothing that was physically violent. Notoriously, they used a famous picture of Geronimo – the one showing him holding a .30-caliber lever-action rifle – and made it a symbol for self-defense and resistance. A poem they wrote had the line "we are all outlaws in the eyes of America" – it became famous when it was used as lyrics for a song called "Volunteers of America" and recorded by Grace Slick and the Jefferson Airplane. One underground newspaper, *The Rat*, found the Motherfuckers so attractive, even sensational, that they let them design their centerfolds. Hence their poetry would reach thousands, generally decorated with smoking guns and scenes of violence, which added to the growing violent tone of "the movement." New Left pacifists, of course, were shocked by their art.

But although the Motherfuckers exuded this kind of violent rhetoric, they didn't engage in any actual violence that I know of, and I knew them very well. Rather than engage in actual terrorist *activity*, they believed that their main job was to "blow" people's minds. Their medium was theater, not serious theoretical disputation, but such disruptive activity has two faces. Admittedly, it can stir people up, but it rarely makes them think, and it can easily get out of control and undermine serious organizations that should be saved and their members educated.

Together with the Yippies, in March 1968 in Grand Central Station the Motherfuckers carried out what was to be a celebration of the spring equinox, a playful protest against the normal daily grind of the commuters who passed through the station every day. But during the celebration a large clock was slightly damaged, and someone, conceivably an agent provocateur, threw a cherry bomb or two into the crowd. The cops closed in and began, with unusual brutality, to club the many kids who had come to the event, beating dozens of them to the ground. They pushed a demonstrator through one of the heavy plate-glass doors that open into the station – I am speaking about glass that was about a half-inch thick – and beat him up in the bargain. All the nerves in his arm were severed. It was a police riot, and it led to widespread outrage, with nonstop discussions on WBAI, a radical New York radio station.

But the Motherfuckers' cultural terrorism left them politically adrift, without a program, without direction, without tangible results. While some of us were trying to give coherence and organization to what we felt was potentially the most important anarchic movement in the United States in decades, we received virtually no support from the other expressly anarchist groups in the country, to the extent that such groups existed. In 1967 I was working with a collective called the *Anarchos* Group, which believed that the New Left and the counterculture could become a unified radical movement directed against all forms of hierarchy and domination and develop a libertarian program, a responsible organization, and a vision that was utopian yet comprehensible to ordinary Americans, free of ultraleftist jargon. The *Anarchos* Group turned out a magazine that tried to spread its ideas – with remarkable influence, in some respects. The two thousand copies of the magazine we published must have reached about 20,000 people in all, and we received a huge amount of mail from all parts of the country.

A major problem that we encountered was the various "national mobilizations" against the Vietnam war, or "mobes," as they were called. Mobilization for Survival, an organization that consisted of fairly respectable middle-class people as well as some rebellious ones, made well-publicized efforts to bring as many people as possible to Washington to demonstrate against the war. It became a year-round effort. They were always engaged in doing only one thing: bringing people to Washington – in buses, in cars, by railroad – gathering them together in huge numbers, and marching in the tens and finally hundreds of thousands in Washington. The problem we faced was that when people were focused on Washington, they put less effort into lasting local work and dealing with other issues that revealed the failings of the system and raised the overall social consciousness of the people. The national mobes simply drained the energy of many militants away from serious organizing and education work *in their own localities* and turned "the movement" into an episodic, single-issue phenomenon at the national level. Once the issue was resolved, the mobes usually disappeared – and that was that!

Was the situation very different in Europe?

I tried to find out in 1967, when I traveled all over the European continent. I visited Provos in Amsterdam and talked with Raoul van Dijn, who was one of the Provo founders, although by 1967 their movement was already waning. They were to return later under the name of Kabouters. I went to Sweden, Norway, and Germany, but I didn't see any active radical political life. In France I met the Situationists: Guy Debord, Raoul Vaneigem, Mustapha Khayati, all the top leaders, with whom I spent a good deal of time. The Situationists had a small, highly centralist organization, guided by Guy Debord, who in effect was their supreme leader. As small as they were, however, the Situationists were highly exclusionary. If the Situationists expelled a member, he became a nonperson, who no one could talk to, which I found very unsavory because it reminded me of Stalinist practices in the 1930s.

Many myths have sprung up about the Situationists since then. Most notably, they are regarded as pioneering cultural revolutionaries, which is very far from the truth. Actually, they were obsessed with the proletariat and with worker's councils, a view that goes back to the council communism of Anton Pannekoek and Hermann Gorter, two Dutch Marxists from the early 1900s. Nor were the Situationists interested in either students or youth; in fact, they regarded the American counterculture and youth movement as politically regressive and petty bourgeois. Their work was basically literary; indeed, Debord was difficult to understand, certainly by the workers who were assigned a hegemonic role in his concept of revolution.

Raoul Vaneigem's *The Revolution of Everyday Life,* written in the mid-1960s, is now the most widely read of all of Situationist works; it is a very buoyant disquisition on the possibilities for the subversion of bourgeois culture, although Vaneigem himself lived a rather middle-class life in Belgium. In fact, I was told it was suburban, and his habits, clothing, and behavior would have been indistinguishable from any middle-class American suburban commuter. The only real flaming revolutionary in the Situationist crowd, frankly speaking, was Mustapha Khayati, who as far as I can recall wanted to return to the Middle East to carry on guerrilla activity.

But they were the most interesting political group that I found in Paris in 1967, between August and October. As minuscule as they were, and for all their failings, they at least were radical and politically informed. Apart from them, no radical politics seemed to exist in France. Many of the French radicals I met wanted to come to the United States, where huge demonstrations were the order of the day and radicalism seemed on the rise. Paris in 1967 seemed dead by comparison, and when I finally left in early November, I did so with a sense of relief. In short, in 1967, apart from Holland, things were pretty dead in Europe.

Did you travel through the United States? What did you find?

Soon after returning to New York, I went to San Francisco, where I visited Haight Ashbury for the first time, symbolically the center of the hippie culture. The scene was incredible: crowds of hippies were disporting themselves in the streets, in the park – and living in communes almost everywhere. The scene was also marked, however, by a certain emotional emptiness. Everyone loved everyone else so much, or so people said, that love became rather meaningless. If you love everyone, love loses its reality, and you don't really love anyone in particular. Although I had hoped to find a strong sense of solidarity in the communes, what I actually found were usually very tenuous bonds between people; in fact, many of the communes in the Haight were really crash pads rather than ongoing communal groups. People entered them and left with dazzling rapidity. There was very little of an organized and permanent political life, still less evidence of any political content. Mysticism – especially Taoism, and mixes of Asian exotica – was prevalent, but these sentiments seemed as thin and transient as the crash pads.

Back in New York, in April 1968 Columbia University exploded, and students occupied the campus in protest against a proposed student gymnasium that the administration was planning to build on a site in Morningside Heights, adjacent to Harlem. Blacks who lived in Harlem used this open area for recreation, but if the gym were built, it would be closed to them. SDS and other radical students justly made the proposed gymnasium into a public issue by demanding that the site be turned over to the people of Harlem. The university refused: legally the area belonged to Columbia, and the administrators claimed the right to do what they wished with it.

It is history now that the students went out on a dramatic strike that attracted nationwide, even international attention. They occupied a number of university buildings, or halls, often according to their ethnicity and politics. For example, Hamilton Hall was occupied entirely by blacks; another hall was taken over by left-leaning middle-class youth; and a third by militant ultrarevolutionaries.

During the occupation the students in these different buildings created a distinctive cultural life for themselves, depending upon their political disposition. The ultrarevolutionaries were said to have spread oil over floors and staircases so that if the police attacked, they would slip all over the place. I heard that they even scattered broken glass around, made clubs out of furniture, and built barricades in the halls to resist an attack. The building occupied by the blacks seemed rather quiet, but I only know what I saw at various times. The middle-class white students turned their occupation into an ongoing party. They showed movies and had concerts, and debated political issues. The book *The Strawberry Statement* is supposed to be based on the events in their hall. In some halls the students went through the university files and found previously undisclosed documents about Columbia's ties with the military-industrial complex.

The police, it seemed, were hesitant to intervene – apparently they were afraid that if they evicted the blacks, Harlem might explode in a riot. Ultimately what happened, to the best of my knowledge, is that black leaders made a deal with the police by which the police quietly removed them from the campus, through little-known tunnels, and released them. Once they were gone, the police suddenly plunged into the university halls with everything they had, clubbing the white left-liberal students with scandalous brutality. It was another police riot. Even the doctors and medical aides who were there – first-aid people in white coats – were beaten by police. *The Strawberry Statement* movie doesn't accurately depict all the events, but it gives some idea of the brutality of the police. As for the ultrarevolutionaries, with their barricades and oiled staircases, they were apparently too frightening for the cops, who finally negotiated a peaceful agreement with them for their removal.

Many students were charged with a variety of crimes, and some faced the prospect of prison terms. Accordingly, money had to be raised for their legal defense. The Living Theater, a radical anarchist theater group, decided to help them out by putting on a fund-raising event. The

Living Theater was well known for its avant-garde theater pieces, in which they used many experimental theatrical techniques that they regarded as anarchistic.

Bill Graham, the owner of the Fillmore East, lent his theater to the Living Theater for one night, for a benefit performance of *Paradise Now* to raise money for the students' legal defense. The Fillmore East, I should explain, was *the* main theater for the youth culture, and all the major rock bands played there. On the night of the benefit, just as the Living Theater was going offstage after finishing its performance, Ben Morea leaped onto the stage, grabbed the microphone, and shouted: "Everybody stay here! We demand that Bill Graham let the whole community and all its friends use the Fillmore East free for one night each week. We're going to occupy this place tonight until he agrees." Graham objected at first, but finally he yielded – it would have been very unsporting not to do so. Thereafter, every Wednesday night, *local* rock bands would play there, until Graham became fed up with the whole business, ended the free night, and closed down the Fillmore East for good.

1968 has the reputation for being the year of revolution in the 1960s. You were in France in late 1967 and nothing much was happening. But what brought about the May-June events of '68?

By early 1968, I would say, a strong sense of unnoticed alienation probably existed in France, especially among university students. They were watching the United States, and the Columbia strike must have had a profound influence on them. After a series of relatively minor incidents, they rose up and occupied Nanterre University buildings in a strike and appealed to students on other French campuses to join them. In fact, they marched to the Sorbonne, essentially sparking a strike in that very important Parisian university. French students, in effect, were actually catching up with what the Americans had been doing for some time. In May an industrial general strike swept across France, from Nantes to Paris. Millions of workers took over factories, raising red flags, while students were talking of revolution almost everywhere, or so it seemed. Paris was in a state of revolutionary euphoria.

Murray Bookchin

How did it happen? First, let me give you the social context, so far as I see it. In the 1960s, I believe, De Gaulle was trying to modernize France, to industrialize it, to break down the traditional patronal economy, in which owners would manage a small number of workers and businesses were handled almost like family affairs. Agriculture was primarily still the work of peasants. The Gaullist technocrats were rapidly transforming France into a more rationalized economy, such as existed in the United States – a *corporate* France based on modern industry and agribusiness. They even created a nationwide police force called the CRS [Compagnies Républicaines de Securité] – a kind of mobile army – initially to control the French peasants, who were prepared to turn to direct action to retain their family farms against large-scale agriculture.

The French working class, in turn, had a long history of revolutions going back 150 years, and even in the 1960s French workers were more the way the American working class had been in the 1930s, sharing their old militant spirit. They were controlled mainly, but not exclusively, by the Communist trade union, the General Confederation of Labor (CGT), and the Communist and Socialist parties were among the largest such parties in Europe.

Nanterre, where the student strike began, was a relatively small university that had been recently built in a Muslim district in the west of Paris, in a North African neighborhood. The initial cause of the student strike there, so I was told, was a regulation, imposed in March 1967, that forbade male students from visiting female dorms. More important, however, by 1968 student discontent with the structure of the university system and with the curriculum had reached a boiling point.

A sociology student at Nanterre named Dany Cohn-Bendit, who was a remarkable orator, became the spokesperson for the left libertarian students. He was called "Dany the Red," but actually he was close to a Parisian anarchist group known as Noir et Rouge, which turned out a kind of mimeographed periodical that was influential among some of the younger French anarchists. The older anarchist organization, the French Anarchist Federation, was anarchosyndicalist – it had very little influence among the workers and was composed mainly of elderly people who lived very much in the past. The younger anarchists of Noir et Rouge were people in their twenties and thirties and were interested in the counterculture and the kind of issues that had been raised in the United States since 1962. Those issues were percolating into France, and Dany and his older brother, who in my opinion was the theoretical brain behind Dany, escalated the situation in Nanterre into a major protest, which finally reached stormy proportions in January 1968, when the dean at Nanterre called in the police to break up student sit-ins and unauthorized meetings.

Now in France, to call the police onto a university campus was a violation of a very revered tradition. For many centuries French society had regarded the university as a special preserve, almost immune from civil authority. In the Middle Ages the universities were controlled by the clergy and were under canon law, not civil law. Of course, the French Revolution had brought the authority of canon law to an end, but the traditional autonomy of the university was so strong in France that during the Second World War, when the Germans occupied Paris and invaded the universities, it produced universal hatred and was an important factor in inciting French students to enter the Resistance. After the war that sanctity of the campus was restored, and the university was expected to police itself. But in January 1968, when the dean at Nanterre called in the police, he turned what might have been a controllable situation into a storm.

The Nanterre students met with the students at the Sorbonne, joined forces, and after the meeting were manhandled by the police. Fighting broke out in the streets outside the university, and before long other parts of the Latin Quarter became involved. Ordinary people joined, and soon there was widespread street fighting – and the police withdrew, leaving most of the Latin Quarter to the students. Students in France were generally quite privileged at the time: only seven percent of the student body was made up of working-class children, in contrast to the United States, where over fifty percent were. Normally, most young people who went to a French university were really children of the bourgeoisie or petty bourgeoisie. This made it all the more remarkable that ordinary Parisians, including working-class youth, also supported their actions. Obviously, the students were expressing widespread public discontent with Gaullist policies, not only their own grievances.

The authorities were completely confused, even the mayor of Paris and the French government. De Gaulle had gone off to Romania, I think, to receive some honorific award, apparently feeling that this trifling incident could be ignored. The students were really quite heroic. They tore up the stone blocks or *pavés* that made up the streets of the Latin Quarter and by May 10 had built larger barricades in several sections of the Quarter, in expectation of a police attack. That night they were assaulted. The battle that exploded went on into the early hours of the morning. The students raised black as well as red flags – presumably signifying a commitment to anarchism as well as traditional socialism.

The principal forces that the government used against them, in the CRS, were dressed in helmets and heavy protective gear. They were armed with tear gas as well as conventional clubs and guns. Everybody in the neighborhood joined in, spilling pails of water on the police, dropping flower pots from windows, and even setting fire to cars. Although some people were very severely wounded, no one was killed. Significantly, the police never pulled out their guns – rather they used tear gas against the students, often directing the canisters at the heads of the defenders, of course, which inflicted serious wounds. But the May 10 assault produced a national uproar in France, due mainly to the courage of the students and the well-publicized cruelty of the hated CRS. Most important, ordinary industrial workers, even clerks, professionals, and others felt a deep sympathy for the students and bitterly resented the behavior of the police. Three days after the "night of the barricades," as it was called, on May 13, about a million people demonstrated in the streets of Paris.

The Communists played a very reactionary role in the events. They were careful to prevent the students and workers from mingling and talking with each other. During demonstrations Communist goons would shepherd students and workers away from each other. I should explain that the Communists were very accommodating to the system and, like the old-time socialists, were mainly interested in gaining governmental positions. Frankly, they did not want an unstable situation to emerge in Paris, and they generally tried to subdue the militancy of the workers.

In fact, in general they were among the most serious obstacles to the May-June "events," trying to contain the general strike that followed as best they could and direct it into parliamentary channels. The students, for example, called a special rally at the Champ de Mars, an open area near the Eiffel Tower, and some workers managed to make their way there after the May 13 demonstration, but the Communists did everything they could to keep the two groups apart. Students and working-class militants alike were furious at these efforts; in fact, the union quickly bused the workers out of the area, as soon as the demonstration came to an end.

What happened then? On May 14, in the coastal cities of Nantes, the Sud-Aviation workers spontaneously went on strike and occupied the Sud-Aviation aircraft plant. It wasn't clear why they struck – certainly it wasn't because of any student activities. But before long the whole city of Nantes and its neighboring city, Saint-Nazaire, went out on general strike. The ships in the harbor raised red flags, as did the factories in both cities. I later learned that workers actually welded bars over the doors of the managers' offices – and serenaded them with songs from the French Revolution and the Paris Commune. The managers were well fed and treated courteously; they were even permitted to use their office telephone – and the radio stations broadcasted what the Sud-Aviation executives said. "The students are treating us very nicely," they declared, "but we can't go home." The strike was marked by a very playful atmosphere, which came to an end only when police attacked the workers.

Farmers too came in from the countryside, which was quite unusual, because there was very little love lost between peasants and workers. They came with their tractors and joined the workers' demonstrations in Nantes. This imagery was absolutely incredible, and within a matter of days – it almost seemed like hours – the general strike had spread across the country into Paris itself, which was completely shut down for weeks. Banks, post offices, insurance firms, department stores, almost everything was closed down except for the television stations, which spread the news of the strike. The TV camera operators and the commentators were generally very sympathetic to the strikers and broadcast favorable footage of all the events to nearly every French hamlet. Thus, rural French people could see footage of Parisians shouting "Strike!" and students throwing *pavés* at the CRS.

The Communists were afraid that a spontaneous strike in a given plant might remove the workers from the CGT's control. Still doing everything they could to keep the students from joining the striking workers who had spontaneously occupied their plants, they now began to pull out the workers in other plants and send them home – occupying the factories with their own people to forestall an uncontrollable popular movement. In Paris the workers at the Renault auto plant, for example, struck on their own – they simply forced Communist officials to support their action. Young workers initiated the strike, and older workers followed in their wake. Faced with a fait accompli, CGT officials essentially tagged along and tried to take over the workers' grievances in union negotiations with the employers.

This was the general pattern, when I came to Paris in mid-July. I visited the Renault plant, and saw signs put up by the Communist hacks that read, "Beware of provocateurs" – presumably meaning students – "who may try to mislead you," or words to that effect. In every possible way, they tried to keep the workers who occupied the Renault plant from talking to students.

The next step of the unions – Socialist as well as Communist – was to try to reduce the workers' demands to strictly economic grievances. For their part, may workers simply wrote up their grievances in *cahiers*, or notebooks, a tradition that dates back to the French Revolution. Many grievances were remarkably noneconomic, even social, such as "We don't like the kind of supervision we get," and "We don't like the alienated atmosphere of the plants." These *cahiers* were not necessarily over issues of pay or vacation time. In a sense, the workers were intuitively challenging the factory culture as such – its overall oppressive and alienating features.

The students, in turn, converted the Left Bank of Paris into a playground, removing fences from parks and producing remarkable posters that, as I saw weeks later, covered the entire sides of multistoried university buildings. They took over auditoriums – even the Opera – and held debates that continued for entire days and evenings. Their slogans are now famous: "Imagination to power," "Be realistic, do the impossible," "Society is a carnivorous flower," "We take our desires to be reality because we believe in the reality of our desires." The man who painted the last slogan was an ex-Situationist who I had come to know in Paris in '67; he had painted it onto a heroic Baroque painting of a horseman in the Sorbonne, and it became very popular. This movement had a tremendous artistic *élan*.

But contrary to the later claims of lifestyle anarchists in the United States, by no means were all of these slogans Situationist. Many were improvised by the students themselves and derive from many different sources. The Situationists, in fact, put up their own posters calling for workers' councils, none of which were ever formed. Indeed, had any such councils been created, I'm certain that they would have been taken over by the Communists, who had a strong organization and still enjoyed the long-term loyalty of many workers. The anarchists lacked an effective movement, so the future of this "proletariat revolution," as the Situationists called it, was for all its drama easily brought under the control of the authorities.

The general strike, to be sure, was massive, finally involving 8 to 12 million workers. I don't think anyone knows how many workers actually occupied factories or went on strike. Almost every workplace was closed down or occupied. Among the few exceptions were the food stores, but even there, the petty-bourgeois owners, who had a reputation for parsimony, were selling food on credit. Nor did the printers of radical periodicals go on strike. *L'Humanité,* the Communist organ, for example, appeared, as did the Socialist and other periodicals; hence their propaganda kept appearing throughout the events.

Eventually, after some two months, the Communists managed to maneuver the workers back to their jobs. One example, I learned, was the way they tricked the Metro workers into resuming subway operations. The Communists told the workers at one subway terminal that the workers at another terminal had returned to work, which of course, induced them to resume operations. Then they went to another terminal and told the workers that the workers at the first terminal were moving their trains – and so it went, from one terminal to another, until the whole Metro was in operation.

The CGT, of course, gained many benefits for the workers; there's no point in deceiving ourselves – in a conflict between bread and ideas, bread usually wins out in the end. Much as I favor ideas over immediate economic aims, I can understand that workers cannot afford to be saints. Today privileged or footloose lifestyle anarchists would have us believe that erotic and artistic impulses govern human behavior at its deepest level, but a two-month strike will create serious economic difficulties for most ordinary workers, especially those who have families. Workers only have each other to rely on, and their unions, so that unless well-organized militants can help them take over society itself, they will always be at the mercy of the bourgeoisie and opportunistic union officials.

I didn't arrive in Paris until July, mainly because no airplanes were landing at Orly Airport during the general strike, and later it took time to get a reservation. I finally arrived with my former wife, Bea, and our two children, in the early afternoon of July 13. It was two weeks after the end of the May-June events, but the city still looked as though it was occupied by an army. CRS buses were zigzagged in many Parisian streets, while CRS loitered around in full battle gear, and ordinary police were everywhere. Some of the "flics," to my amazement, were even walking around with submachine guns. I was resting in my room from my journey, when suddenly, to my astonishment, the neighborhood exploded again. My family went down to the Boulevard St.-Michel, where there had been major street fighting in May and June, and they were suddenly caught up in a street fight between young people and the CRS. Near dusk, Bea and I returned to the boulevard, but things had quieted down, apart from some sporadic fighting. After midnight, we and a group of students were caught up in a group of Africans, and the CRS – which was very racist – chased us into the Rue Soufflot, and we escaped them near the Pantheon. By no means had Paris calmed down, that evening; in fact, there were street fights elsewhere in the city for much of the night.[2]

The '68 events in Paris generated considerable controversy in the Left, and it raised many issues that have yet to be sorted out: questions of organization, a public sphere, theory and practice, and the like. I still struggle with these questions today, but that requires a separate discussion.

Anarchism, Marxism, and the Future of the Left

What did you find when you got back the United States?

As I've said, well into 1968, the American movements were divided against each other. To speak of "*the* movement" as existing in 1968 would be naive. There were many different organizations and tendencies, as I've already described: SDS, the Marxists and Leninists, the anarchists, and the lifestylist Motherfuckers, as well as the decaying counterculture, the students, and the national mobilizations led by pacifists, liberals, and social democrats.

After the assassinations of '68 – Martin Luther King and Bobby Kennedy – and black protests all over the country, my *Anarchos* group and our sympathizers took counsel and asked ourselves what was needed. What was needed, I thought, was a *coherent movement*. I didn't mean a monolithic movement, nor one that suppressed factions. I meant one that had a common purpose, and above all, one that recognized that in 1968, contrary to all appearances, the United States was not facing a revolutionary situation. We were not even in what classical Marxists would call a prerevolutionary situation.

We had yet to win the American people over to our views. To the great majority of people, we seemed either crazy and well-meaning at best, or crazy and dangerous at worst. It was very important, I thought, to reach these people, but from their point of view we were offering nothing but chaos, whereas they wanted stability. They weren't starving to death. Blacks were terribly deprived, and understandably they wanted to participate in the economic upswing, but most of them were not revolutionaries. Workers hated us, not only for cultural reasons but because we wanted to close down war production plants and deprive them of their jobs. Most blacks were, at best, indifferent to anarchistic antics, which were utterly unrelated to their problems. Many middle class people – professionals, technicians, and the like – regarded us as clowns who mocked their way of life and provocatively challenged their values.

In the meantime, the American army seemed to be disintegrating. The war seemed futile, and more and more the soldiers were repelled by what they were being asked to do – largely to slaughter Vietnamese people in order to "save" them from Communism. Officers weren't sure they wouldn't get a bullet from behind if they turned their backs on their men.

Rumour circulated that a lot of "fragging," as it was called, was happening, such as throwing a hand grenade in an officer's tent while he was asleep.

A movement was needed that was seriously concerned with changing society, we thought. It had to have stamina and staying power – very important traits of the much-despised Old Left that were clearly lacking in the New Left and were nonexistent in the counterculture. The 1960s organizations, including SDS, were like a revolving door – people went in and out, frequently not even returning to a second meeting. I often didn't see the same faces from one meeting to the next. Although "teach-ins" about the Vietnam War were common, no emphasis was given to general radical education. Everything was spelled out in terms of *action, action, action,* until the phrase "action faction" came into use. The radicals' politics, apart from opposition to the war, were all too often skin deep, and no attempt was being made to deepen them, let alone to teach ordinary people about the broader connections between the various social dislocations – and explaining those connections is what I mean by *coherence.*

Thus the need for a *coherent* movement was very urgent, a movement that would try to communicate with the American people and, unlike the "action faction," recognize that we were not at a point of revolution nor even in a prerevolutionary situation. People were puzzled by us at best and hateful at worst. We were faced with the task, not only of bringing the war to an end, but of explaining countercultural ideas about communal living and sharing, as well as the emancipation of women, ecology, and the nature of work; we had to explain how we would use the enormous wealth of America in a rational way to satisfy everybody's needs and help meet the needs of third world people as well. But above all we had to explain our basic social vision. The *Anarchos* Group was emphasizing ecology at the time and turning out its magazine, issuing analyses, and disputing with other tendencies in "the movement."

The principal arena for our activities was SDS, which clearly attracted the most radical young people in the United States. The Motherfuckers had essentially abandoned that organization because they regarded students as "shit," and were on their way to becoming a self-destructive street gang. The *Anarchos* Group decided to leave them to their own fate.

Anarchism, Marxism, and the Future of the Left

Most of the factions that were competing for dominance within SDS, however, had nothing constructive to offer. The Communists were living in their own world. Progressive Labor, the Maoists, were trying win people over to their own neo-Stalinist program, which may have been hot news in 1934 but was irrelevant in 1968. PL couldn't even come to an agreement with other ultrarevolutionary groups that favored black nationalism and regarded the Black Panthers and the North Vietnamese as the vanguard. They strictly favored the proletariat, which they didn't have. The Black Panthers were strutting around like inflated cocks in a barnyard; they were also being infiltrated by FBI agents and informers on such a scale that if you were talking to a Panther, it was impossible to know whether the person was really a Panther or an FBI informer. Berkeley was drowning in insane revolutionary hysteria, and the counter-culture was drifting more and more toward mysticism: particularly Taoism and Buddhism.

At the end of 1968, our group's most immediate problem was the need to do something about the next annual SDS convention, which was slated for June 1969. We were not students, nor official members of SDS, but by 1969, SDS was so loose organizationally that anyone could attend its conventions if he or she was a known radical. In preparation for the convention, I hastily wrote a pamphlet titled "Listen, Marxist!"[3] in which I tried to use Marx himself against the Marxists, and in turn explain a serious anarchist approach. I didn't put my own name to the pamphlet – it was simply signed "the *Anarchos* Group," and we presented it as a group work. My friend Jim Lanier, who had printed my "Stop the Bomb" leaflet in 1954, agreed to run it off on a large rotary press. I designed a cover that had pictures of Marx, Lenin, Engels, Mao, with Bugs Bunny in the middle eating a carrot. Jim ran off seven thousand of them in about a few hours. We loaded two thousand into a truck and drove off to the convention.

In Chicago SDS had hired a convention hall, the Chicago Coliseum, that looked like a huge armory. The main hall was some two stories high, crisscrossed by steel girders. It was barren and empty, and the acoustics were such that you could yell and get an echo from all four sides. About two thousand people came to the convention.

When it came to admitting participants, SDS had gone rather insane. PL had demanded that no reporters be allowed to enter the hall, and SDS accepted the demand, which meant that the reporters who were covering the conference could not possibly be accurate but instead were free to present everything negative that their readers wanted to believe about SDS – namely that it was totally confused, Marxist, and dangerous. One couldn't get in without being searched, which didn't prevent the Chicago police from infiltrating the convention in plainclothes, often with small cameras, a very common practice. (One time in New York someone pulled over in a car next to me, stepped out, took a photograph of me, and stepped right back into the car again!) Immigration agents wandered around looking for Europeans who they could remove from the country, and they found a few to expel.

Several factions emerged at the convention. There was PL, Progressive Labor, which by sheer effort was gaining as much control over SDS as it could. PL had bused in quite naive people who were persuaded to support the PL positions and packed the convention with them. They were organized into squads, each of which was led by a reliable PL member, and during the conference proceedings the squad leader would tell the innocents what to do – to yell, to scream, to sit, to stand, how to vote, whatever was necessary to give PL the leadership of SDS.

The rest of SDS was tearing itself apart into factions over how to fight PL. One such faction called itself the Revolutionary Youth Movement, or RYM1, which was also known as the Weathermen; they were led by Bernardine Dohrn, Jeff Jones, and Mark Rudd – all well-known SDS leaders. Their strategy was to build up a revolutionary movement by having students reach out to working-class youth. RYM1 was allied with the Black Panthers, which PL was not. Another faction was called RYM2, or Revolutionary Youth Movement 2. It was headed by Mike Klonsky, another SDS leader, and it differed with RYM1 over some minor issues that escape me today. Both groups professed to be Marxist, admired Castro and Mao, but they seemed to differ mainly over tactics.

This three-part division is the version of the convention that appears in accounts such as Kirkpatrick Sale's constipated account *SDS,* but they seem not to know that there was a fourth faction: the Radical

Decentralist Project. This was the faction that the *Anarchos* Group formed at the convention with the SDS members who supported our ideas. We were with neither the PL people nor RYM1 and RYM2 but were trying to work out an independent radical position that tried to seriously address the issues of the 1960s.

When we first arrived at the conference hall, we immediately laid out a literature table and began to distribute the "Listen, Marxist!" pamphlet. Soon we had given away all of the two thousand copies we had brought with us. Many people who read it approached us with warmly commendatory remarks, especially during the second day of the convention. We and the people who sympathized with us decided to meet in the old IWW hall – which may have been near the Coliseum, but I can't remember – to advance an alternative to the Marxist-Leninist-Maoist orientation of the other factions. Accordingly we formed a caucus and wrote a multipage statement, called "The Radical Decentralist Project,"[4] in which we tried to dispel the myth that students are workers, and that SDS had its hand full trying to win its natural student constituency by addressing their needs and fostering an antihierarchical viewpoint rather than a sectarian third world and proletarian point of view. We argued that SDS should address broader issues like ecology, community, libertarian forms of political organization, and so on. It should orient itself primarily toward American problems, we said, and only try to reach people outside the universities and schools who would be most amenable to its ideas.

We passed out this statement and invited people to join us. Eventually our caucus numbered about 250 members, approximately ten percent of the convention participants. The best way to argue our position before the membership of SDS and advance our program, we decided, would be to put up a slate of candidates for SDS national offices. (Since this was the annual national convention, one of the items on the conference agenda was to elect such an executive body.) By running candidates, we hoped to try to reach rational people who were willing to break away from the insane dogmatic sectarian groups, in which middle-class white students were pretending to be black industrial workers. Some of the SDS members who supported our ideas were willing to run. One of them, if I remember correctly, may have been James Miller, who later wrote a fine book on SDS called *Democracy Is in the Streets*.[5]

These were the factions, and the convention itself became a furious battle between them for the spirit of SDS. In fact, between PL and the two RYM groups, the convention turned into a madhouse. People came in holding their Mao Tse-Tung "little red books," and whenever someone behind the lectern said something that angered them, they would throw their books at the speaker.

Finally a leading Black Panther got up and denounced PL – the Panthers were very hostile to PL since the organization was bitterly opposed to black nationalism. In response, PL started screaming "Read Mao!" while others shouted back "Power to the people!" The fracas went on until Bernardine Dohrn ran up to the microphone and announced, apparently on her own initiative, that the RYM1 group was splitting off. After some discussion RYM2 joined them, and then both factions walked out of the Coliseum.

When I came back the next morning, I found that PL was holding its meeting in the main part of the convention hall. They acted as if SDS were still a viable organization, as if their attempt to take it over hadn't played a decisive role in destroying SDS. But I also heard that a second convention was going to meet in another auditorium directly off the larger hall. The fire doors that separated the two halls were partly open, but before I could enter, two SDS squadristas searched me and asked for my credentials – they wanted to keep all PL people out of their new convention.

This new auditorium was already filled up by the time I arrived. Jeff Jones, a former Motherfucker who was now in RYM 1 and soon became a Weatherman chieftain, stood up before the whole group and said, "I hereby declare the opening of the *real* Students for a Democratic Society convention. Who wants the floor?" I raised my hand and was given the floor immediately. I started to give our program, and the people listening cheered me, "Right on, right on!" Another guy followed and started to say the very opposite of what I'd been saying, but irrespective of what was being said, the audience shouted, "Right on, right on!" to everything. I gave up – I realized that we couldn't do anything here, that the Radical Decentralist Project would have to organize an alternative student movement.

Anarchism, Marxism, and the Future of the Left

What was the basic idea behind your talk?

I said that SDS didn't have the support of the American people, that we
would have to carry on a whole educational campaign to win Americans
over to our ideas. In fact, we had to know what our ideas were, to clarify
them, and give them a libertarian thrust. We had to deal with a wider
range of problems than just the war itself. That is not to deny the importance of ending the war, but we had to offer a broad *social* vision and program. We couldn't just sit around and denounce "Amerikkka" with three
k's, as many people at the convention were doing. Americans weren't
going to listen to mindless denunciations of themselves. If SDS was a student organization, I said, then its real base was the campus. There were
campuses all over America, I argued. There were seven million college
students in the United States. SDS could become a mass, nationwide radical movement if it would earnestly try to reach out to them, educate
them, and provide them with a way to formulate their discontents.

I got nowhere. As for the convention, it turned out to be the last one
SDS ever held, and the organization completely fell apart afterward. After
PL was finally isolated, the Weathermen went off on their own, and
RYM2 all but dispersed. I remained in Chicago with the *Anarchos* Group
for a few days – meeting anarchists, who frankly were doing absolutely
nothing – and returned to New York. We decided to call another convention as soon as possible, because we were now in touch with SDS chapters throughout the country, many of which had ignored the convention
and were interested in our ideas.

Arrangements were made to hold a conference in September, only
three months after the Chicago convention, at Black River, Wisconsin.
The site was an open camping area in a state park in Wisconsin, about
eighty miles north of Madison. Our good friends in Madison were prepared to do the local organizing and handle the logistics.

Unfortunately there were grave problems. First of all, when we got to
Black River, we found out that the convention was going to be held, not
indoors in a meeting hall, but in a campground. A huge canvas-type tent
was erected to accommodate the two hundred or so people who showed
up.

It would have been more sensible to hold a conference indoors, where serious work could be done, but some of the participants were eager to "commune" with nature and decided on the campground, which made it hard to do any work. Second, we were obliged to sit in a "non-hierarchical" circle, which meant that instead of a coherent discussion we had a drifting stream of consciousness. Allow me to say that when it comes to political discussion, which has to sort out positions and ideas, this lack of structure is lethal, because it renders a sequential flow of ideas impossible. Someone would say something that required a response, but instead of a response, the next person would say whatever came into his or her head. Before long fifty, sixty, a hundred different issues were raised, and none of them were being responded to. The result was no dialogue, no exploration of problems, no intelligible discourse, no solutions – and no conclusion; just irrelevant words, rhetoric, and exhaustion.

Another problem that arose was the question of writing a statement. It was very plain to us that the conference had to prepare one. Many "movement" newspapers, we were told, were waiting for the Black River conference to provide an alternative to the dissolution of SDS, based on left-libertarian principles. All the conference had to do was write a statement, and it would be published in the underground press, which had about five million readers around the country.

A perfectly good statement was already available for use: the *Anarchos* statement, the magazine's policy statement. It started out by declaring what we wanted and what we stood for – the conference could have modified it if it chose to, and then all it would have had to do was add a line saying, "We offer this alternative after the breakup of SDS." The new organization could have been called the Student Libertarian League, or Students for a Libertarian Society, or something of that sort. (The word *libertarian* had not yet acquired all the right-wing proprietarian connotations it has today. By the way, the word had been invented in Paris in the 1890s by an anarchist, Sebastian Faure, and it really belonged to the anarchists, not to the proprietarians.)

But the *Anarchos* statement was not used, nor was any other existing statement adopted that the group could have endorsed. There is a certain anarchist type with an overbearing ego who believes that it's wrong for any single individual to draft a statement on behalf of a group – even if the group explores, modifies, and votes in favor of the statement. A statement, we are told, must truly be a collective endeavor, so that each member must contribute to it – maybe put in a verb, an adjective, or a comma. Anarchists who held this view were present in sizable numbers at Black River, and they insisted that we follow their procedure, with the result that no statement was ever written.

As if that weren't enough of a problem, the man who had organized many logistical aspects of the conference turned out to have his own agenda. He was influenced by Situationism, and he believed that sexual desire had to have a central place in the conference proceedings. Now there's nothing wrong with desire, obviously, but it can become a huge problem if you try to make it the focus for politics: "Express your desire, an erection is more important than a clenched fist," or "Through desire [or art] we will transform the world," or "No organization, no program, no politics." This man was basically recruiting people from the group to join a more sybaritic one elsewhere in the campground, which thoroughly disrupted the conference. Perhaps they all had an orgy – I don't know.

The serious people who had come to the conference expecting to create an alternative student organization were visibly disappointed, even shaken by this "creative" anarchic chaos. In turn, the man who had started the erotic subconference based on desire irresponsibly took off for California, but this, "politics of desire" became more and more of a problem in the 1970s and 1980s, and it is an enormous problem to this very day.

Thus the conference simply dissolved, and a remarkable chance to create an alternative to SDS slipped away. After 1969 the New Left too deteriorated quickly – without SDS, it had no organizational framework. When the Ohio National Guard killed four young people at Kent State University in 1970, students went on strike all over the country in protest – but that was the last outbreak of the 1960s. After that strike, when many students returned to their parents' homes, their parents apparently told many of them, "Why were you bothering those poor soldiers in the first place? You brought it on yourselves!" Some students told me that their parents actually reproved them instead of the National Guard. It was a shock for them to find out that the country was not with them after all. When I traveled around and talked to ordinary people, I often asked them what they thought of the killings at Kent State. The typical answer was, "The National Guard didn't shoot enough of them."

Actually, Charles Reich in *The Greening of America* tried to explain to ordinary Americans what the counterculture and the New Left were trying to do. But the super-ultrarevolutionaries condemned that book as too liberal. Most of these superrevolutionaries are now lawyers, doctors, and especially professors. What did they want to tell Americans in the 1960s? "Ho, Ho, Ho Chi Minh, dare to struggle, dare to win"?

Around 1970, Greg Calvert, who had helped introduce the student-as-worker myth into SDS, visited me. As he sat on my sofa finishing off a bottle of vodka, he said, "*I'm* responsible for the Weathermen. Carl Davidson and I brought in this idea that SDS should become Marxist, should think in Marxist categories. I feel responsible for the destruction of SDS." Finally, miserable and drunk, he passed out. When I woke up the next day, he was gone. In his recent memoir about those days, he refers to the Motherfuckers as my "students,"[6] when in fact I was arguing with them almost every time we met.

As for the Motherfuckers, they all went their different ways, many drifting to the West Coast. One was killed holding up a liquor store. It wasn't a political act, it was just a criminal one – which he no doubt excused as political. Another Motherfucker became a businessman. Still others drifted off into artistic endeavors, or scattered among communes in the Far West, but finally they all disappeared from sight. The counter-culture drifted off into the New Age and a personalism that ultimately allowed them to be absorbed by the social system.

What lessons do you think should be learned from the 1960s?

The dominant myth of the 1960s was that it marked the beginning of a revolutionary period. Many people in the 1960s thought that revolution was going to happen in six months. Ben Morea once told me, "We've got 20 million blacks, 40 million poor, and 7 million students." After he had practically tallied up the whole U.S. population, I said, "Then why don't you have the revolution already? You have more people on your side than live in the United States right now. Who's left to fight you? LBJ?"

The fact is that there was no revolutionary situation in the 1960s, not even in Paris in 1968, however much we might have wished otherwise. The Parisian Situationists wrongly concluded that a genuine proletarian revolution had come into existence in France in 1968, as though the students and the French working class were prepared to take power and establish a council republic. In the United States blacks were fighting, as understandably they would, to better their lives. Only a few of them were fighting against capitalism. As for the Trotskyists, they were living in 1930, or even 1917. The Maoists were going mad altogether, and many of them quickly accommodated themselves to the existing social order. The RYM1 faction turned into Weatherman, with a theatrical radicalism that ultimately led to the demise of the New Left altogether. The Weatherman members went underground for a while, but when they surfaced, they went back to school and acquired degrees in law, psychology, and the like. Being quite bright, they often acquired good jobs in the very society that they had so adamantly opposed.

All these tendencies of the 1960s had one thing in common: they performed a great deal of theater, nourished by the goodies of the affluent society. But its postscarcity potential was frittered away on theater. They may have played a role in stopping the war in Vietnam, but even from the standpoint of the bourgeoisie, that was a stupid war – the bourgeoisie had nothing to gain from the American invasion of Vietnam. But the government had put its prestige on the line, and it had to prove that no small Asian country could challenge the American superpower with impunity. So it continued to escalate the war with no strategic results, until finally it had to pull out of Vietnam in disgrace.

There are many lessons to be learned from the 1960s, and if they are ignored, then it will be impossible for left-libertarians to create a libertarian communist society. The new society will not be handed to us on a silver platter; it will have to be fought for with all the vigor and resources at our command.

The first lesson was the desperate need for a serious, relevant, and far-seeing social theory that would have given *meaning* to the torrential events of the decade. Owing to the absence of such a theory, the New Left and the more radical elements in the counterculture lacked any understanding of the nature of the situation they faced and any means of foreseeing how events might unfold. If the vulgar Marxist-Leninist slogans that the Maoists and Trotskyists regurgitated deeply penetrated into the New Left, it was because they at least constituted a *theory*, however inadequate. As a result, even though the American working class wasn't doing what Marxists predicted it would, the Maoists and Trotskyists still had a basis for arguing that the proletariat would play the hegemonic role in the future social revolution.

By contrast, most of the American anarchist groups – very few in number as they were – offered little in the way of theory but contented themselves with ad hoc revolutionism based on blind instinct, impassioned zeal, and inchoate militancy. Street fighting was the tactic and strategy of choice, often organized around extremely narrow issues. The most conspicuous anarchist group of that time, the Motherfuckers, were simply a street gang that linked itself to, maligned, and finally broke with SDS, then simply faded away.

To the extent that American anarchists possessed a theory of social change, it was largely communitarian – a program of changing capitalist society by instituting presumably independent print shops, food coops, head shops, and even libertarian farms, organized along egalitarian and cooperative lines. As it happened, many of these efforts so absorbed the energies of young people that, exhausted, they shut them down and ultimately found jobs in the academy or business. Such enterprises, even when they were kept afloat, became capitalistic enterprises in their own right.

The communitarian strategy may have seemed feasible a century and a half ago, in Proudhon's day – although even then it failed, despite sizable cooperative socialist movements in both England and France. Almost every communitarian venture founded since Robert Owen has either folded up or become a capitalistic enterprise. Today, in an era of transnational corporate mergers and massive capital concentration, no libertarian credit union could possibly challenge Chase Manhattan, and no auto repair coop could possibly dream of undermining a General Motors repair outlet.

During the 1960s a strong revolutionary theory could have reminded young idealists of this dismal history and steered them away from channeling their revolutionary energy into futile endeavors. As it was, however, the 1960s generation fell into this trap once again, just as socialists have fallen into it for 150 years. Even today anarchists all over the place, seemingly oblivious to the lessons of revolutionary history, continue to preach communitarian doctrines.

The next lesson that should be learned as a matter of immense importance is the need for a responsible, committed, clearly structured revolutionary organization. Such an organization is not contrary to libertarian communist goals.

Finally it is vital to learn from the 1960s that we must avoid the marginalization and juvenilization that marked so many aspects of the New Left and the counterculture and instead enter into the public sphere, there to develop a vital libertarian politics. We have to be a living presence in our neighborhoods, cities, and towns, and we have to address problems of social change based not simply on the passing adventures of adolescents but on the real experiences of ordinary people. Such a political presence must be consistent with left-libertarian principles and, as I would later find, it had to be developed out of the communalism inherent in the best traditions of the Left, in such a way that the revolutionary means conform with the ends. Already during the late 1960s I was exploring the institutions that would constitute "The Forms of Freedom," and in the early 1970s I moved on to ideas that foreshadowed libertarian municipalism, in "Spring Offensives and Summer Vacations."[7]

No such left emerged in the United States during the 1960s. The Motherfuckers were a chaotic street gang that faded away after a few years. After the collapse of SDS, the *Anarchos* Group tried to create at least a nationwide network, but these efforts were destroyed by what I would later call lifestyle anarchists, who were to identify their libidinal impulses with politics.

I am deeply concerned to this day that the wrong lessons have been learned from the 1960s: instead of the ones I have named, many libertarian radicals have developed *real* dogmas against organization, theory, and attempts to reach the public in an organized way. Incidents, events, and "happenings" are no substitute for systematic work and organization.

Nor can artistic movements provide a direction for masses of people who are searching for new social perspectives. Innumerable avowedly anarchistic aesthetic groups in the 1960s thought that they would "blow people's minds" with street theater, psychedelic art, "happenings," squats, new lifestyles, and the like. In the end, they were wholly ineffective. Bourgeois clothing designers simply understudied them and commercialized their art for the delectation of the middle classes.

In short, there is no substitute for a well-organized, responsible movement, a coherent body of ideas to guide it, a systematic practice that recognizes the need for patience and persistence – and an awareness that it must provide leadership. I believe all of these needs can be satisfied in a libertarian way. But without such a movement, basic social change will never be achieved, and we will fail again, as in the 1960s. Certainly in its absence, our views will never be taken seriously by oppressed people, and we will be outmaneuvered by the bourgeoisie with little difficulty.

Notes

1. Paul Goodman, "The Black Flag of Anarchy," *New York Times Sunday Magazine*, July 14, 1968, pp. 10ff.

2. On the July 13 skirmishes, see John L. Hess, "De Gaulle Insists on Public Order," *The New York Times*, July 14, 1968, page 1.

3. "Listen, Marxist" is reprinted in *Post-Scarcity Anarchism*.

4. This document was later published as the Radical Decentralist Project, resolution no. 1, "Toward a Post-Scarcity Society: The American Perspective and the SDS," in Howard J. Ehrlich et al., *Reinventing Anarchy: What Are Anarchists Thinking These Days?* 1st ed. (London and Boston: Routledge and Kegan Paul, 1979), pp. 120-26.

5. James Miller, *"Democracy Is in the Streets": From Port Huron to the Siege of Chicago* (New York: Simon and Schuster, 1987).

6. Gregory Nevala Calvert, *Democracy from the Heart* (Eugene, OR: Communitas Press, 1991), p. 245.

7. "The Forms of Freedom" was published in *Anarchos*, no. 2 (Spring 1968) and republished in *Post-Scarcity Anarchism* (1971). "Spring Offensives and Summer Vacations" was published in *Anarchos*, no. 4 (1972).

Part II

The New Social Movements

Deep Ecology, Lifestyle Anarchism, and Postmodernism

Interviewer: Doug Morris

You have been describing the high hopes of the New Left and the countercul-
ture in the 1960s. After the shipwreck of SDS, what happened to all those
hopes?

After the 1960s a sea change occurred that virtually submerged the
intense degree of social commitment of that decade, leaving us with the
reaction, quietism, and mysticism of the 1990s. Gone was the sense of
empowerment, social as well as personal, that had been generated by the
movements of the 1960s and early 1970s. Gone, too, was the fervent
rhetoric in support of social change, indeed of revolution, that New Left
militants and the more politicized elements of the counterculture
expressed to seemingly enthusiastic audiences.

The various tendencies that made up the 1960s "movement" weren't
actually destroyed – they became more particularized. Even as SDS was
falling apart, a new movement was emerging: the feminist movement.
Women in SDS, like women in other areas of American society, refused
to be relegated to deadening office chores. They refused to be mere typ-
ists and mimeograph operators while the men were free to do all the
thinking. For a while SDS men mocked their female colleagues for making these troubling demands, even for having these aspirations. As the
women's movement developed, however, the men, especially Marxists,
attacked it for dividing the proletariat along gender lines.

As young SDS women became more insistent, their ideas began to spread. Shulamith Firestone published *The Dialectic of Sex,* and Kate Millett wrote *Sexual Politics* – Millett's book in particular had an immense impact on many radicals. Soon large numbers of women, outside the student movement and the New Left, were influenced by Betty Friedan's *The Feminine Mystique* and Simone de Beauvoir's formerly neglected *The Second Sex.* Even liberal women wanted to emancipate themselves from the drudgery of the household and from the narrowness of suburban life.

I warmly supported the radical feminist movement, not only for opening up to women the chance for full participation in the same areas of life as men, but most especially *for opposing hierarchy.* In its earliest form radical feminism demanded a nonhierarchical society in which women could achieve their full potential as *people,* not as a particular group.

When the ecology movement appeared after 1970, I hoped it too would become antihierarchical and anticapitalist. I had been advancing precisely such a view since the early 1960s, contending over and over again that there is an intimate relationship between the quality of the environment and the nature of the society in which we live. I argued that human beings have the potential to become self-conscious, rational, and humanistic in the best sense of these words – and in the sense that humanity, although a unique life-form, is still part of natural evolution.

Like the civil rights movement, the feminist and ecology movements began very auspiciously, but over time they began to lose their generous humanism and universalism. Consider the feminist movement, for example – and I'm speaking about feminists who consider themselves radicals, not the liberals, who still make up the overwhelming majority of what are called feminists in this society – that is to say, who simply want to make the existing system more equitable for women. In the late 1970s and early 1980s many radical feminists – by no means all of them, but many – began to retreat into a mystical, supposedly feminist spiritualism that encouraged women to find the hidden goddess within themselves, either within their psyche or within nature at large. These mystical feminists inveighed against the "dualism" of patriarchal religions such as Judaism and Christianity and maintained that through a pantheistic spiritualism, using practices of contemplation and ritual, they would transcend "male" rationalism and discover the mystical forces that bound women to the cosmos. In point of fact neither of these supposed innovations of goddess worship transcended dualism – they simply preserved beliefs in the supernatural, whether within the human psyche or in the world at large. Presumably this feminist spiritualism was to pose a threat to the patriarchal social order. Men were supposed to tremble at the thought of women's elemental and mysterious powers.

Frankly, I have to admit that for a time I wanted to believe that women had a "special" relationship to first nature, or that they were "closer to nature" than men, especially when ecofeminist ideas were on the rise during the 1970s. I had been influenced in this regard by the work of Robert Briffault, a Marxist anthropological writer, as far back as the 1930s. But I no longer agree with this idea, and I retract the statements I made to that effect. First of all, women are not "closer to nature" than men – that's nonsense. Second, the idea that they have some "special" connection to first nature has been used not to create a new Left, a new rationality, a new politics, and a new universalism, but quite to the contrary, to perpetuate patriarchal stereotypes of women's inferiority, to generate this new goddess-worshipping spiritualism, and to create a women's particularism, like the particularism that Black Power had created among blacks in the 1960s civil rights movement.

Such mystifications developed a wide influence in the 1970s and especially the 1980s, resulting in the current plague of "identity politics," in which different ethnic, national, and gender groups cultivated whole outlooks specific to their own kind. Rather than taking a social approach to the world, people were moving into a mystical realm, in which specific ethnic and gender groups viewed the world according to their own "identity." Such groups often wrote or rewrote history to suit their agendas and mysterious, exclusive ways of seeing the world. Identity politics is so pluralistic that it dissolves reality into incoherence, dividing the oppressed against each other, on the basis of gender, skin color, and the like. I do not regard this development as having anything to do with the Left.

As for the ecology movement, about which I've written at length elsewhere: certain Green tendencies drenched in mysticism were turning it from a serious radical social movement that could be part of a new New Left, into a cult of romantic nature-worship. Not only were these tendencies mystical, but they tended to blame human beings as such for the ecological crisis, and they saw their own role as a defense of "the Earth" against human beings. So greatly did they identify themselves with "the Earth" that they become harshly antihumanistic. In effect, they pined after a natural world that had not been altered by human beings, as if human beings were not part of the natural world itself and as if many of their activities were not endowments of natural evolution.

Any idea that tries to elevate other beings to the level of human beings, or give them rights or consciousness or feelings equivalent to those of human beings, by its very nature diminishes the importance of human uniqueness. At the same time, elevating nonhuman beings to a status equal to human beings is absurd anthropomorphism, often attributing to nonhuman life-forms qualities that are specific to human beings. In this respect, deep ecology is implicitly misanthropic. Many people who call themselves deep ecologists today object to this accusation, but I've found that they usually haven't read the literature that deep ecology writers have been producing.

What are your specific criticisms of deep ecology?

What marks deep ecology is its notion of "biocentrism" – the claim that no life-form has any more "intrinsic worth" than any other. I fail to see how one can challenge this view and still be a deep ecologist. Deep ecologists believe that human beings are morally equatable with, say, squirrels in terms of their "intrinsic worth." To deep ecologists, those who raise objections to biocentrism are necessarily anthropocentric – that is, they claim that the world was "created" to meet human needs and that it exists for them to pillage and plunder without compunction. Accordingly, if I reject biocentrism and call upon people to create an ecological society, in which they live cooperatively both with each other and with the natural environment, I'm called anthropocentric for daring to make such a humanistic proposal. I refuse to accept these two choices – biocentrism and anthropocentrism – into which deep ecologists want to classify all ecological ideas. As I have written elsewhere, I do not accept "centricity" – I merely look at the evolutionary qualities that characterize various life-forms.

If human beings are superior to other life-forms, it is because they have more consciousness and therefore more potentiality for innovation and freedom. But saying that doesn't mean giving them a "license" to destroy everything around them, or to be unfeeling about other life-forms. On the contrary, it places upon humans the responsibility to do something that no other species in the natural world does: to look out for the needs of other creatures, even at times when it may conflict with their own self-interest.

When deep ecologists talk about "nature" and defending the "earth," they very often mean "wilderness." That is certainly ironic, because the truth is that wilderness has essentially disappeared. If we have to protect an area by putting a fence around it, either a physical or a legal one, that designates it as "wilderness," then we have already canceled out the reality of authentic wilderness.

Yellowstone Park, for example, is not a wilderness. To begin with, bison don't belong in Yellowstone Park all year round. They are migratory animals that require vast areas in which to live. The vast migrations of millions of bison around the time of Lewis and Clark were one of the great spectacles of the West. They crossed thousands of miles, from one feeding ground to another. To confine several hundred bison to Yellowstone Park is a travesty of "wilderness" – and a quintessential human artifice.

Nor are elk perpetual inhabitants of one area. As for grizzly bears, for a while the ones that lived in Yellowstone Park were dependent on the garbage of tourists for food. When garbage dumps were cleared away, the grizzlies began to wander out of the park, where they were shot, and now all kinds of techniques have to be used to keep them in the park area. So even though wild *animals* still exist, wilderness as an overall *reality* is gone.

You have also spoken vigorously against mysticism.

Today mysticism is not simply confined to the feminist and ecology movements, it's part of the general Euro-American culture. People by the millions are now consulting astrologers and fortune-tellers on a regular basis, often calling up the 900 numbers that they see advertised on cable TV. Maybe they're asking these charlatans how to win at the racetrack or on the stock market – who knows?

It's interesting to examine closely the predictions that many so-called psychics make. They actually phrase them in vague generalities and try to cover all possible bases, with the result that it is difficult to judge whether they are right or wrong. It's a technique that has been used by shamans and priests for thousands of years: they make predictions in such a way that at least *something* will ring true. I found out about it by reading the *I Ching* from beginning to end. A typical entry might read something like, "Today is going to be a good but unhappy day for you in which you are going to be very merry but also sad, and you are going to have wonderful memories, but you will also have to think about your misfortunes." Or: "It's going to be a momentous day for you, although it may seem as if nothing is happening, because you will see the consequences only ten years from now" – and other such nonsense.

Let me assure you that when I criticize eastern religions and popular superstitions, I'm not doing so for the sake of defending Christianity or Judaism, please understand that. I do not believe in any supernatural beings; indeed, as a social ecologist, I believe only in social and natural phenomena.

What about primitivism?

By primitivism, I suspect you mean a kind of spirituality that bases itself on what it regards as the more "natural" or "primal" outlook of human prehistory. During the Pleistocene, exponents of this mysticism tell us, human beings lived in harmony with a pristine natural world, free from civilization's artifices. Civilization was the cause of the ecological crisis, in this outlook, and therefore in order to become more ecological, we should adopt the lifeways or at least the sensibility and consciousness of prehistoric peoples, especially in the Paleolithic, Neolithic, or even Pleistocene eras.

One problem with this argument is that these ancestral peoples are gone forever, so that we know very little about their lifeways. In fact, we can only surmise what prehistoric values and consciousness were. We can draw parallels between prehistoric peoples and existing aboriginal groups that have been studied by anthropologists, but these parallels merely help us make suppositions about the sensibilities that existed among our distant ancestors, or individual tribal groups. I tried to specu-late about prehistoric sensibilities in *The Ecology of Freedom*: within indi-vidual tribes, I wrote, aboriginal peoples probably had a wonderful sense of complementarity, and they carefully tended to the needs of the sick, the elderly, and the weak. They appear to have practiced usufruct and sharing, making certain that each person had enough food and shelter with which to live.

But *between* different tribal groups, this situation was very different. Warfare was fierce, widespread, and chronic. Very few prehistoric people had long lifespans, as the archaeological record shows. Paleopathologists have found no human remains from those eras that support the belief that human beings survived beyond the age of fifty – and most died or were killed much earlier than that. Nor were their relations with nonhu-man nature necessarily the epitome of harmony – people were probably preyed upon by animals as much as they preyed on them. Certainly dur-ing the Paleolithic the night hours were filled with perils from big cats and cave bears. An accident that could be treated very easily using mod-ern methods today would often lead to death.

Those who prescribe mystical neoprimitivism are less concerned about changing society that in changing people's inner lives. They are telling us to look inside ourselves and discover our own "real" selves, our "natural," ecological selves, and tap into our "mysterious" creative powers. To do so, we apparently have to shed the psychic layers that civilization has imposed on us for thousands of years – civilization being responsible for our problems – and peel away our various civilized attributes, much like an onion, until we get to our innermost "core." If we do so, assuming this is possible, we are likely to find very little in the core, if anything, but our barest physical attributes, instincts, and emotions.

Human beings are *social* beings. We have no "natural" inner "self" that exists apart from the society, the civilization, in which we live, whether we accept its values and lifeways or are in revolt against them. This is true for even the most militant individualist. What we do have is the ability to develop intellectually, to absorb knowledge, to become emotionally mature, and above all to *innovate* and *create*. For that we require the presence of other people. We are the most social creatures that ever existed. Our ability to reason and innovate is what makes us uniquely human, in contrast to animals, which are largely guided by instinct and the imperatives of adaptation.

Why has there been, seemingly, such a large rise in spiritualistic and mystical beliefs in the past few decades?

For the same reason that mysticism ran rampant when Rome was falling apart. Even though we're removed from that period by almost two thousand years, we live amidst similar cultural conditions: barbarism, mysticism, and cultural decadence.

Of course, the current decay takes a form that is very specific to our own time. Normally people are tied to one another by their feelings, communities, and a generous capacity for empathy. In precapitalist societies people related to one another through feelings and community ties. Under capitalism, however, commodification severs all the ties created by feeling and community, decomposing them, just as microbes cause a corpse to decay. Capitalism turns the organic into the inorganic, so to speak, and mineralizes our relationships and social lives. It fetishizes commodities as substitutes for genuine social ties.

Thus people come to relate to one another through things. If we're unhappy, we are advised to buy a new outfit or household device, and then we'll feel better. The family mutates into a unit of consumption. Acquiring an education is reduced to training for earning an income; gaining one's livelihood often involves the exploitation of other people and plundering the natural world. Friendships are reduced to relationships designed to advance one's career. Commodification, in short, replaces genuine social ties to such an extent that things seem to preside over human relationships, as Marx observed, instead of human beings administering the disposition of things.

In despair, people turn to belief in a deity, or to their surrogates, to priests or priestesses, or to professional psychics and mystics. It's no wonder that the United States, probably the most consumerist society that has ever existed, is also extremely religious, or at least mystical. Well over ninety percent of Americans claim to believe in God, and an equivalent number in angels. In the vacuous lives of such people – for whom commodities substitute for meaningful relationships – religion is an anodyne.

In the Western industrialized countries, the mystical revival is primarily a substitute for the creation of a politics that would otherwise genuinely empower people. Thus, rather than entering into a political sphere, trying to change the society around them, to destroy the disease – capitalism – and replace it with a new social order, people today are more likely to turn inward, in their despair, and to belief in a god.

But even their gods are commodities! People turn to pathetic designer deities, much as they buy designer jeans. They take Jesus and make him look like a middle-class yuppie, they give him blond hair – as though in Israel two thousand years ago blue-eyed blondes were running around ancient Judea! Jesus was not a Viking, the poor chap was a Jew! And he certainly wasn't a yuppie. But they redesign their Jesuses to look like themselves. They also have their designer beliefs, most of which are tailor made to suit their own needs and images of themselves.

Or perhaps they look for the god or goddess within themselves – pagan, Christian, or otherwise. And again, what they usually find is a psychological vacuum. Capitalism commercializes emotions by placing a dollar sign on everything people believe or feel. It not only creates the desperation that drives people to look within instead of at society, but it also tries to profit from the aspirations that surge within and yearn for meaning and significance.

Any decadent time produces decadent ideologies. In our decadent times the specific decadent ideology is, I believe, a narcissistic individualism, an assertion of autonomy. We have to be autonomous as consumers and autonomously choose from among the various commodities offered to us for sale, if we wish to be fashionable. But of course individuals have no say in which commodities they buy – in the process of choice. Individuals are *not* self-governing, as everyday life very clearly teaches us. Most of us wake up to an alarm clock and work ten or twelve hours a day – the eight-hour day is essentially gone for millions of people. Today the working day keeps growing longer and longer. Many people even take their oppressions home and work for fifteen hours a day at a home office, or they take their work on vacation with them, using laptop computers and cell phones to stay in touch with the office while they lie on a beach.

Today capitalism and commodification are trivializing people to a remarkable extent. We have only to listen to what constitutes "quality" political conversation today, such as public television's "talking heads" shows, to find that they too are trivial, often shockingly so. The egoism, the narcissism, the psychotherapeutic mentality that are all so typical of our society today are symptoms of our trivialization. One of our most important first tasks, as revolutionaries, is to "detrivialize" ourselves and others, so to speak, to recover the great revolutionary traditions that once existed when people devoted their lives to creating a better society.

Is there an active anarchist movement in the United States that people can turn to, and if so, what is its status?

No, not in the United States, if by a "movement" you mean an organiza- tion and a body of social ideas that are even minimally coherent. These are the worst of times in the history of anarchism, worse than any I have either read about or experienced. At best there is an anarchist "scene," but there's no movement.

The real question we face is, what *is* anarchism?

Today anarchism is more of an ambience than an organized move- ment. There are many people who call themselves anarchists and simply rush into streets with bricks, smash windows, or try to beat up cops – and usually get beaten up mercilessly by cops. They set garbage cans on fire, wave black flags, and proclaim that they are doing something impor- tant – and then disappear, having had absolutely *no* impact on the com- munity in which they live.

It seems to me that these kinds of anarchists are basically having fun. By throwing bricks, by making "temporary autonomous zones," they create the illusion that they are free for a single moment. They go from one sporadic action to another. I'd like to think that Bakunin or Kropotkin would have been shocked by this kind of nonsense and rejected it firmly. Certainly capitalism can live comfortably with these "happenings." They are really forms of release from the monotony of life and, however meagerly, they supply an outlet for the frustration it produces.

In time, many of these anarchists grow up and become CEOs or stockbrokers or corporate lawyers, as Jerry Rubin did in the later years of his life. As a man I knew who was a Parisian '68-er told me, "We had our fun in '68, and now it's time to grow up" – by which he meant enter into the system. This person was in his early twenties in May-June 1968 and was an activist who helped build barricades – and at that time he pompously declaimed how "revolutionary" he was by comparison with other people. Now he is in his forties, well-off financially, and says '68 was merely "fun."

In fact, I strongly disagree with some of the people who call themselves anarchists today as much as I disagree with Marxists. I disagree with them very fundamentally, even if they claim, like me, to be against the State. Antistatism isn't enough. Many reactionaries and even corporate bandits are against State intervention too. In my view, unless socialism is an integral part of anarchism, then anarchism becomes self-indulgence. Anarchists who aren't socialists might as well just call themselves individualists. Hakim Bey even invokes Max Stirner, who believed that the concerns of the ego – the "I" – should be the guide of all human action.

Anarchist Stirnerites today tend to call for autonomy, notably personal autonomy, a word that is easy to misconstrue. In ancient Greek, *auto* means "self" and *nomos* means "law"; *autonomos* means "self-regulation." *Autonomy* today usually means the individual's right to do as he or she pleases, as though one's very wishes and desires were independent of cultural factors. The word often expresses the bourgeois claim to have the right to use the world as one pleases. Presumably this bourgeois right is qualified by the restriction that, in the process, one cannot impinge on someone else's autonomy. But it's never quite clear what someone else's autonomy is. If you make a mere *judgment* about what their autonomy is, then you may very well be restricting their autonomy, according to some anarchists – and bourgeois.

I prefer the word *freedom,* in which the full development of individuality rests on the richness of the communal social structure in which a person lives. This kind of individuality long existed in Spanish villages, for example, where the people developed considerable individuality through a rich community life, joined with an intense sense of mutual responsibility and mutual aid. This freedom was born not out of anarchist theory but out of the whole tradition of the cohesive Spanish village. When I traveled in Spain, in second-class train cars, each person I met seemed to me to be a deeply etched, rich, unique individual. All together, their uniqueness was a product of the collectivity into which they were born and was nourished by the support of the community. The word *freedom* embraces that sense of collectivity as well as the individuality it can produce.

Stirner viewed the autonomous ego as existing in an asocial world. In my view, the ego is in great part the result of historical development, and the emergence of its modern form resulted from a process that required centuries of social evolution. Whether individualistic anarchists want to admit it or not, Western culture, including its radical culture, draws from ancient Greek and Hebrew traditions – and it is also drawn from the Christian tradition, in which all people's souls are considered equal in the eyes of God. At least the idea of equality has been retained within Christian doctrine, if only as a vision if not a reality, and in some periods it became a very important revolutionary vision. Many Christian revolutionaries during the late Middle Ages turned the medieval world upside down with peasant insurrections, and the like.

Stirner's individual ego, existing in an ahistorical, asocial vacuum, is, in my opinion, pure rubbish and could be used to justify *any* behavior, even reactionary behavior. Yet today anarchists like Hakim Bey invoke Stirner's name with admiration. Such people have every right in the world to call themselves anarchists (which may be a major unresolved problem with anarchism itself). Indeed, a lot of them even think anarchism is incompatible with democracy. They, as well as other anarchists, identify democracy with majority rule, and when they hear the word, they leap almost reflexively to the conclusion that democracy is oppressive – that when people vote to make a decision on an issue, the majority "dominates" the minority, even if majority rule is designed to foster fairness in collective decision-making, with the widest latitude of expression. They therefore conclude that democracy is incompatible with anarchism.

Others believe that organization itself is incompatible with anarchism. I have seen anarchists disrupt meetings and even break them up because they objected to orderly discussion. This may be marvelous Dadaism, but it's political disaster. What *is* compatible with their anarchism, I wonder: a temporary autonomous zone? the expression of one's inner self and desires? in effect, allowing one's bourgeois ego to express itself "imaginatively"?

Inasmuch as many anarchists now are not in any sense socialists or communists, it is no longer presupposed that anarchism is a kind of socialism. To those who want their anarchism to involve something more than an assertion of personal autonomy, I strongly advise them to place a qualifying adjective in front of the word. I would suggest that socialistic anarchists call themselves "social anarchists" or "socialist anarchists" or "communist anarchists," to distinguish themselves from these individualistic anarchists who are on the rise within anarchism today.

Another problem is the anarchist tendencies that follow a markedly antitechnological direction. This is absurd – especially at a time when science and engineering are rushing ahead in an unending technological revolution. We now have ongoing industrial revolutions, gaining knowledge of the secrets of life, using instantaneous communication networks, and developing automated technologies that, used to serve human needs instead of those of capital, could free all humanity from onerous and deadening toil.

Technophobes, be they anarchists or not, believe that technology as such is the primary source of social ills, that its uses are not determined by the society in which it exists but rather that it has autonomous imperatives of its own. These alleged imperatives are invariably viewed as socially destructive. But technology, or "industrial society," is not the primary source of our social ills – what drives technology in a destructive direction is not technology itself but the capitalist economic system in which that technology is embedded. Capitalism already existed and was doing a great deal of harm even before the Industrial Revolution, even before the steam engine came into wide use. What we should blame on the marketplace and competition – on the capitalist system of accumulation and production – the technophobes blame on technology.

You have recently been accused of being a technocrat. What is your response?

This is pure nonsense. I do not mindlessly or reverentially accept all technological development. Technology can definitely be used to oppress people. What concerns me is damning technology *as such* – as the cause of all contemporary social ills. This simple-minded view obscures more than it reveals. Technology is basically a function of society, and the uses of most technologies are overwhelmingly conditioned by the society in which they exist. I'm not saying that *all* technologies are socially neutral. Nuclear power plants are inherently bad because of their wastes, and they should be eliminated. I would also like to see the advanced weaponry that we have in the world today disappear in a free and rational society.

But other technologies that many people criticize, I would actually preserve – after getting rid of the economic system that today drives their use to the maximum. Motor vehicles, for example, are very useful. What I would change is the social system that markets them to us incessantly, that arranges life so that they seem necessary, at the expense of public transportation. I would certainly change the energy source that powers them – I'd convert them from fossil fuels to nonpolluting or renewable fuels. And I don't think they should be used as conventional forms of transportation. I'd rethink the American urban and suburban landscape so that people are no longer dependent on motor vehicles but instead could use mass transportation. I'd like to see far fewer people cooped up in their own little vehicle-capsules and encourage much closer integration of home, work, and recreation, so that people could walk or bicycle to their workplaces. But for some purposes, motor vehicles are indispensable, like getting a sick person to the emergency room, for example, or traveling in the byways of the countryside.

And when an important message has to be transmitted quickly, electronic communications technology is indispensable. And to keep masses of people from having to perform arduous labor from childhood until they sicken at an early age, highly productive and automated technologies are also indispensable.

The antitechnological tendency in contemporary anarchism is actually antidemocratic in certain respects. Advanced technologies in a rational society could allow people the free time they require to actively participate in self-managing political institutions. Thousands of years ago Aristotle said very perceptively that when looms can weave by themselves, and when lyres can play music by themselves, we will no longer need slaves. Of course, slavery disappeared in the Western world before the Industrial Revolution, but Aristotle's statement was one of the most profound that that very profound thinker ever made. Today, not only can looms weave by themselves, and not only can lyres play by themselves, but we have technologies that relieve most forms of toil, which potentially gives people the free time they need to manage their own communities, instead of handing power over to elites to run their lives for them. When technophobes object to technologies that diminish human toil, then of necessity they're asking for a restoration of that toil, with all its attendant miseries, including a surrender of political power.

The claim is sometimes made that, far from freeing people from toil, machines are actually forcing people to work intensively. But that, like the denunciation of technology, is preposterous. Capitalism is responsible for the fact that the machines are used to make people work intensively. When Jerry Mander blames a machine for the fact that a worker works intensively, for example, he is obscuring the fact that behind that machine is a CEO and a board of directors that is trying to make a profit at the expense of labor, rather than serve human needs.

You have also been accused of being a Western hyperrationalist. How do you answer this accusation?

Yes, I'm a product of Western culture, I believe in the importance of rationality, and yes, I believe that science is a way of arriving at the truth about objective reality. That hardly means that I think the world should be turned into a huge factory or a scientific laboratory, or even that science is the exclusive way to learn about reality. It's true that scientists can be bought and sold as easily as stockbrokers and lawyers, but science is also a very solid way of learning about reality, and it can't be regarded as totally conditioned by social factors, including bourgeois interests.

Today I find it particularly necessary to emphasize the importance of reason because a tide of irrationality is sweeping over our society. Remember what irrationality produced in earlier times: it gave Germans the Nazi Nuremburg rallies, in which thousands of uniformed men shouted "Sieg heil" to Hitler, revered the folk community of the Nordic race, and viewed all other people – especially Jews – as inferior to themselves. Irrationalism in politics is one of the major preconditions for fascism, given its "blood and soil" notions and beliefs in racial superiority. Neither the ecology movement nor other allegedly radical movements are immune to authoritarian developments, and some of their ideas have a frightening kinship to reaction. I already see radicals who fetishize nature and a spiritualism that leads to a loss of rationality, with marked parallels to some of the thinking that fed into National Socialism. Regressions back to the mystical, the mythic, the irrational, and the primitive frighten me – and they are all too common today among eco-anarchists and eco-feminists.

And that you favor civilization.

As I wrote in *The Ecology of Freedom,* the failings of civilization have been enormous and have claimed a ghastly toll in blood. But let us recognize that civilization has also had a progressive side: it emancipated us, to a great extent, from social arrangements based on blood ties, and it has freed us, to some extent, from ideas rooted in the sinister demonic forces that long haunted the human imagination and that gave rise to religious and political persecution and bloody wars.

Our problem today is not that human beings are too civilized – rather, our problem is that *they aren't civilized enough*. It's not that people are anthropocentric – it's that they are not really humanistic. We fail to recognize our own human potentialities; we have not yet risen to the level

of that compassion, understanding, ethical behavior, and rationality that
would lead to the creation of a new society and a rich, fecund relationship with the natural world.

*Bakunin said that "the two most precious human qualities are the power to
reason and the power to rebel." In the intellectual world these days, rebellion
seems to have turned to texts, to something called postmodernism, which, as
far as I can tell, has little to do with reason but is highly irrational. What's
your take on postmodernism?*

To begin with, there's no single unified body of postmodernist ideas, no
one text that give us the last word on postmodernism, just as there's no
single *text* that is the definitive work on communism: Marx had his version, as did Kropotkin and other people, and some of them wrote books
and essays on the subject long before Marx and Kropotkin. The same is
true of postmodernism.[1]

Before I can talk about postmodernism, I have to say something
about modernism. Prior to 1968, the word *modernity* generally referred
to the Enlightenment and its social and political elaboration after the
mid-seventeenth century: not only to the industrial capitalist social
order that it accompanied but also to the socialist and other revolutionary movements that tried to translate Enlightenment ideas into an alternative, noncapitalist social order. The Enlightenment had many
shortcomings, but it was nonetheless a tremendous movement in civiliz-
ing humanity and making it aware of the importance of reason.

While the Enlightenment made possible so-called bourgeois-demo-
cratic states, as well as the rationalization and instrumentalization of life
that we associate with the more oppressive aspects of modernity, it also
advanced the ideal of a rational society, which was spelled out either in
political terms, such as the French slogan "Liberty, equality, fraternity," or
in socialist and communist terms, such as the maxim "From each according to ability, to each according to need." In all these forms, the
Enlightenment gave expression to the ideal of a society that would be
guided by reason, a world based on justice and equality before the law.

These ideals scored a decisive advance over the pre-Enlightenment mentality, which had believed that some people are innately inferior to others and, accordingly, must obey their superiors. The Enlightenment favored technological development, even the control of natural forces, in the interest of human progress. It was thus a glorious project, notwithstanding its flaws, which are understandable within the context of its time.

The earliest major reaction against the Enlightenment project occurred in the early nineteenth century. The Romantic movement was anti-Enlightenment in that it rejected rationality, technology, and a belief in progress. Instead of rationality, most Romantics placed great emphases on emotions and intuitions as ways of apprehending reality; instead of looking to science for ways to improve human welfare, they often looked to religion – including pantheism, paganism, and mysticism – for ways to care for the soul; and instead of looking toward the more advanced and enlightened future that human beings were capable of creating, they revered the Middle Ages – Sir Walter Scott's *Ivanhoe* and other such stories recreated a colorful but naive image of the glories of medievalism. Another part of the Romantic movement was aesthetic in that it endowed the individual artist with quasi-mystical attributes.

Postmodernism is the latest incarnation of the Romantic rejection of the Enlightenment. Its roots lie in the antirational, implicitly antitechnological outlook of the early nineteenth century, although some postmodernist texts date the origins of postmodernism as far back as Montesquieu and Rousseau. In any event, the floodgates of postmodernism were opened in France after the May-June 1968 events: the uprising of the students and the two-month general strike in which some 8 to 12 million workers went out.

The appearance of postmodernism in France, especially after '68, is a story that has yet to be fully told. The Stalinists, as I've said in my discussion of the 1960s, opposed the '68 uprising, and in all practical respects they proved to be collaborators with Charles De Gaulle against the workers and students. The Communist trade union, the CGT (General Confederation of Labor), tried to keep the students separated from the workers – and it tried to control the workers, bringing them back to work and trying to turn an essentially social general strike into a narrowly economic one. Many French radicals who were Marxists of one sort or another – either dissidents or those who had rejected Marxism altogether in favor of a different kind of socialism – were terribly shaken by the Communists' behavior, and by the queasiness of the Socialists. I am reminded in particular of the "Socialism or Barbarism" group, which had dissolved by 1968 but whose members played a much greater and more creative role in '68 than the widely touted Situationists.

Some of these people – not exclusively "Socialism or Barbarism," but others associated with dissident Marxist groups – were so revolted by the behavior of the Communists that they made what was nearly a 180-degree reversal in their thinking away from Communism. Not only did they become anti-Communists; they rejected Marxism itself. And not only did they reject Marxism, but in some cases they rejected the entire Enlightenment project, of which Marxism was a vital part. For example, since Marxism was, in part, a theory of history, they didn't just provide a different theory of history or a different account of history; they rejected the very legitimacy of seeing history as a meaningful development. They found it impossible to sort out the progressive from the regressive aspects of history, let alone see in history any dialectic or continuity. And since Marxism was a theory of progress and was grounded in rationality, they generally repudiated progress and the role of rationality in historical development. I am only too aware of the fact that many postmodernists have since modified these strong denials – and as I pointed out, one cannot pick out an *ultimate* postmodernist text, and postmodernists vary considerably in the details of their views.

But they also share certain essentials. Instead of breaking with the Stalinists and developing a more advanced radical perspective out of the ruins of socialism, they denied the existence of reason in history and progress, indeed quite often the legitimacy of rationality itself. They identified any kind of coherence with totalitarianism: thus, if one tries to be intellectually consistent – *note this twisted reasoning* – one is a potential totalitarian!

Instead, they hypostatized spontaneity. Wherever the Communists said yea, in a sense, they said nay. Even when the Communists said something that was true, perhaps something sound from the writings of Marx, they often rejected it. As a result they dissolved history, rationality, progress, the individual, and the author, into a series of unrelated fragments that verged on cultural, social, and political nihilism.

One can play many games with nihilist ideas, as Michel Foucault essentially did. But whether the postmodernist message is cast in psychological, intellectual, or sensuous terms, it's still basically nihilistic and can usually be reduced to a highly subjective outlook that nourishes individual hedonism. Many postmodernists, such as Foucault and Baudrillard, I should point out, tried to be anarchistic albeit without calling their ideas anarchistic.

Eventually many postmodernists found that all the rejections they had made of other ideologies were insupportable. Toward the end of his life, for example, Foucault turned back to history again as a meaningful development in his *History of Sexuality,* which he left incomplete upon his death. Baudrillard gave up on radical social change altogether and went back into bourgeois society, advising his readers, in effect, that they couldn't change anything in this society, so they should have a good time.

Still another group that was involved in 1968 was the Situationists, who came out at the time with demands for workers' councils. The original Situationists were for the most part merely repeating slogans whose social meaning was already long dead, as I've already pointed out. If workers' councils had been established in 1968, I have no doubt that they would have been controlled by the Communists.

But the Situationists also emphasized that society turns people, things, and events into spectacularized phenomena or epiphenomena of the commodity. For the Situationists, capitalism was no longer premised only on the fetishism of the commodity; they viewed it as the fetishism of the spectacle, and between these two fetishizations – of the commodity and the spectacle – they eventually made any prospect of overthrowing this society a hopeless endeavor. Since the commodity has invaded every part of life, as they argued, resistance is all but impossible.

I agree that the commodity is invading all aspects of life, of course, but capitalism is by no means a stable social order, and the ability of the commodity to take full command of social life comes up against very real countervailing phenomena, such as environmental breakdown, vast disparities of wealth and income, possibly economic crisis, and violations of human rights and freedom.

Anarchism, Marxism, and the Future of the Left

Why do you think postmodernism has become so popular in the universities?

For one thing, postmodernism is professionally very rewarding for academics. It has produced a sizable industry with innumerable books, papers, periodicals, courses, conferences, positions, and other goodies that have made it immensely profitable to its acolytes.

As for the students, they find postmodernism to be a convenient mix of contradictory ideas. On the one hand, it promotes a cynicism that makes it possible for them to come to terms with the system, and on the other, it gives them an ideological warrant to "do their thing" and say to hell with society. In fact, postmodernism tends very frequently to attract individualistic anarchists. Many of them see in postmodernism anarchic characteristics such as the notion that any organization must eventually produce a bureaucracy and hence any movement for change must be purely spontaneous or rest on "happenings" – chaotic and unrelated incidents. But spontaneity that isn't informed by theory only produces mere *events*, such as the 1960s countercultural explosions – riots, street theater, and squats that quickly die down and have no lasting effect upon society. Spontaneity that isn't informed, that doesn't produce its own libertarian program and organization, frequently burns itself out and disappears.

A number of feminists have turned to postmodernism as an expression of their antipatriarchal position. Other students have turned to postmodernism because it ostensibly represents a total break with the past, and sometimes with civilization as a whole. In a strange parallel with primitivist anarchism, this kind of postmodernism denies civilization, but are the brutalities that have accompanied its advance sufficient reason to conclude that all civilization is a fraud? And who ever said that *this* society is a fulfillment of the potentialities of civilization, let alone of reason and humanity?

For postmodernists, as I've said, coherence is totalitarian, which means that incoherence is regarded as a virtue – in fact, it has become rather chic, a way to insult authority. While authority must certainly be challenged at the very minimum, incoherence is no substitute for organization, for a theory of society and social change that can provide a direction in creating a new society. Postmodernism offers *no* political direction, no program for social action, and no clear focus on society.

In fact, in some places it has gone wild – absolutely wild. It argues that language has an autonomy of its own, a life of its own, and that in point of fact there is no objective reality apart from texts. There is only language. It has turned experience into a process of linguistic, syntactic, and textual deconstruction. The text assumes authority over the author, who, for postmodern criticism, does not really exist. Now if the author does not exist, then the author has no responsibility – either for the truth of what he or she has written. Socially, in effect, postmodernism is a grossly irresponsible set of often conflicting ideas.

Do you think that there is a canon of works with which people should be familiar?

Absolutely, although I dislike the word *canon*. I do not believe that the great tradition of European intellectuality must be rejected because it was created by "dead white males." I am shocked by statements of that sort. What would life be, for any educated person, without a knowledge of Plato and Aristotle, always bearing in mind the times in which they lived?

We have to see how ideas develop over the course of history. I am not going to stop reading Aristotle, who was a genius, indeed truly one of the most monumental thinkers of Western history as a whole, because he accepted slavery. Nearly all the ancient Athenians accepted slavery in their day as a natural fact. They couldn't conceive of a world without it – as did most ancient societies, including Chinese and Indian ones. It took thousands of years for the world to come to think of slavery as a monstrosity – and even today society still hasn't freed itself from the existence of slavery.

I regard it as the height of arrogance to look at European civilization, or what is best in it, as dead, just as it would be to regard great works from other civilizations as irrelevant and lacking in a wealth of ideas. Is Aristotle worthless because he lived not only in a slave society but in a patriarchal society, as though the whole ancient Mediterranean world were not patriarchal? We are duty bound to put great works in their historical context and, above all, see what is *unique* about them, what is *remarkable* about them, how people went beyond and *transcended* the limiting circumstances of their time, as well as the extent to which they can still nourish us. I certainly think the "canon" should be expanded to include works by people of color and women and people from non-European cultures. I would no more want to see the European tradition frozen into a sacred canon than I would want to see the social anarchist and socialist traditions turned into a dogma, fixed eternally. But should that really mean we throw out Shakespeare's poetry because he didn't use politically correct language?

The postmodern deluge reflects the seeming relativism, fragmentation, and irrationality of our age. Yet you maintain a belief in reason, as well as civilization and progress. Why is that?

For one thing, I understand that there are at least two very different kinds of reason, and I look at the strengths and limitations of both. The most common is the conventional analytical reason we require to build a bridge or a house, or to balance a checking account. That is the ordinary instrumental reason that we need for dealing with everyday life. It's the kind that is used by the physical sciences to try to understand the nature of inorganic matter, both on the earth and in the cosmos. It's very necessary for understanding the world, and we can't do without it. This is the kind of reason that was promulgated by the French Enlightenment, and it is the kind that postmodernism rejects. And for good reason, since while it is useful for ordinary practical life and for physical science, it is limited in trying to understand *developmental* phenomena: that is, the evolution of organic life and human societies.

The second, more overarching kind of rationality, in my view, is suited for understanding *processes*. It's a broader way of thinking that traditional philosophy calls dialectical reason. Dialectical reason, although it had its origins in ancient Greece, gained its fullest expression in nineteenth-century Germany, especially with Hegel and Marx. It is based on the notion that what exists is always in a state of becoming and undergoing transformation, in contrast to conventional reason, which takes things as very fixed. I would suggest that when one talks about how the natural and social worlds are developing, one is using dialectical reason, often quite unconsciously. It's a process of deriving one concept from another – not arbitrarily, by using fantasy and passion (which certainly is not to say that I am "against" fantasy and passion), but by *educing* one mode of development from its predecessors. I've written in some detail about dialectical reason in *The Philosophy of Social Ecology*, so I won't go into it in any detail here. But I think it's important that people who are concerned with ecologizing the dialectic, with humanizing it, read this book.

Postmodernism – like individualistic or primitivistic anarchism, and like deep ecology – rejects reason because it identifies all intellection solely with conventional reason. But dialectical reason doesn't deal with the same kind of problems that conventional reason does. And I would argue that dialectical reason is the kind that is most important for forming a new Left today, because it is most suited for exploring the development of new social forces.

Dialectical development emphasizes the concept of potentiality. This concept, again, is very important for the development of a new Left, because we must explore the potentiality in a given situation to create a rational society. We are products of natural evolution, with uniquely human attributes – our abilities to think, foresee, and rationally intervene in the world. We acquired our intelligence not from some external artificer but from our mammalian, primate evolution.

Many deep ecologists and other eco-primitivists, by contrast, believe that human intervention into the nonhuman world – or first nature, as I call it – is what is destroying the biosphere. I encounter people who believe that anytime we engage in agriculture, we are interfering with pristine natural processes. There are people today who insist that all our ecological sins arose from agriculture, possibly even from linguistic communication! They argue that the moment human beings put a plow to the soil, they immediately began to despoil the natural world and alienate themselves from it.

These writers seem to want human beings to be like the lotus-eaters in Homer's *Odyssey*. On his way home from the Trojan War, Odysseus stops by an island where human beings blissfully eat the lotus, which makes them forget everything. They recall no past, and as such they have no future. With no yesterday and no tomorrow, they have only an eternal "now," the eternal present, in which spring follows winter, and summer follows spring, and so on, into eternity. They know nothing but what they immediately experience. They "live lightly on the land," to be sure – but they do nothing, nor do they try to create a society in which their potential as human beings is developed to the fullest. Rather, they are drugged into a state of everlasting immediacy, in asocial bliss.

Basically what I am trying to say is that human beings are capable not only of *adapting* to the world but of *innovating* in the world. As I have already pointed out, innovation is a fundamental trait of being human: to engage in practices beyond everyday eating, sleeping, reproducing, excreting, and even playing. This capacity to go beyond the animal level, to inquire about the future, to alter the world, to use language – all are fundamentally human attributes. Creativity is in great measure the capacity to intervene in the natural world with an intelligence that animals do not possess and are incapable of developing. These capacities come with the evolution of rationality, certainly in a strictly biological sense – due to our larger brain, our larger cerebral cortex, our ability to talk, due partly to Broca's area in our brain, and other parts of our head and neck. Another product of natural evolution is our inherited ability to talk in a very complex syllabic language, in a complex symbolic syntax.

All these capacities, to create, to think, and to talk, have given us the potentiality to become insightfully cooperative and rational beings, and to become creative beings. Our rationality endows us with the ability to modify the world, to recreate it, to use it to meet our needs instead of adapting to the terms that our environment presents to us, in order merely to survive. As a result, we can go beyond mere survival imperatives and act more rationally in altering the world than "Mother Nature" can – presumably in "her" primal wisdom. This is not something that we should be ashamed of or eschew, as deep ecologists and various conservationists would have it.

The problem for the Left is to create a society in which we can live humanely. We're not going to behave rationally, either toward ourselves or toward the natural world, unless we have a rational society. If our society is irrational, the people within it will also, for the most part, be irrational. We must have, therefore, a standard that determines what is rational and what is not, and as a corollary, what is good and evil, what constitutes virtue and vice. In short, we need criteria for determining what is rational, in a logic of development whose internal consistency gives us the basis for ethical behavior and an ethical direction toward which society should advance.

Human beings emerged socially out of animality, out of societies organized according to biological realities like blood ties, gender differences, and age differences that formed the real structure of aboriginal societies, and they developed the concept – *as yet unfulfilled in practice* – that we share a common humanity. This idea was made possible with the emergence of the city, because the city made it possible for people from different tribes that were formerly hostile to each other, to live together without conflict. City culture made it possible for us to begin to communicate with each other as human beings, not as tribal members, and to shake off in varying degrees the superstition, mystification, illusion, and particularly the authority of the dream world, which had ideological priority in tribal society. This eminently rational development created a greater sense that we all belong to the same species, that we need not go to war with each other because of our different blood ties and distrustful relations with outsiders.

These developments, both of rationality and of the city, gave a new reality to ideas of justice and freedom. They provided them with greater meaning and expanded their definition. The system of justice that had existed in primal society was one of vengeance, not of rational adjudication based on weighing real evidence. Rationality and the city also gave rise to hopes for emancipation in a free society, a society that would regard all people, however unequal they might be physically and mentally, as deserving compensation for their limitations. Real freedom ultimately consists in the recognition of differences and inequalities, and in the attempt to compensate for them, according to an ethics of complementarity.

Building on the best of the Western heritage, *which has yet to be realized*, the great democratic revolutions insisted that each individual has real worth, and that no one should be more privileged, at least in the political or civil realm, than any other person. Finally, modern socialism, social anarchism, and communism emerged and waged revolutionary struggles to achieve these goals.

Anarchism, Marxism, and the Future of the Left

These basic concepts are all essential to the formation and creation of a new Left. Yet postmodernism has challenged every one of them. It subverts them and offers us instead the nihilistic idea that all knowledge is a matter of one's individual perspective, and if we follow the logic of the earlier Foucault, we arrive at the pessimistic conclusion that power, like gravity, exists everywhere, from language to the authority of the State. Anarchists and Marxists who are inspired by Foucault are entirely confused about what to do with power. Eliminate it? But how, if it is ubiquitous? Power always exists; the question is, *who has* it. I believe that power must exist for the masses of people who are disempowered today. The notion that power is ubiquitous, without any social or political centrality, simply sidetracks the revolutionary problem of gaining power for all people.

If we permit postmodernism to set the terms of a new Left, then it will undermine the potentialities of the Left, not to speak of the two centuries of the international revolutionary tradition. It is vital that we produce social change in the most fundamental and rational sense, by building on the best in civilization while eliminating its horrors. If we are to distinguish the best from the worst, we can do so only by using our reason. Moreover, no new Left can have hopes for the future unless it believes, in some sense, in progress. Otherwise that Left's existence would have no basis, no purpose, and no principle of hope.

What disturbs me most is that all the tendencies in postmodernism that I've named accept the fragmented reality that capitalism has finally produced. What could be more fragmenting than the market, with its competition between buyer and seller? Not only does postmodernism accept fragmentation, it provides no ideological basis for opposing hierarchy, class exploitation, and oppression, in pursuit of freedom. Its tendency to transform reality into texts that have to be deconstructed verges on the preposterous; its attempt to recover our unity with Being, as Heidegger would have us do, is a return to a prelapsarian world, before the Fall; and Foucault's view of power as ubiquitous makes it impossible for us to know where to aim our thrusts against it, or even where to find the specific forms of power that have to be reclaimed so that people can become really empowered.

Postmodernism, as well as lifestyle anarchism and deep ecology – all these prelapsarian ideologies – are significantly undermining the possibility for the reemergence of a Left. They redirect our attention away from the social question, class exploitation, and capitalism toward the self and a relativistic outlook toward the human condition, just as deep ecology redirects our attention away from the social causes of the ecological crisis, and toward conservation and a biocentric, often misanthropic sensibility.

Capitalism has no problem at all with postmodern academics and disenchanted Leftists, or with a lumpen Left that wants to create "temporary autonomous zones" and peddle technophobia, irrationalism, and spiritualism. Faced with such critics, capitalism is quite secure and can comfortably continue to debase humanity and the natural world with impunity.

Note

1. I have written my full critique of postmodernism in *Re-enchanting Humanity* (London: Cassell, 1995).

Communalism
The Democratic Dimension of Social Anarchism

Seldom have socially important words been subject to more confusion, or been more divested of their historic meaning, than they are at present. Two centuries ago, *democracy* was deprecated by monarchists and republicans alike as "mob rule." Today, democracy is hailed, but only in the sense of "representative democracy," an oxymoronic phrase that refers to little more than a republican oligarchy of the chosen few who ostensibly speak for the powerless many.

Communism, for its part, once referred to a cooperative society that would be based on an ethics of mutual respect and on an economy in which each contributed to the social labor fund according to his or her ability and received the means of life according to his or her needs. Today, communism is absurdly associated with the Stalinist gulag and wholly rejected as totalitarian. Its cousin, *socialism* – which once denoted a politically free society based on various forms of collectivism and equitable material returns for labor – is wrongly interchangeable today with a somewhat humanistic bourgeois liberalism.

During the 1980s and 1990s, as the entire social and political spectrum has shifted ideologically to the right, *anarchism* has been no more immune to redefinition than these other words. In the Anglo-American sphere, anarchism is being given an emphasis on personal autonomy, an emphasis that is divesting it of its social meaning and draining it of its historic vitality. A Stirnerite individualism – marked by an advocacy of lifestyle changes, the cultivation of behavioral idiosyncrasies, and even an embrace of outright mysticism – has become increasingly prominent. This personalistic "lifestyle anarchism" is steadily eroding the socialistic core of anarchist concepts of freedom.

Let me stress that in the British and American social tradition, *autonomy* and *freedom* are not equivalent. Autonomy, by insisting on the elimination of personal domination, focuses on the individual as the formative component and locus of society. By contrast, freedom, despite its looser usages, denotes the absence of domination in society, of which the individual is obviously an integral part. This contrast becomes very important when individualist anarchists unthinkingly reject collectivism as such as the tyranny of the community over its members.

Today, if an anarchist theorist such as L. Susan Brown can assert that "a group is a collection of individuals, no more and no less," thereby rooting anarchism in an abstract ahistorical individual, we have serious reason to be concerned.[1] Not that this view is entirely new to anarchism; various anarchist historians have described it as implicit in the libertarian outlook. But then as now, it presents the individual as appearing *ab novo*, endowed with natural rights and bereft of either roots in society or historical development. Here autonomy consists merely in a refusal to impair the liberties of others – or negative liberty, as Isaiah Berlin called it.

But whence does this "autonomous" individual derive? What is the basis for its "natural rights," beyond a priori premises and hazy intuitions? What role does historical development play in its formation? What social premises give birth to it, sustain it, indeed nourish it? How can a "collection of individuals" institutionalize itself, so as to give rise to substantive freedom constructed along socialistic lines?

In the history of ideas, autonomy, in the strict sense of personal self-rule, found its ancient apogee in the imperial Roman cult of *libertas*. Under the rule of the Julian-Claudian Caesars, the Roman citizen enjoyed a great deal of autonomy to indulge his own desires – and lusts – without reproval from any authority, provided that he did not interfere with the business or the needs of the state. In the more theoretically developed liberal tradition of John Locke and John Stuart Mill, autonomy acquired a more expansive sense that was opposed ideologically to excessive state authority.

During the nineteenth century, if any single subject gained the interest of classical liberals, it was political economy, which they often conceived not only as a system of production of goods and services and their distribution but as a system of morality as well. Still, liberal thought generally reduced the social to the economic, opposing excessive state authority in favor of a presumed economic autonomy. In their defenses of economic liberty, ironically, liberals often invoked the word *freedom*, using it in the sense of "autonomy," as they do to the present day.[2]

Despite their assertions of autonomy and their distrust of state authority, however, classical liberal thinkers did not in the last instance hold to the notion that the individual is entirely free from lawful guidance. Indeed, their interpretation of autonomy actually presupposed a quite definite social arrangement beyond the individual – notably, the marketplace. Individual autonomy to the contrary, the marketplace and its laws constitute a social system that places all "collections of individuals" under the sway of the famous "invisible hand" of competition. Paradoxically, the laws of the marketplace override the exercise of "free will" by the same sovereign individuals who otherwise constitute the "collection of individuals."

If a society were ever to emerge that was really only merely a "collection of individuals, no more and no less," it would simply dissolve. No rationally formed society can exist without institutions. Liberals nonetheless cling to the notions of a "free market" and "free competition" guided by the "inexorable laws" of the marketplace.

Alternatively, *freedom*, a word that shares etymological roots with the German *Freiheit* (for which there is no equivalent in Romance languages), takes its point of departure not from the individual but from the community or, more broadly, from society as a whole. In the eighteenth and nineteenth centuries, as Enlightenment thought and its derivatives brought the idea of the mutability of institutions to the foreground of social thought, the individual came to be seen as mutable.

In the last century and early in the present one, the great socialist theorists greatly sophisticated the idea of freedom, seeing the individual as consciously intertwined with social evolution. For these thinkers, a "collection of individuals" would have been alien as a way of conceiving society; they properly considered individual freedom to be congruent with social freedom and, very significantly, they defined freedom as such as an evolving, as well as a unifying, concept.

145

As social revolutionaries, moreover, socialist theorists asked a key question: What would constitute a *rational* society? This question is uniquely ethical in that it abolishes the centrality of economics in a free society. Where liberal thought had generally reduced the social to the economic, non-Marxian socialisms (among which Kropotkin denoted anarchism the "left wing") dissolved the economic into the social.[3]

In short, both society and the individual were historicized, as parts of an ever-developing, self-generative, and creative process in which each existed within and through the other. This historicization was to be accompanied by the establishment of ever-expanding rights and duties. The First International, in fact, demanded, "No rights without duties, no duties without rights" (a demand that later appeared on the mastheads of anarchosyndicalist periodicals in Spain and elsewhere well into the present century).

Thus, for classical socialist thinkers, to conceive of the individual without society was as meaningless as to conceive of society without individuals. They sought to realize both in rational *institutional* frameworks that fostered the greatest degree of free expression in every aspect of social life.

II

Individualism, as it had been conceived by classical liberalism, thus rested on the presupposition of a social "lawfulness" maintained by marketplace competition, a presupposition that meant its "autonomous" individual was far indeed from sovereign. With even fewer presuppositions to support itself, the woefully undertheorized work of Max Stirner shared a similar disjunction: the ideological disjunction between the ego and society.

The pivotal issue that reveals this disjunction – indeed, this contradiction – is the question of democracy. By democracy, I do not mean a type of representative government but rather face-to-face, direct democracy. In a tradition originating in classical Athens, democracy as I use it is the direct management of the *polis* by its citizenry in popular assemblies. (Which is not to downplay the fact that Athenian democracy was scarred by patriarchy, slavery, class rule, and the restriction of citizenship to males of putative Athenian birth. What I am referring to is an evolving tradition of institutional structures, not a model for a free society.[4]) Democracy generically defined, then, is the direct management of society in face-to-face assemblies, in which *policy* is formulated by the resident citizenry and *administration* is executed by mandated and delegated councils.

Many libertarians consider democracy, even in this sense, as a form of rule, since when a democratic assembly makes decisions, the majority view prevails and thus "rules" over the minority. As such, democracy is said to be inconsistent with a truly libertarian ideal. So knowledgeable a historian of anarchism as Peter Marshall observes that, for anarchists, "the majority has no more right to dictate to the minority, even a minority of one, than the minority to the majority."[5] Scores of libertarians have made this objection to democracy time and again.

What is striking about these assertions is their highly pejorative language. Majorities, it would seem, neither decide nor debate: rather, they "rule" and "dictate," and perhaps command and coerce. But a free society would be one that not only permitted but fostered the fullest degree of dissent; its podiums at assemblies and its media would be open to the fullest expression of all views, and its institutions would be true forums for discussion. When such a society had to arrive at a decision that concerned the public welfare, it could hardly "dictate" to anyone. The minority who opposed a majority decision would have every opportunity to dissent, to work to reverse that decision through unimpaired discussion and advocacy.

By what alternative means do libertarians intend for their society to make necessary collective decisions about public affairs? The means of decision-making that is most commonly proposed is the process of consensus. In consensus decision-making a group seeks to attain unanimity, or as close to unanimity as possible, in voting a given issue. Everyone must agree with a decision (or else withdraw from voting on that issue) before it can be adopted. Thus a minority – even a "minority of one" – has an unconditional right to *abort* a decision by a "collection of individuals."

I do not deny that consensus decision-making may be appropriate for small groups whose members are thoroughly familiar with one another. But my own experience has shown me that when larger groups try to make decisions by consensus, the process usually obliges them to arrive at the lowest common intellectual denominator: the least controversial or even the most mediocre decision that a sizable assembly of people can attain is the one that is adopted. More disturbingly, I have found that it permits manipulation and an insidious authoritarianism, even when used by movements that advocate autonomy or freedom.

To take a very striking case in point: The largest consensus-based movement in recent memory in the United States (involving thousands of participants) was the Clamshell Alliance, which was formed to oppose the Seabrook nuclear reactor in the mid-1970s in New Hampshire. In her recent study of the movement, Barbara Epstein has called the Clamshell the "first effort in American history to base a mass movement on nonviolent direct action" after the 1960s civil rights movement. As a result of the Clamshell's apparent organizational success, many other regional alliances against nuclear reactors were formed throughout the United States.

I can personally attest that within the Clamshell Alliance, consensus was fostered by a clique of often-cynical Quakers and by members of a dubiously "anarchic" commune that was located in Montague, Massachusetts. This small, tightly knit faction, unified in service to its own hidden, opportunistic agendas, was able to manipulate many Clamshell members into subordinating their goodwill and idealistic commitments to those agendas. During the lifetime of the Clamshell, its de facto leaders overrode the rights and ideals of the innumerable individuals who entered it and undermined their morale and will.

In order for that clique to create full consensus on decisions that it wished the Clamshell to pass, they often subtly urged or psychologically coerced dissenters to decline to vote on a troubling issue, inasmuch as their dissent would essentially amount to a one-person veto. This practice, called "standing aside" in American consensus processes, all too often involved intimidation of the dissenters. So that rather than make an honorable and continuing expression of their dissent by voting, even as a minority, in accordance with their views, they withdrew from the decision-making process. Having withdrawn, they ceased to be political beings – so that a "decision" could be made.

More than one "decision" in the Clamshell Alliance was made by pressuring dissenters into silence, and through a chain of such intimidations, "consensus" was ultimately achieved only after dissenting members had nullified themselves as participants in the process.

On a more theoretical level, consensus silences that most vital aspect of all dialogue, *dissensus*. In majority decision-making, dissent plays a creative role, valuable in itself as an ongoing democratic phenomenon. Even after a minority temporarily accedes to a majority decision, the minority can dissent from the decision on which they have been defeated and work to overturn it. They are free to openly and persistently articulate reasoned and potentially persuasive disagreements. Their dissent may be ongoing, and a passionate dialogue may persist.

Consensus, for its part, honors no minorities but mutes them in favor of the metaphysical "one" of the "consensus" group, with its gray uniformity. It stifles the dialectic of ideas that thrives on opposition, confrontation and, yes, decisions with which everyone need not agree and should not agree, lest society become an ideological cemetery. Any libertarian society that allowed Marshall's "minority of one" to block the majority of a community, indeed, of regional and nationwide confederations, from making decisions, would essentially mutate into a Rousseauean "general will," in a nightmare world of intellectual and psychic conformity. In more gripping times, it could easily "force people to be free," as Rousseau put it – and as the Jacobins practiced it in 1793-94.

In the Clamshell Alliance dissent was replaced by dull monologues – and the uncontroverted and deadening tone of consensus. Its de facto leaders were able to get away with their behavior precisely because *the Clamshell was not sufficiently organized and democratically structured,* such that it could countervail the manipulation of the well-organized clique. The de facto leaders were subject to few structures of accountability for their actions. The ease with which they cannily used consensus decision-making for their own ends has been only partly told,[6] but consensus practices finally shipwrecked this large and exciting organization, with its Rousseauean "republic of virtue." (It was also ruined, I may add, by an organizational laxity that permitted mere passersby to participate in decision-making, thereby destructuring the organization to the point of invertebracy.) It was for good reason that I and many young anarchists from Vermont who had actively participated in the Alliance for some few years came to view consensus as anathema.

III

I have dwelled on consensus at some length because it constitutes the individualistic alternative to democracy, commonly counterposed against "majority rule" as "no rule" – in what amounts to a free-floating personal autonomy. Inasmuch as libertarian ideas in the United States and Britain are increasingly drifting toward affirmations of personal autonomy, the chasm between individualism and antistatist collectivism is becoming unbridgeable, in my view.

A personalistic anarchism has taken deep root among young people today, who increasingly use the word *anarchy* to express not only a personalistic stance, but an antirational, mystical, antitechnological, and anticivilizational set of views that makes it impossible for anarchists who anchor their ideas in socialism to apply the word *anarchist* to themselves without a qualifying adjective. Howard Ehrlich, one of our ablest and most concerned American comrades, uses the phrase *social anarchism* as the title of his magazine, apparently to distinguish his views from an anarchism that is ideologically anchored in liberalism and possibly worse.

But far more than a qualifying adjective is needed if we are to elaborate our notion of freedom more expansively. It would be unfortunate indeed if the general culture had reached such a low point that libertarians had to explain that they believe in a *society,* not a mere collection of individuals! A century ago, this belief was presupposed; today, so much has been stripped away from the collectivistic flesh of classical anarchism that it is on the verge of becoming a personal life-stage for adolescents and a fad for their middle-aged mentors, a route to "self-realization" and the seemingly radical equivalent of encounter groups.

Today, there must be a place on the political spectrum where antiauthoritarian thought that advances humanity's bitter struggle to arrive at the realization of its authentic *social* life – the "Commune of communes" – can be clearly articulated *institutionally* as well as ideologically. Socially concerned anti-authoritarians must have a program and a practice for attempting to change the world, not merely their psyches. There must be an arena of struggle that can mobilize people, help them to educate themselves, and develop an anti-authoritarian *politics,* to use this word in its classical meaning, indeed that pits a new public sphere against the State and capitalism.

In short, we must recover not only the socialist dimension of anarchism but its political dimension: democracy. Bereft of its democratic dimension, anarchism may indeed come to denote little more than a "collection of individuals, no more and no less." Even anarcho-communism, by far the most preferable adjectival modification of the libertarian ideal, nonetheless retains a structural vagueness that tells us little or nothing about the institutions necessary to expedite a communistic distribution of goods. It spells out a broad desideratum – one that, alas, has been terribly tarnished by the association of "communism" with Bolshevism and the State – but its public sphere and forms of institutional association remain unclear at best and susceptible to a totalitarian onus at worst.

I wish to propose that the democratic and potentially practicable dimension of the libertarian goal be expressed as *communalism,* a word that, unlike those that have lost their former radical social and political meanings, has not been historically sullied by abuse. Even ordinary dictionary definitions of communalism, I submit, capture to a great degree the vision of a "Commune of communes" that is being lost by current Anglo-American trends that celebrate anarchy variously as "chaos," as a mystical "oneness" with "nature," as self-fulfillment, or as "ecstasy," but above all as personalistic.[7]

One dictionary defines *communalism* as "a theory or system of government [sic] in which virtually autonomous [sic] local communities are loosely in a federation."[8] No English dictionary is very sophisticated politically, and I would take issue with some of the words in this definition. But the presence of *government* and *autonomous* here does not commit communalists to an acceptance of the State and parochialism, let alone individualism. Further, *federation* is often synonymous with *confed-*

eration, the word that I regard as more consistent with the libertarian tradition.

What is remarkable about this (as yet) unsullied term is its extraordinary proximity to libertarian municipalism, the political dimension of social ecology that I have advanced at length elsewhere. In *communalism,* libertarians have an available word that they can enrich as much by experience as by theory. Most significantly, the word can express what communalistic anarchists are *for,* namely democratic libertarian social institutions. It is a word that can tear down the ghetto walls that are increasingly imprisoning anarchism in cultural exotica and psychological introversion. It stands in explicit opposition to the suffocating individualism that sits so comfortably beside bourgeois self-centeredness and a moral relativism that renders any social action irrelevant, indeed, institutionally meaningless.

It is important to emphasize that libertarian municipalism – or communalism, as I have called it here – is a developing outlook, a politics that seeks ultimately to achieve the "Commune of communes." As such, it tries to provide a directly democratic confederal alternative to the State and to a centralized bureaucratic society. To challenge the validity of libertarian municipalism, as many liberals and ecosocialists have, on the premise that the size of existing urban entities raises an insurmountable logistical obstacle to its successful practice is to turn it into a strategy and freeze it within the given conditions of society, then tally up debits and credits to determine its potential for success, effectiveness, levels of participation, and the like.

Libertarian municipalism – communalism – is not a form of social bookkeeping for conditions as they are but rather a *transformative* process that starts with what can be *changed* within present conditions as a valid point of departure for achieving what *should be* in a rational society. It is above all a politics, to use this word in its original Hellenic sense, that is engaged in the process of remaking what are now called "electoral constituents" or "taxpayers" into active citizens, and of remaking what are now urban conglomerations into genuine communities related to each other through confederations that would countervail the State and ultimately challenge its existence. To see it otherwise is to reduce this multifaceted, processual development to a caricature.

Nor does libertarian municipalism intend to eliminate private association as such – without the familial and economic aspects of life, human existence would be impossible in any society.[9] It is rather an outlook and a developing practice for recovering and enlarging the presently declining public sphere, which the State has invaded and in many cases virtually eliminated.[10]

If the large size of municipal entities and a diminished public sphere are accepted as unalterable givens, then we are left with no hope but to work with the given in every sphere of human activity – in which case, anarchists might as well join with social democrats (as quite a few have, for all practical purposes) to merely reform the State apparatus and alleviate the brutalities of the market. Indeed, on the basis of such common-sensical reasoning, a far stronger argument could be made for preserving the state, the market, the use of money, and global corporations than could be made for decentralizing urban agglomerations. In fact, many urban agglomerations are already groaning physically and logistically under the burden of their size and are reconstituting themselves into satellite cities before our very eyes, even though their populations and physical jurisdictions are still grouped under the name of a single metropolis.

Strangely, many lifestyle anarchists, who, like New Age visionaries, have a remarkable ability to imagine changing everything, tend to raise strong objections when they are asked to actually change anything in the existing society – rather than cultivate greater self-expression, experience more mystical reveries, and turn their anarchism into an art form, retreating into social quietism. When critics of libertarian municipalism bemoan the prohibitively large number of people who are likely to attend municipal assemblies or function as active participants in them – and question how "practical" such assemblies could be – in large cities like New York, Mexico City, and Tokyo, may I suggest that a communalist approach raises the issue of whether we can indeed change the existing society at all and achieve the "Commune of communes."

If this communalist approach seems terribly formidable to lifestyle anarchists, I can only suspect that for them the battle is already lost. For my part, if anarchy came to mean merely an aesthetic of self-cultivation, a titillating riot, spraycan graffiti, or the heroics of personalistic acts nourished by a self-indulgent "imaginary," I would have little in common with it. Theatrical personalism came too much into fashion with the 1960s counterculture, which in the 1970s turned into the New Age culture and became a model for bourgeois fashion designers and boutiques.

IV

Anarchism is in retreat today. If we fail to elaborate its democratic dimension, we will miss the opportunity not only to form a vital movement but to prepare people for a revolutionary social praxis in the future. Alas, we are presently witnessing the appalling desiccation of a great tradition, such that neo-Situationists, nihilists, primitivists, antirationalists, anticivilizationists, and avowed "chaotics" are closeting themselves in their egos, reducing anything resembling public political activity to juvenile antics.

I do not mean to deny the importance of creating a libertarian culture, one that is aesthetic, playful, and broadly imaginative. The anarchists of the last century and part of the present one justifiably took pride in the fact that many innovative artists, particularly painters and novelists, aligned themselves with anarchic views. But behavior that verges on a mystification of criminality, on asociality, intellectual incoherence, anti-intellectualism, and disorder for its own sake, is simply lumpen. It feeds on the dregs of capitalism itself.

However much such behavior invokes the "rights" of the ego as it dissolves the political into the personal or inflates the personal into a transcendental category, it has no origins outside the mind to even potentially support it. As Bakunin and Kropotkin argued repeatedly, individuality has never existed apart from society, and the individual's own evolution has been coextensive with social evolution. To speak of "The Individual" apart from its social roots and social involvements is as meaningless as to speak of a society that contains no people or institutions.

Merely to exist, institutions must have *form,* as I argued some thirty years ago in "The Forms of Freedom," lest freedom itself – individual as well as social – lose its definability. Institutions must be rendered functional, not abstracted into Kantian categories that float in a rarefied academic air. They must have the tangibility of structure, however offensive the term *structure* may be to individualist libertarians: concretely, they must have the means, policies, and experimental praxis to arrive at decisions. Unless everyone is to be so psychologically homogeneous and society's interests so uniform in character that dissent is simply meaningless, there must be room for conflicting proposals, discussion, rational explication, and majority decisions – in short, democracy.

Like it or not, such a communalist democracy, in order to be libertarian, will have to be given institutional form, in such a way that it is face-to-face, direct, and grassroots. Only then can it advance a rational society beyond negative liberty to positive liberty. A communalist democracy would oblige us to develop a public sphere – and in the Athenian meaning of the term, a *politics* – that grows in tension and ultimately in a decisive conflict with the State.

Confederal, antihierarchical, and collectivist, with the means of life municipally managed rather than controlled by any vested interest (such as workers, private industry, or more dangerously, the State), it may justly be regarded as the processual actualization of the libertarian ideal as a daily praxis.[11]

A communalist politics entails participation in municipal elections – based on an unyielding program that demands the formation of popular assemblies and their confederation. Entry into existing village, town, and city councils, however, does not involve participation in State organs, any more than establishing an anarchosyndicalist union in a privately owned factory involves participation in capitalist production. In the French Revolution of 1789-94, the Parisian municipal district assemblies, established by the monarchy in 1789 to expedite elections to the Estates General, were transformed in only four years into revolutionary sectional assemblies, or "sections," calling for the establishment of a "Commune of communes" throughout France. Their movement for sectional democracy met with defeat during the insurrection of June 2, 1793 – not at the hands of the monarchy, but by the treachery of the Jacobins.

Capitalism will not generously provide us with the institutions for popular democracy. Its control over society today is nearly ubiquitous, not only in what little remains of the public sphere but in the minds of many self-styled radicals. A revolutionary people must either assert their control over the institutions that are basic to their public lives – which Bakunin correctly perceived to be their councils – or else they will have no choice but to withdraw into private life, as is already happening on an epidemic scale today.[12]

It would be tragic indeed if individualistic anarchism and its various mutations, from the academic and transcendentally moral to the chaotic and the lumpen, having rejected democracy in favor of a "minority of one," were to further raise the walls of dogma that are steadily growing around the libertarian ideal, and if, wittingly or not, anarchism were to turn into just another narcissistic cult that fits snugly into a secure niche in an alienated, commodified, introverted and egocentric society.

September 18, 1994

Notes

1. L. Susan Brown, *The Politics of Individualism* (Montreal: Black Rose Books, 1993), p. 12. I do not question the sincerity of Brown's libertarian views; she regards herself as an anarcho-communist, as do I. But she makes no direct attempt to reconcile her individualistic views with communism in any form. Both Bakunin and Kropotkin would have strongly disagreed with her formulation of what constitutes "a group," while Margaret Thatcher, clearly for reasons of her own, might be rather pleased with it, since it is so akin to the former British prime minister's notorious statement that there is no such thing as society – there are only individuals. Certainly Brown is not a Thatcherite, nor Thatcher an anarchist, but however different they may be in other respects, their common ideological filiation with classical liberalism makes possible their shared affirmations of the "autonomy" of the individual. I cannot ignore the fact, however, that neither Bakunin's, Kropotkin's, nor my own views are treated with any depth in Brown's book (pp. 156-62), and her account of them is filled with serious inaccuracies.

2. Liberals were not always in accord with each other, nor did they hold notably coherent doctrines. Mill, a free-thinking humanitarian and utilitarian, in fact exhibited a measure of sympathy for socialism. I am not singling out here any particular liberal theorist, be he Mill, Adam Smith or Friedrich Hayek, each of whom had or has his or her particular eccentricity or personal line of thought. I am speaking of classical liberalism as a whole, whose general features involve a belief in the "laws" of the marketplace and "free" competition.

3. See Kropotkin's widely read "Anarchism," his *Encyclopaedia Britannica* article, republished in Roger N. Baldwin, ed., *Kropotkin's Revolutionary Pamphlets: A Collection of Writings by Peter Kropotkin* (Vanguard Press, 1927; reprinted by Dover, 1970).

4. I have *never* regarded the classical Athenian democracy as a model, let alone an ideal, to be restored in a rational society. I have long admired Athens for one reason: the *polis* around Periclean times pro-vides us with striking evidence that direct-democratic structures *can exist*, an assembly that makes policy, public offices that are rotated and limited, and a nonprofessional armed citizenry for defense. The Mediterranean world of the fifth century B.C.E. was largely based on monarchical authority and repressive custom. That all Mediterranean societies of that time included patriarchy, slavery, and the State (usually an absolutist State) makes the Athenian experience all the more remarkable for what it *uniquely* introduced into social life, including an unprecedented degree of free expression. It would be naîve to suppose that Athens could have risen above the most basic attributes of ancient society in its day, which, from a distance of 2,400 years we now have the privilege of judging as ugly and inhu-man. Regrettably, no small number of people today are willing to judge the past by the present.

5. Peter Marshall, *Demanding the Impossible: A History of Anarchism* (London: HarperCollins, 1992), p. 22.

6. Barbara Epstein, *Political Protest and Cultural Revolution: Non-Violent*

Direct Action in the 1970s and 1980s (Berkeley: University of California Press, 1991), especially pp. 59, 78, 89, 94-95, 167-68, 177. Although I disagree with some of the facts and conclusions in Epstein's book – based on my personal as well as general knowledge of the Clamshell Alliance – she vividly portrays the failure of consensus in this movement.

7. The association of chaos, nomadism, and cultural terrorism with "ontological anarchy" (as though the bourgeoisie had not turned such antics into an ecstasy industry in the United States) is fully explicated in Hakim Bey (aka Peter Lamborn Wilson), *T.A.Z.: The Temporary Autonomous Zone* (New York: Autonomedia, 1985). The Yuppie *Whole Earth Review* has celebrated this pamphlet as the most influential and widely read "manifesto" of America's countercultural youth, noting with approval that it is free of conventional anarchist attacks upon capitalism. Such 1960s detritus is echoed in one form or another by most American anarchist tabloids that pander to youth who have not yet "had their fun before it was time to grow up" and become real estate agents and accountants.

8. Quoted from *The American Heritage Dictionary of the English Language* (Boston: Houghton Mifflin Co., 1978).

9. History provides no model for libertarian municipalism, be it Periclean Athens, or any tribe, village, town, or city – or a hippie commune or Buddhist ashram. (My incessant repetitions of this caveat have not prevented my critics from saying that my model for a libertarian city is Athens.) Nor is an "affinity group" a model of the institutional basis for a libertarian society. Rather, the Spanish anarchists used this word interchangeably with "action group" to refer to an *organizational* unit for the FAI.

10. For a detailed discussion of the differences between the social domain, which includes the ways in which we associate for personal and economic ends; the public sphere or political domain; and the State in all its phases and forms of development, see my book *From*

Urbanization To Cities (1987; London: Cassel, 1995).

11. I should emphasize that I am not counterposing a communalist democracy to such enterprises as cooperatives, people's clinics, communes, and the like. But we should have no illusions that such enterprises are anything more than *exercises* in popular control and ways of bringing people together in a highly atomized society. Under capitalism, no food cooperative can replace a giant retail food market, and no clinic can replace a hospital complex, any more than a craft shop can replace a factory. I should observe that as early as the 1880s the Spanish anarchists took full note of the limits of the cooperativist movement, at a time when such movements were in fact more feasible than they are today, and they significantly separated themselves from cooperativism programmatically.

12. For Bakunin, the people "have a healthy, practical common sense when it comes to communal affairs. They are fairly well informed and know how to select from their midst the most capable officials. This is why municipal elections always best reflect the real attitude and will of the people." *Bakunin on Anarchy*, Sam Dolgoff, ed. (New York: Alfred A. Knopf, 1972; republished by Black Rose Books: Montreal), p. 223. I have omitted the queasy interpolations that Dolgoff inserted to modify Bakunin's meaning. It may be well to note that anarchism in the last century was more plastic and flexible than it is today.

Whither Anarchism?

A Reply to Recent Anarchist Critics

> *Liberty without socialism is privilege and injustice.*
> *Socialism without liberty is slavery and brutality.*
> – Mikhail Bakunin

What form will anarchism take as it enters the twenty-first century?
What basic ideas will it advance? What kind of movement, if any, will it
try to create? How will it try to change the human sensibilities and social
institutions that it has inherited from the past?

In a fundamental sense these were the issues that I tried to raise in
my 1995 polemic *Social Anarchism or Lifestyle Anarchism: An Unbridgeable
Chasm.*[1] The title and especially the subtitle were deliberately provocative. In part, I intended them to highlight a profound and longstanding
contradiction within anarchism, an ideology that encompasses views
that are basically hostile to each other. At one extreme of anarchism is a
liberal ideology that focuses overwhelmingly on the abstract individual
(often drawing on bourgeois ideologies), supports personal autonomy,
and advances a negative rather than a substantive concept of liberty. This
anarchism celebrates the notion of *liberty from* rather than a fleshed-out
concept of *freedom for.* At the other end of the anarchist spectrum is a
revolutionary libertarian socialism that seeks to create a free society, in
which humanity as a whole – and hence the individual as well – enjoys
the advantages of free political and economic institutions.

Between these two extremes lie a host of anarchistic tendencies that
differ considerably in their theoretical aspects and hence in the kind of

practice by which they hope to achieve anarchism's realization. Some of the more common ones today, in fact, make systematic thinking into something of a bugaboo, with the result that their activities tend to consist not of clearly focused attacks upon the prevailing social order but of adventurous escapades that may be little more than street brawls and eccentric "happenings." The social problems we face – in politics, economics, gender and ethnic relations, and ecology – are not simply unrelated "single issues" that should be dealt with separately. Like so many socialists and social anarchists in the past, I contend that an anarchist theory and practice that addresses them must be *coherent,* anchoring seemingly disparate social problems in an analysis of the underlying social relations: capitalism and hierarchical society.

It should not be surprising that in a period of social reaction and apparent capitalist stabilization, the two extremes within anarchism – the individualistic liberal tendency and the socialistic revolutionary one – would fly apart in opposing directions. At best, they have previously existed only in uneasy tension with each other, submerging their differences to their common traditions and ideological premises. During the late nineteenth and early twentieth centuries, the liberal tendency, with its strong emphasis on individual rights and sensibilities, gave greater emphasis to individual self-expression, ranging from personal eccentricities to scandalous or even violent behavior. By contrast, the socialistic tendency placed its greatest emphasis on popular mobilizations, especially in syndicalist organizations, working-class strikes, and the everyday demands of opposition to capitalism in the public sphere.

Supporters of the socialistic tendencies in anarchism, which I have called social anarchism, never denied the importance of gaining individual freedom and personal autonomy. What they consistently argued, however, was that individual freedom will remain chimerical unless sweeping revolutionary changes are made that provide the social foundations for rounded and ethically committed individuals. As social anarchism has argued, the truly free individual is at once an active agent in and the embodiment of a truly free society. This view often clashed with the notion, very commonly held by individualistic or, as I have called them, lifestyle anarchists, that liberty and autonomy can be achieved by

making changes in personal sensibilities and lifeways, giving less attention to changing material and cultural conditions.

It is not my intention to repeat my exposition of the differences
between social and lifestyle anarchism. Nor do I deny that the two tendencies – the liberal and the social – have often overlapped with each
other. Many lifestyle anarchists eagerly plunge into direct actions that are
ostensibly intended to achieve socialistic goals. Many social anarchists, in
turn, sympathize with the rebellious impulses celebrated by lifestyle
anarchists, although they tend to resist purely personal expressions.

Not surprisingly, the ability of social anarchism to make itself heard
in the public sphere has generally fluctuated with the economic times. In
periods of capitalist stability, social anarchism is often eclipsed on the
Left by reform-oriented social-democratic and liberal ideologies, while
lifestyle anarchism emerges as the embodiment of anarchism par excellence. During these periods anarchism's cranks, often more rebellious
than revolutionary, with their exaggerated hostility to conventional lifeways, come to the foreground, constituting a cultural more than a revolutionary challenge to the status quo. By contrast, in times of deep social
unrest, it is social anarchism that, within anarchism, has usually held center stage. Indeed, during revolutionary situations in the past, social anarchism has enjoyed a great deal of popularity among the oppressed and in
some cases was responsible for organizing the masses in such a way as to
pose a serious threat to the social order.

The varying fortunes of social and lifestyle anarchism belong to a
long history of revolutions and counterrevolutions, of rebellion and conformity, of social unrest and social peace. When the rebellious 1960s
bubbled up after a decade of social quiescence and numbing mediocrity,
lifestyle anarchism enjoyed great popularity among the countercultural
elements, while social anarchism exercised a measure of influence with
some New Leftists. During the political apathy and social conformity of
the 1970s and 1980s, as the counterculture was absorbed into New Age
narcissism, lifestyle anarchists moved increasingly to the fore as the pre-
dominant expression of anarchism.

The America of the mid-1960s that had seemed to be weighing new,
indeed utopistic possibilities opened by ferment among people of color,
students, women, gays, and community activists, has been replaced, in

the 1990s, by an America that is narcissistic and self-absorbed, moved by
mystical, antirational, often otherworldly, and decidedly personal concerns. The visionary pursuit of social change that was so widespread a
mere quarter-century ago has yielded, as the German social theorist
Joachim Hirsch observes, to a "fatalistic and radically anti-utopian consciousness." Social activity, such as it is, focuses overwhelmingly on single issues and seeks to reform the existing social order rather than
challenge its basic institutions and economic relationships. Not only is
today's consciousness fatalistic and radically anti-utopian; it is derisively
antirevolutionary and even antiradical. The enormous change in social
and moral temper is reflected by the conventional ideology of the present
time, with its emphasis on trivial concerns, financial markets, consumerist escapes, and personal psychology. It has all but eliminated, for
the present, any principle of hope, to use Ernst Bloch's phrase. Where
social criticism does exist, it tends to focus on the abuses of specific corporations or on the defects of specific governmental actions (all valuable
work, to be sure) rather than on the capitalist and state system that produces them. Cynicism about the possibility of social change now prevails, as well as an appalling narcissism in everyday life.

Despite Hirsch's verdict, even this jaded public temper – a temper
that prevails no less among young people than among their parents –
needs compensatory escapisms to soften a life without inspiration or
meaning. It is not easy to accept a gray world in which acquisition, self-
absorption, and preoccupation with trivia are the main attributes of
everyday life. To improve the "comfort level" of middle-class life, Euro-
American society has witnessed an explosion of mystical, antirational,
and religious doctrines, not to speak of innumerable techniques for personal self-improvement. The personalistic form of these anodynes makes
self-expression into a surrogate for a politics of genuine empowerment.
Far from impelling people to social activism, these nostrums are infected
with an ancient Christian virus: namely, that personal salvation precedes
political change – indeed, that in every sense the political is reduced to
the personal, and the social to the individual.

Not only have lifestyle anarchism and social anarchism diverged very
sharply, but their divergence reflects an unprecedented development in
capitalism itself: its historic stabilization and its penetration into ever

more aspects of everyday life. This development, not surprisingly, engulfs even the ideologies that profess to oppose it, so that in the end they actually work to justify those changes. More than any society that preceded it, capitalism (to use Marx and Engels's phrase in *The Communist Manifesto*) "turns everything solid into air" – and polluted air at that. Rock 'n' roll, the music of countercultural rebellion, has long entered the liturgical ceremonies of modern churches, while radical folksinger Woody Guthrie's "This Land Is Your Land" appears in television commercials for a giant airline. The "culture war" that created so many professorial jobs in major universities is rapidly drawing to a close. As Thomas Frank, editor of a recent anthology, *Commodify Your Dissent,* has observed, "The countercultural idea has become capitalist orthodoxy. . . . However the basic impulses of the countercultural idea may have disturbed a nation lost in Cold War darkness, they are today in fundamental agreement with the basic tenets of Information Age business theory."[2]

In *Social Anarchism or Lifestyle Anarchism (SALA)*, I tried to show that lifestyle anarchism is well on its way to becoming just this kind of rebellious chic, in which jaded Americans rakishly adorn themselves with the symbols and idioms of personal resistance, all the more to accommodate themselves to the status quo. Anarchism's lifestyle tendencies orient young people toward a kind of rebellion that expresses itself in terms of narcissism, self-expression, intuition, and personalism – an orientation that stands sharply at odds with the socialistic core of anarchism that was celebrated by Bakunin, Kropotkin, and Malatesta, among so many others.

Lifestyle anarchism thus *recasts the spirit of revolt itself* – however residual it may be today – and *subverts the very basis for building the radical social opposition that will be needed in times more propitious for a rational social development.* Lifestyle anarchism, in effect, eats away at the traditions, ideas, and visions upon which anarchism as a *socialist* movement rests and that form its point of departure for the development of future revolutionary libertarian movements. In effect, its growing influence threatens to derail anarchism, with its rich implications for society as a whole, and redirect it toward the self as the locus of rebellion and reconstruction. In this respect, lifestyle anarchism is truly regressive. If a space is to be preserved on the political spectrum for serious left-libertarian discussion and activity – for use in the future, if not always in the present – then the growing influence of lifestyle anarchism must be earnestly resisted.

It is not only anarchism that is plagued by the advent of a an anti-Enlightenment culture with psychologistic, mystical, antirational, and quasi-religious overtones. Some of the ostensibly new reinterpretations of Marxism are patently psychologistic and even mystical in nature, while the ecology movement risks the prospect of becoming a haven for primitivism and nature mysticism. Goddess worship has invaded feminism, while postmodernism reigns in the formerly radical portions of the Academy. Indeed, the attempt to displace Enlightenment values of reason, secularism, and social activism with an emphasis on intuition, spiritualism, and an asocial psychologism pervades society as a whole. In this respect *SALA* may be seen as an appendix to my larger book, *Re-Enchanting Humanity*, which critiques the more general cultural manifestations of these tendencies.

Sorting Out the Issues

Nothing more strikingly supports my contention that lifestyle anarchism reflects present trends in bourgeois culture – its psychologism, antirationalism, primitivism, and mysticism – than the replies that lifestyle anarchists themselves have written to *SALA* since its publication. As of this writing (February 1998), two books, one pamphlet, and several articles have been published, all decrying my essay, yet all serving overwhelmingly as evidence to bolster my case against this tendency.

Consider, for example, a review of my essay in the journal *Social Anarchism,* written by Kingsley Widmer, an anarchist who harbors strong sympathies for primitivism and technophobia.[3] The critical thrust of his piece is that I insist on standing "in lonely splendor" on the "*ghostly* shoulders of Bakunin, Kropotkin, and their descendants in such as the Spanish anarchists of more than two generations ago," which makes me a proponent of an "antique left-socialism," a "*narrow* and *thin* libertarianism of a different time and place and conditions."

I collapse to the floor in shame. Never did I expect that the day would come when an anarchist – in fact, a member of *Social Anarchism*'s advisory board – would regard this lineage as "ghostly" and "thin"! Perhaps it would be more relevant to our time, in Widmer's view, if I ended my "lonely isolation" and adopted today's fashionable technophobia? Perhaps he believes I should join those who mystify the preindustrial age (which was already going into eclipse several generations ago)? Or those who mystify the Neolithic era of four hundred generations ago? Or the Paleolithic of some 1,200 generations ago? If being up to date is the standard for social relevance, then the mere two generations that have passed since the Spanish Revolution undoubtedly give me the edge over the primitivists whom Widmer defends (although in all fairness to him, he appears to be not quite certain where he stands on primitivism anymore).

Despite its brevity, Widmer's review touches on substantive issues concerning primitivism and technology that other critics have argued at greater length and which I will address later in this essay. Suffice it to note here that Widmer also makes use of a polemical technique that my longer-winded critics also use – namely, to demonize me as a "dogmatic" Leninist or even Stalinist. Widmer, however, makes this insinuation in a rather convoluted way: he reproves me for using the words "infantile" and "fascistic" in describing certain aspects of lifestyle anarchism – his objection being that "'political infantilism' was a favorite epithet of Leninists," and "'social fascism' of Stalinist and fellow-traveling 'progressives' in the Thirties."

This would be a damning criticism indeed if I had used these words in any sense that is relevant to Lenin, still less Stalin's characterizations. Nowhere did I suggest that my opponents are infantile leftists, as Lenin did, or designate any of my opponents "social fascists," as the Third Period Stalinists did. Am I to understand from Widmer that the words "infantile" and "fascistic" must be excised from the vocabulary of critical discourse today simply because Lenin and Stalin's Communist International used them nearly seventy years ago? If my ideas really do constitute an "antique left-socialism" that belongs to "dogmatically exclusionary political movement," then it is remarkable that Widmer can find a place on the anarchist spectrum at all for this "old socialist anarchist."

Anarchism, Marxism, and the Future of the Left

What troubles me about this polemical strategy, as many of my current critics use it, is that by its own terms, commitment to principle comes to be chastised as "dogma"; support for revolution over reform is condemned as "sectarian"; fervent objections to opponents' arguments are castigated as "authoritarian"; and polemical argumentation is designated as "Marxist" or "Leninist." In my own case, even my authorship of more than a dozen books becomes evidence of my agenda to "dominate" or "master" anarchism. At the very least, such methods reflect the ugly personalism that pervades this highly individualistic and trivialized culture.

This polemical techniques and many others are also put to use in Robert C. Black's *Anarchy After Leftism* (*AAL*), another response to *SALA* that is pervaded with a far more intense and personalistic vilification.[4] Black, the reader should be warned, is no mere author; he is a psychic who apparently can read my demonic mind, divine all my self-serving intentions, and unearth the Machiavellian meanings hidden in *all* of my writings, which are part of my devilish master plan to gain power and prestige, enrich my own wealth, and imperialistically colonize the entire anarchist scene as my own private fiefdom. Did I say that Black is a psychic? Actually, he is also an *exorcist*, and a cabalistic study of his book will surely free Anarchy (as distinguished from that lowly ideology "anarchism") from the Great Bookchin Conspiracy to take over that flourishing galactic realm.

To be serious about Black's endeavor – which his publisher, Jason McQuinn (aka Lev Chernyi) called "brilliant" in a recent issue of *Anarchy* – this ugly book is transparently motivated by a white-hot animosity toward me. So cynical, so manipulative, and so malicious are its invectives, even by the lowest standards of gutter journalism, that I will not dignify them with a reply. As I indicated in the subtitle to *SALA*, the chasm between people like this author and myself is unbridgeable.

Indeed, so numerous are the falsehoods in Black's book that to correct even a small number of them would be a waste of the reader's time. One sample must suffice to demonstrate the overall dishonesty of the tract. Black seems to establish early on that I am a "dean" at Goddard College (*AAL*, p. 18), a position that, he would have his readers believe, endows me with the very substantial income that I need in order to advance my nefarious ambitions. Consummate scholar that Black is, he sedulously documents this claim by citing Goddard College's *1995 Off-Campus Catalog*. Thereafter, throughout the book, I am referred to as "Dean Bookchin" or "the Dean," presumably on the assumption that mere repetition will make my title a reality.[5]

Goddard's *1995 Off-Campus Catalog* is a rare document, one that even I had difficulty acquiring – a fact upon which Black is apparently relying. Those few individuals who are able to find it, however, will learn that Black's claim is an outright fabrication. My name appears nowhere in that catalog nor in any other recent edition, for the very good reason that I ended my professional connections with Goddard College (as well as Ramapo College, which he also mentions) in 1981. Anyone who cares to find out my status as an employee of Goddard is invited to telephone the college and ask them.

Far from enjoying the material wealth that Black attributes to me, I live on a pension and Social Security, both of them paltry, supplemented by occasional lecture fees and book advances. I shall conclude this obligatory sketch of my economic status by noting that my supplemental income has diminished considerably in recent years because the physical infirmities caused by advanced age prevent me from traveling or writing easily any longer. Some of Black's followers will no doubt prefer to believe his statement that I am a well-to-do dean at Goddard, irrespective of the facts. I have neither the time nor the disposition to disenchant people who want to believe in his book.[6]

The Long, Dark Road Back

The second full-size book that contains a response to *SALA is Beyond Bookchin: Preface to a Future Social Ecology (BB)* written by David Watson (more widely known by his pseudonym George Bradford).[7] The leading writer for the Detroit anarchist periodical *Fifth Estate*, Watson is an individual whose writings I criticized in *SALA* for technophobia, anticivilizationism, primitivism, and irrationalism. In *BB* Watson, in turn, not only defends his positions, as he doubtless ought to do, but radically confirms my claim that the chasm between his ideas and mine is unbridgeable.

Indeed, what puzzles me about his work is that he ever found my writings interesting at all, especially given our incommensurable views on technology, or that they even influenced him, as he says they did.

The fact is that *BB* is not merely a reply to my criticisms – it is also a sweeping critique of almost everything I have ever written. "It is the intent of this essay," Watson declares early on, "to reveal how seriously limited Bookchin's work was *from the very beginning*" (*BB*, p. 10, emphasis added). Nor is *BB* simply a sweeping critique of my work "from the very beginning"; it is a scandalous hatchet job on my thirty years of writing to create a body of ideas called social ecology. By the end of the book we learn that Watson's true purpose is to "abandon [Bookchin's] idea of social ecology" altogether (*BB*, p. 245). Or as Steve Welzer advises in his laudatory introduction to the book, "social ecology itself must be liberated from Bookchin" (*BB*, p. 4).

In this 250-page indictment, Watson pokes into the smallest crevices in my writings while omitting the aspects of my writings that, on his own admission, allowed him to set himself up as an libertarian thinker. Divesting all my writings of their contexts – spanning some forty years in social movements – he wantonly tosses together my casual observations and polemical exaggerations with my more considered writings on social theory, ecology, urban development, politics, and philosophy. Running through almost every paragraph of Watson's book are vituperative attacks, manic denunciations, ad hominem characterizations, and even gossipy rumors. In time, the reader becomes so drenched in Watson's outpouring of trivia, distortion, and personal venom that he or she may well lose sight of the basic differences between Watson and myself – the very issues that motivated my critique of his views in *SALA*.

What, after all, are the views that Watson is really trying to advance as the "future social ecology" that he advertises as an advance over my own? What precisely does it consist of? Amid the thickets, thorns, and weeds of personal invective that proliferate in his book, I find four basic tenets that he is promoting – each of which, if adopted by anarchists, would radically remove anarchism from the liberating realm of Enlightenment thought and entomb it in the mystical realm of anticivilizationism, technophobia, primitivism, and irrationalism.

Murray Bookchin

Civilization and Progress

For many years, in many different essays, as I pointed out in *SALA*,
Watson has sharply rejected civilization, presumably in its Western form
(although he devotes little space to denunciations of Oriental despotisms, with their megamechanical armies of serflike gang laborers). Thus,
he told us in 1991: "Civilization is coming to be regarded . . . as a maladaption of the species, a false turn or a kind of fever threatening the
planetary web of life" (*CIB*, p. 10).* It has been little more than "a labor
camp from its origins" (*CIB*, p. 12); it is "a machine, an organization," "a
rigid pyramid of crushing hierarchies," "a grid expanding the territory of
the inorganic" (*CIB*, p. 12). Its "railroad leads not only to ecocide, but to
evolutionary suicide" (*CIB*, p. 13).

Nor is it merely one or several aspects of civilization that exhibits
these qualities: it is civilization *as such*. In 1988 he wrote that civilization
is "destructive in its essence to nature and humanity" (*HDDE*, p. 3). In
1984 he wrote that we must be "willing to confront the entirety of this
civilization and reclaim our humanity" (*SDT*, p. 11). While considering
the mystical pap of Monica Sjoo and Barbara Mor (in their book *The
Great Mother Goddess*) to be "fascinating," he nonetheless reproaches them
for placing quotation marks around the word *civilization* because it suggests "a reverse or alternative perspective on civilization rather than . . .
challenge its terms altogether" (*CIB*, p. 14, n. 23).

Metaphors for civilization as a unitary, monolithic grid or railroad,
whose nature is necessarily destructive, are shallow, unmediated, and in
fact reactionary. By putting quotation marks around "civilization," a
writer can at least acknowledge civilization's advances without accepting
its abuses.[8] If Watson will not allow even this concession to civilization's
role, then it becomes clear that for him, redemption can be achieved only
by regression. The rise of civilization becomes humanity's great lapse, its
Fall from Eden, and "our humanity" can be "reclaimed" only through a
prelapsarian return to the lost Eden, through recovery rather than discovery – in short, through a denial of humanity's advance beyond the
horizon of prehistory.

This sort of rubbish may have been good coin in medieval monasteries. But in the late Middle Ages, few ideas in Christian theology did more to hold back advances in science and experimental research than the notion that with the Fall, humanity lost its innocence. One of the Enlightenment's great achievements was to provide a critical perspective on the past, denouncing the taboos and shamanistic trickery that made tribal peoples the victims of unthinking custom as well as the irrationalities that kept them in bondage to hierarchy and class rule, despite its denunciations of Western cant and artificialities.

Nor does Watson have the least use for the idea of progress; indeed, he even denigrates the development of writing, disparaging the "dogma of the inherent superiority of the written tradition" over nonliteracy as "embarrassingly simplistic" (*BB*, p. 24) and "an imperial tale" (*BB*, p. 100), and praises the oral tradition. Before the written word, it should be noted, chiefs, shamans, priests, aristocrats, and monarchs possessed a free-wheeling liberty to improvise ways to require the oppressed to serve them. It was the written word, eventually, that subjected them to the restrictions of clearly worded and publicly accessible laws to which their rule, in some sense, was accountable. Writing rendered it possible for humanity to record its culture, and inscribing laws or *nomoi* where all could see them remains one of the great advances of civilization. That the call for written laws as against arbitrary decisions by rulers was a age-old demand of the oppressed is easily forgotten today, when they are so readily taken for granted. When Watson argues that the earliest uses of writing were for authoritarian or instrumental purposes, he confuses the *ability to write* with what was *actually written* – and betrays an appalling lack of historical knowledge.

On the subject of modern medicine, our poet – as he styles himself – delivers himself of the sublime view that "it could conceivably [!] turn out to be medicine which extinguishes humanity rather than ecological disaster or human conflagration" (*BB*, p. 115). Not nuclear war? Not a terrifying and rampant epidemic? Not even "ecological disaster" – but *medicine?*[9]

Watson's rejection of "civilization in bulk" and his denial of even the most obvious advances of progress leaves us with the conclusion that, for him, civilization as such must either be accepted or rejected in its entirely.

Such mental rigidity, such unitary determinism, gives us no choice but to define civilization exclusively by its evils. Accordingly, while Watson concedes that my defense of civilization's achievements "might represent in some sense what is 'best' in Western culture," ideas of civilization and progress "have also typically served as core mystifications concealing what is *worst*" (*BB*, p. 9). For Watson, then, the idea of progress is merely a cover-up for the sins of civilization.

That the "official story" of progress contains both good and evil, indeed that civilization is "Janus-faced" (*RS*, p. 180) and constitutes a subtle dialectic between a "legacy of freedom" and a "legacy of domination" (which I elaborated for nearly fifty pages in *The Ecology of Freedom*) is conveniently ignored in Watson's discussion of this subject. Instead, he debases my account of civilization's substance and form, divests my discussion of history's interacting dialectic of all its development, flesh, bone, and blood, leaving only a straw man: a blind champion of *all* aspects of civilization, the unmediated reverse of his own radically simplistic rejection.

Which is not to say that Watson is unaware of his butchery of ideas. Much later in his book, and in an entirely different context, he lets slip the fact that I see the "city" as "Janus faced . . . in its look toward the prospect of a common humanity as well as in its look toward barbarities in the name of progress" (*BB*, p. 171; quoting *RS*, p. 180). Unfortunately, in the original passage from which he draws this quote, I wrote that "civilization," not the "city," is Janus-faced – a distortion that should warn Watson's readers about the need to refer back to my writings whenever he undertakes to quote from me.

Having inserted this misquotation at the book's end, Watson feels free to describe me as the "lone defender of civilization" (*BB*, p. 7), at the very beginning the book. This honor, however, is too great for me to bear alone. I must share my laurels with Lewis Mumford, who (even more than Langdon Winner, Lao-Tzu, and Fredy Perlman) seems to be the supreme guru of Watson's "future social ecology." As it turns out, Mumford also posited a dual legacy for civilization – and, like Mor and Sjoo, put quotation marks around "civilization" to cite one of them.[10]

In fact, Mumford explicitly condemned anticivilizationist positions like the one Watson espouses, describing them as a "nihilist reaction."

"The threatened annihilation of man by his favored technological and institutional automatisms," he once lamented, ". . . has in turn brought about an equally devastating counter-attack – an attack *against civilization itself*."[11] Mumford bluntly repudiated "the notion that in order to avoid the predictable calamities that the power complex is bringing about, one must destroy the whole *fabric of historic civilization* and begin all over again on an entirely fresh foundation."[12] He objected to "a revolt against *all historic culture* – not merely against an over-powered technology and an over-specialized, misapplied intelligence, but against any higher manifestations of the mind."[13]

The only person here who would seem to have difficulty accepting the existence of ambiguities in civilization appears to be Watson himself, the unwavering denouncer of "civilization in bulk."

Technophobia

If Watson claims that the good that civilization offers is merely a veil for its evils, it is not likely that he and I will ever agree on so provocative an issue as technology. My conviction is that productive and communications technologies will be needed by a rational society in order to free humanity from toil and the material uncertainties (as well as natural ones) that have in the past shackled the human spirit to a nearly exclusive concern for subsistence. Watson, by contrast, is an outright technophobe.

What makes this disagreement particularly abrasive, however, is his persistent tendency to misrepresent my views. Consider, for example, his assertion that because my "notion of social evolution is clearly linked [!] to technological development and an expansion of production" (*BB*, p. 96), I am an icy technocrat who rhapsodizes about the technics of the "megamachine," especially the chemical and nuclear industries.[14] Watson, who seems to have difficulty acknowledging the existence even of a mere "link," as he puts it, between technological and social development, performs the kind of fabrication at which he most excels and turns a "link" into sufficient cause:

Only [!] technological development, [Bookchin] says, would bring "a balance . . . between a sufficiency of the means of life, a relative freedom of time to fulfill one's abilities in the most advanced levels of human achievement, a degree of self-consciousness, complementarity, and reciprocity that can be called truly human in full recognition of humanity's potentialities" [EF: 67-68]. (*BB*, p. 96)

In fact, the reader who consults the whole passage from which Watson has cynically clipped this quotation will find that I made no statement that "technological development" *alone* creates these marvels. Quite to the contrary, by inserting the word "only" and clipping the words after "balance," Watson grossly distorts my claim. What I actually wrote was not that technology will bring such a "balance" but that a "balance *must be struck* between a sufficiency of the means of life" and self-consciousness, complementarity, reciprocity, and so on. That is, *technological development, far from "bringing" these features, must "strike a balance" with them!*

The same misquoted passage from *The Ecology of Freedom* leads into a discussion of the fact that material scarcity is not only the result of physically limiting conditions but is also "*socially* induced" and "*may occur even when technical development seems to render material scarcity completely unwarranted.* . . . A society that has enlarged the cultural goals of human life may generate material scarcity *even when the technical conditions exist for achieving outright superfluity in the means of life*" (*EF*, p. 68, emphases added). Expressed in more general terms: technics is a *necessary* condition for progress, but it is not a *sufficient* one. Let me emphasize quite strongly, as I have repeatedly argued, that without moral, intellectual, cultural, and, yes, spiritual progress, a rational society will be impossible to achieve.

In the same passage, I then went on to discuss the "fetishization of needs" that capitalism creates, and which a rational society would eliminate. That is, capitalism creates artificial needs by making people feel they must buy the most status-elevating motor vehicle or the fastest computer in the market.

Watson's distortion of my views cannot be written off as accidental; indeed, it is hard to believe that it is not cynically deliberate, leading me to conclude that he is a demagogue who regards his readers as gullible fools.

What is basic to my views is that the ecological crisis is more the result of the capitalist economy, with its grow-or-die imperatives, than of technology or "mass technics." Capitalist enterprise employs technologies to produce on a wide scale for the market, but in the end these technologies remain the instruments of capitalism, not its motor, amplifying the effects of a grow-or-die economy that is ruinous to the natural world. Yet as devastating as the effects of technology can be when driven to maximum use by capitalist imperatives, technologies *on their own* could not have provided the imperatives that produced the ecological damage we are now witnessing.

Nor do the technologies that capitalism drives to the point of wreaking ecological destruction need always be sophisticated industrial ones. The romantic heaths of Yorkshire that excite such wonder in travelers today were once covered by stately forests that were subsequently cut down to produce the charcoal that fueled the making of metals even before capitalist development in Britain got under way. European entrepreneurs in North America used mere axes, adzes, and hammers to clear forested land. A nearly Neolithic technology deforested much of Europe in the late Middle Ages, well in advance of the "megamachine" and the impacts Watson assigns to it.

To distinguish his own view of the relationship between technology, capitalism, and the rest of society from mine, Watson turns philosophical. He disparages my ostensibly simplistic ways of thinking in favor of his supposedly more dialectical mental processes. I am not at all sure what Watson thinks dialectics is; instead of standing on his own philosophical ground, he turns to John Clark for a quick philosophy lesson. Clark, whose philosophical insights I have always found to be less than trenchant, advises Watson that mere causal notions, presumably of the kind I advance concerning capitalism, are "uni-directional." Dialectics, he advises us, must instead be understood in the following terms: "If the [social] totality is taken as the whole of society, rather than the superstructure, and if reciprocity is extended to encompass *all* relations,

including the economic ones, then this represents a model for a dialectical social theory in the full sense" (quoted in *BB*, p. 157; emphasis
added). Put in less pompous language: We can identify no single cause
as more compelling than others; rather, all possible factors are mutually
determining.

This morass of "reciprocity," in which everything in the world is in a
reciprocal relationship with everything else, is precisely what dialectical
causality is *not,* unless we want to equate dialectics with chaos. Dialectics
is a philosophy of development, not of mutually determining factors in
some kind of static equilibrium. Although on some remote level, everything does affect everything else, some things are in fact very significantly
more determining than others. Particularly in social and historical phenomena, some causes are major, while others are secondary and adventitious. Dialectical causality focuses on what is *essential* in producing
change, on the *underlying* motivating factors, as distinguished from the
incidental and auxiliary. In a forest ecocommunity, for example, all
species may affect all others, however trivially, but some – the most
numerous trees, for example – are far more prominent than the ferns at
their base in determining the nature of that forest.

In Clark's befuddled understanding of dialectic, however, a potpour-
ri of causes are so "interrelated" (a magic word in modern ecobabble)
with one another that major and secondary causes are impossible to distinguish. Watson nonetheless accepts Clark's wild mix of "reciprocity"
not only as serious thinking but as true dialectics and blandly incorpo-
rates it into his own position on technics. "It makes no sense," he saga-
ciously muses, "to layer the various elements of this process in a
mechanistic [!] hierarchy of first [!] cause and secondary effects" – that
is, to assign greater potency to either capitalism or even technology as
generating the ecological crisis. "There is no simple or single etiology to
this plague, but a synergy of vectors" (*BB*, p. 128).

Watson then goes on to offer us his version of a "synergy of vectors":
the megamachine. This is a concept he borrows from Mumford, in which
technics, economics, politics, the military, bureaucracy, ideology, and the
like are one giant monolithic "machine," all of them so closely interrelated
as to be causally indistinguishable. In this universe etiology is indeed

meaningless; everything is part of the "synergy of vectors" known as the megamachine.

Still, in some passages of *BB*, etiology sneaks back into Watson's rarefied dialectical cogitations: "*Technology also forms a matrix,*" (*BB*, p. 125), he tells us, "by way of a synergistic tendency to reshape the pattern within which it emerged" (*BB*, p. 125). Not only do "technological relations" (whatever they may be) "*shape* human action"(*BB*, p. 120), but in some societies "technology has thoroughly *shaped and redefined* the social imaginary" (*BB*, p. 124).

Far from advancing a "synergy of vectors," in fact, Watson advances a very clear "etiology," with one very clear determining cause: technology. A decade and a half of Watson's writings show that he has been consistent (might one even say dogmatic?) on this score:

> "The technological apparatus has transformed human relations entirely, *recreating us in its image.*" (*ATM*, p.5)

> "Technology is not a tool but an environment, a *totality* of means enclosing us in its automatism of need and production and the geometric runaway of its own development." (*SDT*, p. 11 emphasis added in this and the next five quotations)

> Our "form of social organization, an interconnection and stratification of tasks and authoritarian command" is "*necessitated* by the enormity and complexity of the modern technological system in all of its activities." (*SDT*, p. 11)

> "The direction of governance flows from the technical conditions to people and their social arrangements, not the other way around. What we find, then, is not a tool waiting passively to be used but a technical ensemble that *demands* routinized behavior." (Winner quoted in *SDT*, p. 11)

> Mass technics is "a *one-way* barrage of mystification and control." (*SDT*, p. 11)

"Mass technics have become . . . 'structures whose conditions of operation *demand* the restructuring of their environments.'" (Winner quoted in *SIH,* p. 10)

These quotations give "uni-directional" determinism a bad name. So habituated is Watson to making such all-encompassing statements that, even while he was writing *BB,* he sometimes forgot about Clarkean "dialectics." Technology, he writes, "bring[s] . . . about *imperatives* unanticipated by their creators, which is to say: technological means come with their own repertoire of ends" (*BB,* p. 120; the emphases here and in the next paragraphs are mine). "Technicization" is "now *extinguishing* vast skeins in the fabric of life" (*BB,* p. 126). The technological system *"requires"* people to operate within it (*BB,* p. 143). Technics makes "hierarchy, specialization, and stratified, compartmentalized organizational structures . . . *inescapable"* (*BB,* p. 144).

A similar intellectually paralyzing reductionism is also reflected in passages Watson quotes from other authors. Jacques Ellul is trotted in to say that technology is establishing "a new *totality"* (*BB,* p. 144). Ivan Illich remarks on "the industrially *determined* shape of our expectations" (*BB,* p. 142). Langdon Winner observes that all tools "evoke a *necessary* reaction from the person using them" (*BB,* p. 126) and that "the technical ensemble *demands* routinized behavior" (144). And:

> "Ultimately," [Winner] explains, "the steering is inherent in the functioning of socially organized technology itself," which is to say that the owners and bosses *must* steer at the controls their technology provides. As the monster says to Doctor Frankenstein, "You are my creator, but I am your *master."* (*BB,* p. 143)[15]

Not only does Watson single out technology as a determining cause, he explicitly regards capitalism as secondary, a mere expression of a supposed technological imperative. "Market capitalism," he writes, "has been everywhere the *vehicle* for a mass megatechnic civilization" (*BB,* p. 126). Accordingly, it is not simply "capitalist greed" that produces oil spills; "not only capitalist grow-or-die economic choices, but the very nature of the complex petrochemical grid *itself* makes disasters inevitable" (*BB*, p. 120).

I have often written that, because capitalism is still developing so rapidly, we cannot be sure what actually constitutes mature capitalism. Watson puts his own spin on my formulation and offers a redefinition of capitalism that is so broad as it strip it of its specific features and submerge it to the megamachine altogether:

> We need a larger definition of capitalism that encompasses not only market relations and the power of bourgeois and bureaucratic elites [!] but the very structure and content of mass technics, reductive rationality and the universe they establish; the social imaginaries of progress, growth, and efficiency; the growing power of the state; and the materialization, objectifications and quantification of nature, culture and human personality. (*BB*, p. 126)

So much is included within this "larger" definition of capitalism that capitalism in its specificity and in all its phases is completely lost. Elsewhere, in a quintessential example of his obscurantism, Watson tells us with finality: "Technology is capital" (*ATM*, p. 5). Farewell to two centuries of political economy and debates over the nature of capitalism: over whether it is a social relation (Marx), machines and labor (Smith and Ricardo), a mere factor of production (neoclassical economists) or, most brilliantly, the teeth of a tiger (H. G. Wells)! Farewell to the class struggle! Farewell to an economics of social and class relations! When Watson slows down his dervishlike whirl and gives us a chance to examine his ecstatic spinning, we find that it leads to the elimination of the social question itself, as a century of socialist thought called it. Watson is now tries to apprise us that the great conflict that has beleaguered history is not really workers and bosses, or between subjects and elites. Fools that we have been – *it is between human beings and their machines!* Machines are not the embodiment of alienated labor but in fact are the "social imaginary" that looms over them and controls their lives! And all this time, Marx, Bakunin, Kropotkin, et al. foolishly labored under the illusion that the social question stems from exploitation and domination, scarcity and toil!

If my conclusion seems overstated, then I would suggest that readers follow Watson himself down into his dark valley of technological absurdity. Approvingly quoting Langdon Winner, Watson enjoins us to practice "epistemological luddism" as a "method of inquiry" (*BB*, p. 132). To those who notice that these phrases are empty, Watson concedes that they are "inchoate and embryonic" (*BB*, p. 132) – so why present them? But only three paragraphs later, we learn that Watson's luddism is not merely "epistemological" or a "method of inquiry." Rather, it is a concrete agenda to achieve a good society. We will require, he enjoins, "a careful negotiation with technics" and (approvingly quoting the mystic Theodore Roszak) "the selective reduction of industrialism" (*BB*, p. 133).

Roszak, at least, was sensible enough to speak of a *selective* reduction of industrialism. For Watson, however, selectivity all but disappears, and his "negotiated" dismantling of industry becomes nothing less than spectacular. "Let's begin dismantling the noxious structures," he has enjoined; "let's deconstruct the technological world" (*BPA*, p. 26). We have to "dismantle mass technics" (*SIH*, p. 11) – that is to say, all those "vectors" that make up the "megamachine" and civilization.

What is Watson's opening "negotiating" position? For the most part, in his other writings, he has long avoided naming *which* technologies he would keep and *which* he would dispose of, even airily disparaging the question. But for one who wishes to "negotiate," the necessity for him to identify the technologies he favors and disfavors should be self-evident. These other writings give us some idea of Watson's alternative to the cage of megamechanical civilization.

"Let's reforest and refarm the cities," he counsels; "no more building projects, giant hospitals, no more road repair" (*BPA*, p. 26). I may be simple-minded, but this seems to be a call to pull down cities and reduce them to forests and farmland. In the absence of cities and roads, Watson seems to want us to return to small-scale farming, "a clear context where small scale, the 'softness' of technics, labor-intensiveness, and technical limits all crucially matter" (*BB*, p. 138). Clearly tractors and the like will be excluded – they are patently products of the megamachine. But I would hope Watson's brave new world will not be so extreme as to exclude the plow and horses – or are we being domineering if we put horses into harnesses?

"Stop the exponential growth of information, pull the plug on the communications system" (*BPA*, p. 26). We would thus have to eliminate computers and telecommunications; farewell, too, to telegraphs, radios, and telephones! It is just as well we do so, since Watson doesn't understand telephones: the work of telephone line workers, he says, is "a mystery" to him (*BB*, p. 146). So good riddance! He has also written that "the wheel is *not* an extension of the foot, but a simulation which *destroys* the original" (*MCGV*, p. 11, emphasis added). So away with the wheel! Away with everything that "simulates" feet! And who knows – away with the potter's wheel, which is a "simulation" of the hand!

As to energy sources, Watson really puts us in a pickle. He disapproves of "the elaborate energy system required to run" household appliances and other machines, since it renders people "dependent" (Christopher Lasch quoted in *BB*, p. 141). So – away with the mass generation of electricity, and every machine that runs on it! Needless to say, all fossil as well as nuclear fuels will have to go. Perhaps we could turn to renewable energy as an alternative – but no, Watson has also voiced his sovereign disapproval of "solar, wind and water technologies" as products of "an authoritarian and hierarchical division of labor" (*NST,* p. 4). All of this leaves us with little more than our own muscles to power our existence. Yes, "revolution will be a kind of return" (*BB*, p. 140), indeed!

To be sure, we will eliminate such noxious products of the megamachine as weapons, but if we also dispense with roads (clearly if we do not repair them, they will disappear), typewriters and computers (except the computer owned by *Fifth Estate,* presumably, for otherwise how will Watson's golden words reach the public?), any form of mechanical agriculture (which Watson seems to confuse with agribusiness), et cetera ad nauseam. The reader has only to walk through his or her home, look into each room, and peer into closets and medicine chests and kitchen cabinets, to see what would be surrendered in the kind of technological world that Watson would "negotiate" with industrialism.

Let it be noted, however, that a return to the economic conditions of twelfth-century Europe would hardly *create* a paradise. Somehow, even in the absence of advanced technology to generate them, oppressive social relations still existed in this technological idyll. Somehow feudal hierarchies of the most oppressive kind (in no way modeled on ecclesiastical hierarchies, let alone "shaped" by technology) superimposed themselves. Somehow the peasant-serfs who were ruled and coerced by barons, counts, kings, and their bureaucratic and military minions failed to realize that they were free of the megamachine's oppressive impact. Yet they were still so unecological as to drain Europe's mosquito-infested swamps and burn its forests to create meadows and open farmland. Happily spared the lethal effects of modern medicine, they usually died very early in life of famine, epidemic disease, and other deadly agents.

Given the demands of highly labor-intensive farming, what kind of free time, in the twelfth century, did small-scale farmers have? If history is any guide, it was a luxury they rarely enjoyed, even during the agriculturally dormant winters. During the months when farmers were not tilling the land and harvesting its produce, they struggled endlessly to make repairs, tend animals, perform domestic labor, and the like. And they had the wheel! It is doubtful that, under such circumstances, much time would have been left over for community meetings, let alone the creation of art and poetry.

Doubtless they sowed, reaped, and did their work joyously, as I pointed out in *The Ecology of Freedom*. The workman's song – proletarian, peasant, and artisan – expresses the joy of self-expression through work. But this does not mean that work, bereft of machinery, is an unadulterated blessing or that it is not exhausting or monotonous. There is a compelling word for arduous labor: *toil!* Without an electric grid to turn night into day, active life is confined to daylight hours, apart from what little illumination can be provided by candles. (Dare I introduce such petroleum derivatives as kerosene?) It is one of the great advances of the modern world that the most arduous and monotonous labor can often be performed entirely by machines, *potentially* leaving human beings free to engage in many different tasks and artistic activities, such as those Charles Fourier described for his utopian phalansteries.

But as soon as I assign to technology the role of producing a society free of want and toil, Watson takes up the old dogmatic saw and condemns it to perdition as "the familiar marxist version" (*BB*, p. 129). Watson may enjoy appealing to unthinking political reflexes that date back to the Marx-Bakunin battles of the First International, but the merit of an idea interests me more than its author. Instead of directly addressing the problem of scarcity and toil in any way, however, Watson settles the issue, at least in his own mind, by quoting his guru, Lewis Mumford: "The notion that automation gives any guarantee of human liberation is a piece of wishful thinking" (quoted in *BB*, p. 130) – as though a technological advance *in itself* were a "guarantee" of *anything* under capitalism, apart from more exploitation and destruction. (It is astonishing that one has to explain this concept to a former Trotskyite like Watson, who should have some knowledge of Marx's ideas.)

Alas, Mumford does not serve him well. In *The Pentagon of Power* (the same work from which Watson quotes), Mumford himself actually gives what Watson would be obliged to dismiss as "the familiar marxist version." Mumford notes, first quoting from an unattributed source:

> "The negative institutions . . . would never have endured so long but for the fact that their positive goods, even though they were arrogated to the use of the dominant minority, were ultimately at the service of the whole community, and *tended to produce a universal society of far higher potentialities, by reason of its size and diversity*." If that observation held true at the beginning, it remains even more true today, now that this *remarkable technology* has spread over the whole planet. The only way effectively to overcome the power system is to *transfer* its more *helpful* agents to an organic complex.[16]

Elsewhere in the same book, speaking of "the decrepit institutional complex one can trace back at least to the Pyramid age," Mumford says that "what modern technology has done is . . . . rehabilitate it, perfect it, and give it a global distribution." Then, more significantly: "The *potential* benefits of this system, under more humane direction" are "immense." Indeed, elsewhere he speaks of "our genuine technological advances."[17] Now what does Watson have to say about that?

How should the technological level of a free society be determined? Watson's thoughts on this question are such as to render his libertarian views on technics and human needs more authoritarian than is immedi-

ately evident. Suppose, for example, that nonindustrialized and even tribal people actually *want* not only wheels, roads, and electric grids, but
even the material goods, such as computers and effective medications,
that people in industrialized countries enjoy – not least of all, Watson
himself and the *Fifth Estate* collective. I have argued in *The Ecology of
Freedom* that no one, particularly in a consumption-oriented country
such as the United States, has any right to bar nonindustrialized societies
from choosing the way of life they wish. I would hope that they would
make their choices with full awareness of the ecological and even psychological consequences of consumption as an end in itself, which have been
amply demonstrated for them by the course of developed nations; and I
would engage in a concerted effort to persuade all peoples of the world to
live according to sound ecological standards. But it would be their indu-
bitable right to acquire what they believe they need, without anyone else
dictating what they should or should not acquire.

Not only is my proposal intolerable in Watson's eyes, he cannot even
paraphrase it correctly. He must distort it in order to make it seem ridiculous: "What are we to make of the proposal to develop mass technics and
a combination consumer-producer utopia [!] *in order to reject them*?"
(*BB*, p. 107). The implication of this distortion is, I believe, that poor
societies must develop capitalism and technology in order to know the
consequences of doing so, irrespective of the fact that the consequences
of doing so are quite clear and the information is widely available, not
least of all because of communications technology.

For Watson, however, the ecological crisis is too urgent to wait for a
policy as slow as mine. "Neither ecological wisdom nor the health of the
planet can wait for this grotesque overindulgence [that I supposedly
advocate] to have its curative effect," he firmly declares (*BB*, p. 108). How,
then, would our lifestyle anarchist handle this very real problem himself?
He doesn't tell us, but he does call on people in the industrialized countries to seek "a new relationship to the phenomenal world – something
akin to what [Marshall] Sahlins calls 'a Zen road to affluence, departing
from premises somewhat different from our own'" (*BB*, p. 108). May I
suggest that this is dodging the issue? If the urgency of resolving the ecological crisis is the paramount factor, Watson's own solution would seem
rather inadequate as well, requiring as it does an ethereal spiritual revolu-

tion on the basis of one-by-one conversion. Nor is such an approach likely to succeed, any more than Christianity succeeded in creating a loving, self-sacrificing, and all-forgiving world in two thousand years of one-by-one conversions – and the Church, at least, promised pie in the sky (as the old IWW song has it) in the next world if not in this one.

As for people in the industrial-capitalist world, Watson, who has tried to prejudice his readers against my views as "marxist," "authoritarian," and "dogmatic," suddenly mutates into an ideological despot in his own right. He finds it inconceivable that people could actually make conscious decisions about the use of technology, still less place moral constraints upon it. Quite to contrary, inasmuch as, in his view, technology governs people rather than the other way around, we can scarcely hope to spring the trap and decide for ourselves. Watson ridicules the notion that "a moral society . . . could sit down and decide how to 'use'" a technology (bioengineering is cited here) "without catastrophic results" (*BB*, p. 125). He arrogantly forecloses democratic decision-making by ordinary people on the proper use of advanced technologies, because open civic discussions would *"inevitably"* result in "compliance with the opinion of experts" and "would of *necessity* be based on persuasion and faith" (*BB*, pp. 146-47, emphasis added). Lest we have any doubt that Watson means what he says, he reiterates the same disdainful view: "It's ludicrous [!] to think that citizen assemblies could make informed decisions about chemical engineering strategies, communications grids, and complicated technical apparatus" (*BB*, p. 180).

One may modestly ask: why should this be "ludicrous"? Expert knowledge is by no means necessary to make general decisions about the uses of technology: a reasonable level of ordinary competence on the part of citizens is usually quite adequate. In fact, today legislators at the local, state, and national levels make such decisions every day, and ordinary people can clearly do the same. Watson's argument that such decisions are beyond the ken of ordinary people is (possibly unknown to him) *precisely* the argument that Lenin advanced in 1918 against workers' control of factories (which, of course, Watson would abandon wholesale) and in favor of one-man management (to use Bolshevik terminology). Does our poetic lifestyler really have so little faith in the competence of ordinary people? Doubtless workers, technicians, and farmers need someone with higher wisdom – perhaps Watson himself – to specify their appropriate level of technology for them?

Actually, Watson seems to be suffering from a memory lapse. Somewhat later in his book he gives us the very opposite message, notably that "people have the capacity, in fact the duty to make rational and ethical choices about technics" (*BB,* p. 203). How, then, will they avoid all the "inevitable" and "necessary" obstacles that Watson himself earlier raised? One gets the distinct impression that, no matter what specific issue is under discussion, if I say yea, Watson is certain to say nay – even if it means he must reverse himself on a later occasion.

Primitivism

There is nothing new about the romanticization of tribal peoples. Two centuries ago, denizens of Paris, from Enlighteners such as Denis Diderot to reactionaries like Marie Antoinette, created a cult of "primitivism" that saw tribal people as morally superior to members of European society, who presumably were corrupted by the vices of civilization. This romanticization later infected not only the early nineteenth-century Romantics but thinkers so disparate as Marx and Engels, Jacob Bachofen and Lewis Morgan. These and others wistfully thought that humanity had exiled itself from a benign, "matriarchal," caring, and cooperative world to a civilization filled with immoral and egoistic horrors.

The more urbanized and suburbanized bourgeois culture of the 1960s was far from immune to this trend. During the 1960s anthropologists celebrated the "noble savage" in his or her pristine paradise, which more than ever seemed like a refuge, however imaginary, for jaded urban (and suburban) dwellers of the industrial capitalist world. Inhabitants of American cities and suburbs, from San Francisco to New York, were completely enchanted by myths of primal naïveté, particularly members of the youth culture, who stressed the virtues of innocence and passivity and harbored a basic sympathy for "noble savage" anthropology.

This anthropology, contrary to less sanguine views of primitive lifeways, argued that foraging peoples were compelled to work at hunting and food-gathering for only a few hours each day. Wrote anthropologists Richard B. Lee and Irven DeVore:

> Even some of the "marginal" hunters studied by ethnographers actually work short hours and exploit abundant food sources. Several hunting peoples lived well on two to four hours of subsistence effort per day and were not observed to undergo the periodic crises that have been commonly attributed to hunters in general.... [Some ethnographers] speculate whether lack of "future orientation" brought happiness to the members of hunting societies, an idyllic attitude that faded when changing subsistence patterns forced men to amass food surpluses to bank against future shortages.[18]

It was most notably Marshall Sahlins who argued that aborigines lived in an "affluent society."

> By common understanding an affluent society is one in which all the people's wants are easily satisfied; and though we are pleased to consider this happy condition the unique achievement of industrial civilization, a better case can be made for hunters and gatherers.... For wants are "easily satisfied," either by producing much or desiring little.... A fair case can be made, that hunters often work much less than we do, and rather than a grind the food quest is intermittent, leisure is abundant, and there is more sleep in the daytime per capita than in any other conditions of society.[19]

During the late 1960s and 1970s I myself shared an excessive enthusiasm for certain aspects of aboriginal and organic societies, and in *The Ecology of Freedom* and other writings of those years I gave an overly rosy discussion of them and speculated optimistically about aboriginal subjectivity. I never accepted the preposterous theory of an "original affluent society," but I waxed far too enthusiastic about primitive attitudes toward the natural world and their compassionate outlook. I even maintained that the animistic qualities of aboriginal subjectivity were something that Westerners could benefit from emulating.

I later came to realize that I was wrong in many of these respects. Aboriginal peoples could have no attitude toward the natural world because, being immersed in it, they had no concept of its uniqueness. It is true that individual tribes had considerable compassion for their own members, but their attitudes toward nontribal members were often indifferent or hostile. As to animism, in retrospect, I regard any belief in the supernatural as regressive. As I discussed in detail in *Re-Enchanting Humanity* (pp. 120-47), much that passes for pristine "primitivism" is based on fictions, and what can be authenticated from the paleontological record is not as benign as some 1960s-oriented anthropologists would have us believe. Aboriginal societies were hardly free from such material insecurities as shortages of game animals, diseases, drudgery, chronic warfare, and even genocidal acts against communities that occupied coveted land and resources. Such a prevalence of premature death, given their level of social and technological development, bears comparison with some of Western civilization's worst features.

Having been too gullible about "organic society" in *The Ecology of Freedom,* I was at pains to criticize my own work on this score when the book was republished in 1992. At that time I wrote a lengthy new introduction in which I distanced myself from many of the views expressed in the first edition of the book.[20] It was not my intention, however, nor is it now, to disparage aboriginal societies. Quite to the contrary, I still stand by the core issues in these societies that I identified in *The Ecology of Freedom* as sources of valuable lessons for our own time. In the best of cases organic societies organized their economic and cultural lives according to a principle of usufruct, with a system of distribution based on an "irreducible minimum" (a phrase I borrowed from Paul Radin), as well as an ethic of complementarity, for all members of the community, regardless of their productive contribution.

Not only does Watson ignore my criticism of my own earlier position, he himself advances a primitive romanticism whose rosy scenarios far surpass anything I wrote in my book. He serves up all the 1960s myths, indeed, all the puerile rubbish, about aboriginal lifeways of that time – not only Sahlins's "original affluence" economics but the most absurd elements of animistic spirituality. Primitivity, for this man, is essentially a world of dancing, singing, celebrating, and dreaming. The subjectivity that I came to reject is precisely what Watson still extols: primitive people, in his version, seem to be all mystics at some counter-cultural "be-in." In fact, they seem to be free of most human features, as if they were festive "imaginaries" that stepped out of a psychedelic mural. That they also do such mundane human things as acquire food, produce garments, make tools, build shelters, defend themselves, attack other communities, and the like, falls completely outside the vision of our Detroit poet. In fact, although tribal society is extremely custom-bound, straitjacketed by taboos and imperative rules of behavior, Watson nonetheless decides, gushingly, that even when aborigines are "living under some of the harshest, most commanding conditions on earth" – no less! – they "can nevertheless do what they like when the notion occurs to them" (*BB*, p. 240).[21] One can only gasp: Really!

In *SALA*, while I was arguing against the primitivism of lifestyle anarchists like Watson, I summarized my criticisms of aboriginal society, calling into question the theory of an "original affluence" as well as the idea of a "noble savage." Yet even as I criticized the romanticization of primitive lifeways, I was careful to qualify my remarks: "There is very much we can learn from preliterate cultures ... their practices of usufruct and the inequality of equals are of great relevance to an ecological soci-ety" (*SALA*, p. 41).

This reservation is entirely lost on our arch-romanticizer, for just as Watson glorifies aboriginals beyond recognition, he now portrays me, beyond recognition, as hostile to aboriginal peoples altogether. Bookchin "no longer seems to have *anything* good to say about early societies" (*BB*, p. 204), he declares with finality. He even pulls off the old Maoist and Trotskyist stunt of asking, not whether my observations are true or not, but whose interests they serve! In my case, since I fail to romanticize primitive peoples according to Watson's prescription, I clearly aid and abet the bourgeois-imperialist destroyers of primal cultures: "Bookchin's social ecology," he huffs, shares "the assumptions of bourgeois political economy itself" (*BB*, p. 215). I encountered this level of argumentation some fifty years ago, and whoever can be persuaded by these con-temptible methods is welcome to share Watson's polemical world.

Like other primitivists in the lifestyle zoo, Watson argues for the sustainability of primitive lifeways by maintaining that in the history of humanity, hunting-gathering societies existed far longer than the societies that followed the rise of written history. He recycles Lee and DeVore's claim that "for ninety-nine percent of human existence [by which Lee and DeVore meant two million years] people have lived in the 'fairly loose systems of bonding' of bands and tribes" (*BB*, p. 30). It is worth noting that two million years ago, modern-type humans – *Homo sapiens sapiens* – with their enlarged mental capacities and hunting-gathering lifeways, had not yet emerged on the evolutionary tree. The hominids that populated the African savannahs were Australopithecines and *Homo habilis*, who most likely were not hunter-gatherers at all but scavengers who lived on game killed by larger carnivores. Like all hominids and members of the genus *Homo* (including Neandertalers), they probably lacked the anatomical equipment for syllabic speech (a feature that some primitivists, to be sure, would see more as an advantage than as a deprivation).

The earliest proto-*Homo sapiens sapiens* did not appear in Africa until only 200,000 to 150,000 years ago. And even then they did not forage in an organized fashion such as Watson envisions: as Robert Lewin has noted, "recent archeological analysis indicates that true hunting and gathering – as characterized by division of labor, food sharing, and central place foraging – is a rather recently emerged behavior," dating from the retreat of the last Ice Age, beginning only some 12,000 to 15,000 years ago.[22] The origins of civilization in the Near East date back to approximately 10,000 to 8,000 years ago. If we calculate using the earliest date that Lewin suggests for the rise of hunting and gathering – 15,000 years ago – we must conclude that civilization has occupied at least half – or perhaps a third – of our species's cultural history.

In any case, what difference does it make if human beings lived as hunter-gatherers for one percent of their existence or fifty? Such a level of discussion is juvenile. The fact remains that, although it took a long time for our species to advance beyond the level of Australopithecine scavengers on the African veldt, they evolved culturally with dazzling rapidity over the past 20,000 years.

Anarchism, Marxism, and the Future of the Left

Almost invariably, discussions of an "original affluence" enjoyed by hunting and foraging peoples focus on the San people of the Kalahari desert, especially the !Kung "Bushmen," who, until very recently, it was frequently assumed, were living in a pristine state that reflected the life-ways of prehistoric foragers. The studies that are most commonly invoked to support the "affluence" thesis are those generated by anthropologist Richard B. Lee. Writing in the 1960s, Lee noted that it took the !Kung only a few days in a week to acquire all the food they needed for their well-being, ostensibly proving that affluence or, more precisely, free time is one of the great rewards of primitivity. (I may add that by this standard, anyone who chooses to live in a shack, bereft of a sophisticated culture, could be said to be affluent. If this is affluence, then the Unabomber Ted Kaczynski was a wealthy man indeed.)

In recent years, however, strong doubts have arisen that the !Kung were quite as affluent as 1960s anthropologists made them out to be. As anthropologist Thomas Headland summarizes the current research, "The lives of the !Kung are far from idyllic. An average lifespan of thirty years, high infant mortality, marked loss of body weight during the lean season – these are not the hallmarks of an edenic existence." Moreover:

> Data testifying to the harsher side of !Kung life have steadily accumulated. Lee himself has acknowledged shortcomings of his 1964 input-output study. For one thing, his calculations of the amount of work the !Kung devoted to subsistence ignored the time spent in preparing food, which turned out to be substantial. Other researchers established that even though the Dobe !Kung may have appeared well nourished when Lee encountered them, at other times they suffered from hunger and disease. Meanwhile, the theoretical underpinnings of the original-affluence model collapsed. It became clear that while many tribal groups were adapted to their environment at the population level, existence was often harsh for individuals in those groups.[23]

Even in Elizabeth Marshall Thomas's narrative of their culture, *The Harmless People,* the !Kung encounter very harsh situations; her own descriptions of them contradict her enthusiasm for their way of life. In

SALA, drawing on the work of Edwin Wilmsen, I noted that the lives of the San were actually quite short, that they do go hungry at times, especially during lean seasons, and that they lived in the Kalahari not because it was their habitat of choice from time immemorial but because they had been driven into the desert from their erstwhile agricultural lands by more powerful invaders who coveted their original territory.

Moreover, I wrote, "Richard Lee's own data on the caloric intake of 'affluent' foragers have been significantly challenged by Wilmsen and his associates.... Lee himself has revised his views on this score since the 1960s" (*SALA*, pp. 45-46). Watson's reply to these observations is worth noting: he telephoned Lee himself to query him on this point.

> He replied that he modified his findings on caloric intake very slightly in the late 1970s – "no more than five percent either way" – but that Bookchin's claim was otherwise spurious. "I stand by my figures," he said. (*BB*, p. 209).

Note well, however, that the change in Lee's work to which I was referring took place between the mid-1960s and the late 1970s, not *since* the late 1970s. (Watson might have understood this had he read the page in Wilmsen that I cited in my note 32 in *SALA*.) In fact, in his 1979 book *The !Kung San,* Lee dispelled the excessively rosy image he gave of the San in the 1960s by giving evidence of malnutrition among the "affluent" Zhu (a San-speaking people). Adult Zhu, he wrote, "are small by world standards and ... this smallness probably indicates some degree of undernutrition in childhood and adolescence." When Zhu individuals are raised "on cattle posts on an essentially Bantu diet of milk and grains," he acknowledged, they "grow significantly taller" than foraging Zhu.[24]

Moreover, in the same book, Lee provided us with evidence that these foragers experience severe hardship: "We admire the !Kung from afar, but when we are brought into closer contact with their daily concerns, we are alternately moved to pity by their tales of hardship and repelled by their nagging demands for gifts, demands that grow more insistent the more we give."[25]

In fact, even during the 1960s, Lee's image of the "affluence" enjoyed by the San was already marred by significant indications of hunger.

During the lean months of the year, he noted in 1965, the Zhu "must resort to increasingly arduous tactics in order to maintain a good diet.... it is during the three lean months of the year that Bushman life approaches the precarious conditions that have come to be associated with the hunting and gathering way of life."[26] Finally, Lee has greatly revised the length of the workweek he formerly attributed to the Zhu; the average workweek for both sexes, he wrote in 1979, is not eighteen but 42.3 hours.[27] Irven DeVore, the Harvard anthropologist who shared Lee's conclusions on the Bushmen in the 1960s and 1970s, has observed: "We were being a bit romantic. .... Our assumptions and interpretations were much too simple."[28]

Not even Watson can deny that foraging societies experienced hunger, although it contradicts his own image of "original affluence": he acknowledges that hunter-gatherer societies "periodically suffered" (*BB*, p. 110).[29] But his justification for their suffering is astonishingly callous. In societies such as our own, he points out, only some sectors of the population starve during times of hunger. But "during tough times in most aboriginal societies," he writes with amazing sang-froid, "generally, *everyone starves or no one does*" (*BB*, p. 94). Indeed, "even when primal people starve, 'the whole group as a positive cohesive unit is involved. In consequence, there is generally no disorganization or disintegration either of individual or of the group as such, in stark contrast with the civilized" (*BB*, p. 95). They *all* starve to death – and that is that! Are we expected to admire a situation where "everyone starves" because they do so in an organized fashion?

Allow me to suggest that this is anything but a consolation. Scarcity conditions – conditions of generalized want and hunger – that could result in famine are precisely those that, historically speaking, have led to competition for scarce goods and eventually the formation of class and hierarchical societies. Far more desirable to develop the productive technologies sufficiently to avoid famine altogether! If such technologies were sufficiently developed, then put to use ethically and rationally in a libertarian communist society, *everyone* could be freed from material uncertainty. This condition of postscarcity would give us the *preconditions* for one day achieving a truly egalitarian, free, and culturally fulfilling social order.

It might be supposed that, in weighing these two alternatives – scarcity, with the possibility of a community's entire extinction, against postscarcity, with the potentiality to satisfy all basic human needs – Watson might choose the latter prospect over the former. But far be it from Watson to agree with anything Bookchin has to say! Watson, it seems, would prefer that "everyone starve" together rather than that they have sufficient means to enjoy well-being together. So cavalier is his attitude about human life, that when I object to it, he reproaches me for being "utterly affronted by affirmative references to death as part of the ecological cycle" (*BB*, p. 114).

As a humanist, allow me to state categorically that I am indeed "utterly affronted" by such references, and by Watson's blatant callousness. It is this kind of stuff that brings him precariously close to the thesis of his erstwhile antihero, Thomas Malthus (in *HDDE*), namely that mass death would result from population growth, whose geometric increase would far outstrip a merely arithmetically increasing food supply. Indeed, it was *precisely* the productivity of machines that showed thinking people that the Malthusian cycle was a fallacy. Yes – better machines than death, in my view, and Watson is welcome to criticize me for it all he likes!

If Watson is callous toward the objective aspects of primitivism, his attitude toward its subjective aspects, as I have noted, resembles the vagaries of a flower child. An essential feature is his belief that the mental outlooks of aboriginal peoples can override the material factors that might otherwise alter their lifeways. "Most, if not all, aboriginal peoples practiced careful limits on their subsistence activities," he tells us, "deliberately underproducing, expressing gratitude and consideration in their relations with plants and prey" (*BB*, p. 52).[30] Moreover, "Primal society ... refused power, refused property" (*CIB*, p. 11). In effect, for Watson, social development was a matter of conscious selection, choice, and even lifestyle, as though objective realities played no role in the shaping of social relations. 1

In *SALA* I tried to correct this romantic, idealist, and frankly naive view by pointing out that among most tribal peoples – indeed, among most peoples generally – not only economic life but even much of spirituality is oriented toward obtaining the means of life. "With due regard for their own material interests – their survival and well-being," I wrote, "prehistoric peoples seem to have hunted down as much game as they could, and if they imaginatively peopled the animal world with anthropomorphic attributes, . . . it would have been to communicate with it with an end toward manipulating it, not simply toward revering it" (*SALA*, p. 41).

Not only does Watson take issue with this statement as economistic, he rejects *any* economic motivations in aboriginal society: "Economic motivation," he declares, "is the motive within class societies, not aboriginal communities" (*BB*, p. 63). Presumably people whose societies are structured around dancing, singing, and dreaming are immune to the problems – social as well as material – of acquiring and preparing food, fending off predators, building shelter, and the like. Where I present contradictory evidence – such as the many cases of foragers "stampeding game animals over cliffs or into natural enclosures where they could be easily slaughtered," or "sites that suggest mass killings and 'assembly-line' butchering in a number of American arroyos," or the Native American use of fire to clear land, or the likelihood of Paleoindian overkills of large mammals (*SALA*, p. 42) – he maintains a prudent silence. In fact, the demanding endeavor to gather the means for supporting everyday life may well be the major preoccupation of aboriginal peoples, as many of their myths and cosmic dramas reveal to anyone who examines them without romantic awe.

At some point, clearly, primal peoples in prehistoric Europe and the Near East stopped "refusing" power and property, and from their "loosely knit" band and tribal societies, systems of domination developed – hierarchies, classes, and states – as part of civilization itself. Why this happened is by no means an academic question; nor is the approach we take to understanding the processes of social change generally a matter of trivial concern.

Social changes, both major and minor, do not come about solely as a result of choice or volition. Even in inspired moments, when people believe they are creating an entirely new world, their course of action, indeed their thinking, is profoundly influenced by the very history from which they think they are breaking away. To understand the processes by which the new develops from the old, we must closely examine the conditions under which human beings are constrained to work and the various problems with which they must contend at particular moments in history – in short, the inner dialectic of social development. We must look at the factors that cause apparently stable societies to slowly decompose, giving rise to the new ones that were "chosen" within the limitations of material and cultural conditions.

I followed this approach in *The Ecology of Freedom,* for example, when I examined the nature and causes of the rise of hierarchy. There I tried to show that hierarchy emerged from within the limitations and problems faced by primal societies. I made no pretense that my presentation constituted the last word on this problem; indeed, my most important goal was to highlight the importance of trying to understand hierarchical development, to show its dialectic and the problems it posed.

Watson not only dismisses this vitally important issue but arrogantly rejects *any* endeavor to look into "the primordial community to find the early embryonic structure that transformed organic society into class society" (*BB,* p. 97). Needless to say, he claims that I fail to understand power in aboriginal societies, "where the so-called chief is usually a spokesman and a go-between" (*BB,* p. 98). This was probably true at one time in the early development of chiefdoms, but it is evidence of Watson's static, absolutist mentality that he fails to see that many chiefdoms gradually and sometimes even precipitously transformed themselves, so that chiefs became petty despots and even monarchs long before there were "megamachines" and major technological advances.

Watson's reckless farrago of obfuscation merely beclouds his own ignorance. The fact is that he himself simply cannot answer the question of how social development occurs. Although the pages of *BB* are bereft of an explanation for the origin of domination, in an earlier work he once brightly suggested: "Somehow [!] ... the primal world unravel[ed] as the institutions of kingship and class society emerged. How it happened remains unclear to us today" (*CIB,* p. 10). I hate to think how desiccated social theory would become if all its thinkers exhibited the same paucity of curiosity and speculative verve that this off-handed remark reveals. Instead of making any attempt to account for social evolution, Watson merely times the passage of millennia of hominid and human evolution with his stopwatch ("ninety-nine percent"), as though timing were more important than examining the causes ("which remain unclear for us today") that impelled hominids and humans to make those major decisions that eventually removed them from their simple lifeways and landed them in the complex coils of the "megamachine." If we ever do arrive at the "revolution [that] will be a kind of return" (*BB*, p. 154), then with Watson to guide us, and lacking any understanding of the processes of change, we will have little or nothing to prevent our new society from once again, during the next historical cycle, recapitulating the rise of hierarchical and class society.

If there is one thing on which everyone – Watson, the anthropologists, and myself – agrees, it is that among foraging peoples today, their subjectivity has failed to prevent either the invasion of commodities from the industrialized world or its colonization of material life. But it is worth asking how much deliberate resistance tribal societies have put up against this invasion. For their part, the !Kung, the flagship culture of "original affluence" theorists, seem to be greatly attracted to modern "goodies." As John E. Yellen, to cite only one of several accounts, found when he visited Dobe in the mid-1970s, !Kung were planting fields and wearing mass-produced clothing; indeed, they had given up their traditional grass huts for "more substantial mud-walled structures." Significantly, their hearths, which had formerly been located in the front of their huts – where they were "central to much social interaction" – were now located away from the community center, and the huts themselves, once spaced close together, were now farther apart.[31]

Moreover, the acquisition of commodities has now become of major importance. Where once, as Lee put it, the charge of "stinginess" was one of "the most serious accusations one !Kung [could] level against another,"[32] commodities are now shamelessly hoarded:

> With their newfound cash [the !Kung] had also purchased such goods as glass beads, clothing and extra blankets, which they hoarded in metal trunks (often locked) in their huts. Many times the items far exceeded the needs of an individual family and could best be viewed as a form of savings or investment. In other words, the !Kung were behaving in ways that were clearly antithetical to the traditional sharing system. Yet the people still

spoke of the need to share and were embarrassed to open their trunks for [the anthropologist]. Clearly, their stated values no longer directed their activity.[33]

It must be supposed that the !Kung think so little of their "original affluence" that, even in the decades since the 1960s, many of them have discarded primitive lifeways for the amenities of the "megamachine" and exhibit an eagerness to obtain more than they already have. It may also be that the bourgeois commodity has an enormous capacity to invade primitive economies and undermine them disastrously – Watson's certainties to the contrary notwithstanding.

Reason and Irrationalism

As a man whose vision is turned to the past – whether it be the technology of the Middle Ages, or the sensibility of the Paleolithic or Neolithic – it should come as no surprise that Watson favors the more primal imperatives of intuition over intellectual reflection and has very little to say about rationality that is favorable. In this respect, he is nothing if not trendy: the current explosion of interest in irrational charlatans – psychics, divinators, mystics, shamans, priestesses, astrologers, angelologers, demonologers, extraterrestrials, et cetera ad nauseam – is massive. Humorless though I may be – as Watson tells his readers, on the authority of someone who "knows" me "intimately" (surely not John Clark!) (*BB*, p. 39) – I would regard this irrationalism as laughable, were it not integral to his anarchism and to his gross misrepresentation of my own views.

I have long been a critic of mythopoesis, spiritualism, and religion. Yet as the author of "Desire and Need" and *The Ecology of Freedom,* I have also fervently celebrated the importance of imagination and the creative role of desire. As an admirer of utopian thinking at its best, I have celebrated the importance of emotion and even intuition in developing ideals for a utopian society that would ultimately fulfill humanity's potentiality for freedom and self-consciousness. My writings on reason contain numerous critiques of conventional or analytic (commonly known as instrumental) reason, important as it is in everyday life and experience. I have long maintained that the analytical forms of scientific rationality leave much to be desired for understanding developmental phenomena, such as biological evolution and human social history.

These fields are better comprehended, I have argued, by dialectical reason, whose study, practice, and advocacy have been my greater interest. Dialectic is the rationality of developmental processes, of phenomena that self-elaborate into diverse forms and complex interactions – in short, a secular form of reason that explores how reality, despite its multiplicity, unfolds into articulated, interactive, and shared relationships. It provides a secular and naturalistic basis for bold speculation, for looking beyond the given reality to what "should be," based on the actualization of rationally unfolding potentialities – and, if you please, for formulating utopian visions of a society informed by art, ecology, cooperation, and solidarity. I have devoted a volume of essays, *The Philosophy of Social Ecology,* to elucidations of the limits of analytic reason and the importance of dialectic.

Thus, in reading *BB,* I was shocked to find that Watson, descending to the depths of demagoguery, writes not only that I am a promoter of "reified hyper-rationality and scientism" (*BB,* p. 45) but that I "adhere to *repressive* reason" (*BB,* p. 68) – no less!

Coming from a philosophical naif such as Watson, this distortion could well be attributed to the kind of arrogance that often accompanies fatuity. But Watson does not restrict his attack to me; rather, he proceeds to mount an attack upon the validity of reason itself by attacking its very foundations. "Discursive reason and rational analyses," we learn, are merely "dependent on intuition" (*BB,* p. 59), while an underlying kind of knowing is somehow more profound: "the 'sage-knowledge' or 'no-knowledge' of Zen and Taoism, for example, which passes beyond the 'distinction between things' to the 'silence that remains in the undifferentiated whole'" (R.G.H. Siu quoted in *BB,* p. 60).

It is possible to dismiss this ineffable wordplay as nonsense; an assertion of the significance of insignificance, for instance, would make more sense than this passage, leaving the reader no wiser about the nature of reality. What is more important, however, is the sheer arbitrariness and reductionism of Watson's nonmethodology. Having brought us into a black hole of "no-knowledge," Watson is free to say *anything* he wants without ever exposing it to the challenge of reason or experience. As Paul Feyerabend once wrote: "Anything goes!" With this approach, Watson is at liberty to freight his readers with nonhistorical histories, nontheoretical theories, and irrational rationalities.[34]

Indeed, the lifelines provided by rationality and science that anchor us to reality and the natural world itself come unmoored as Watson proceeds with his exposition. Complaining that "social ecology demands explanation," he argues that "nothing, not even science or social ecology, explains anything definitively. All explanations are matters of credibility and persuasion, just as all thinking is fundamentally metaphorical" (*BB*, p. 50).

Neither Nietzsche nor the postmodernists who currently follow in his wake can have formulated a more disastrous notion, fulfilling precisely my analysis in *SALA*. Even science, we learn, has not given us knowledge: to my colleague Janet Biehl's observation that "we [knowledgeable human beings] do know more about the workings of nature than was the case with earlier societies," Watson brightly responds, "Even scientists don't seem to agree on . . . the definition of what is *alive*" (*BB*, p. 58), which is supposed to indicate that science can't tell us much of anything at all. Yet eight pages earlier Watson noted with sparkling originality, "This doesn't mean that scientific reasoning can't help us to know or explain anything, only that there are other ways of knowing" (*BB*, p. 50) – a point I emphasized years ago in *The Ecology of Freedom* (pp. 283-86).

As to science (more properly, the sciences, since the notion of a science that has only one method and approach is fallacious): it (or they) do not claim to "explain anything definitively," merely to offer the best and most rational explanations (dare I use this word?) for phenomena based on the best available objective data – explanations that are subject, happily, to change, when better data come to light, rather than to Watsonian "no-knowledge."

If Biehl and I object to the "extrarational and irrational facets of the human personality" (*BB*, p. 22) and "judg[e] extrarational modes of thought worthless" (Biehl quoted in *BB*, p. 49), it is not these faculties in themselves that we criticize but the employment of them in arenas for which they are not suited. For gaining an understanding of the natural and social worlds, emotions and intuitions (they are by no means the same thing) are both worse than useless, while for general communal endeavors like politics, they can even be positively harmful, as the irrationalistic messages of fascism indicate.

But neither Biehl nor I ever condemned them as inappropriate for the emotional dimensions of human life, such as friendships and families, aesthetics and play. In fact, I defy my irrationalist critics to show me a single quotation from my work in which I disdain the use of metaphor or mythopoesis for creating poetry and works of art. By trundling out my objections to their misuse in political and social matters, Watson cannily creates the illusion that I am hostile to them altogether, in all arenas of life.

The subject-matter of my own work – indeed, the subject-matter that Watson seems to be debating with me – is neither psychology nor the processes of artistic creation but *politics*, an endeavor to understand the social world and, in community, to exert conscious choice over forms of social relations. This endeavor demands an entirely different category of subjective processes from those demanded by artistic creation.

In common with science, rationality (as it is commonly understood) emphatically seeks explanations whose truth is confirmed by observation and logical consistency, including speculation. That this requirement is not always enough to arrive at truth does not mean that rationality should be abandoned in favor of the metaphors, psychobabble, and "no-knowledge" precepts that spew from Watson's heated imagination. Few things have greater potential for authoritarianism, in my view, than the guru whose vagaries stake out a claim to truth that is beyond logical and experiential scrutiny.[35]

The nightmarish consequences of irrationalism, from Cossack pogroms to the killing fields of Cambodia, from endless religious wars to the genocides of Hitler and Stalin, from Klan lynchings to the Jonestown mass suicide, are the fruits of mythopoesis at their demonic worst when it is adopted as a guide to political and social affairs, just as the works of Shelley and Joyce are among the fruits of mythopoesis at its best in artistic affairs. In the arts mythopoesis is a way to sharpen and deepen human sensibility; but in politics – a realm where people and classes struggle with each other for power and the realization of their most important communal hopes in the force field of tension between the

dominated and their dominators – mythopoesis, as a substitute for rational inquiry, often becomes demonic, appealing to the lowest common
denominator of impulse and instinct in the individuals in a community.
Impulses and instincts, while very commonplace, cannot guide us to the
achievement of a better and more humane world; indeed, the use of
myth in politics is an invitation to disaster.

Watson's rejoinder is to argue that reason, too, has contributed to the
slaughterbench of history: "Plenty of blood has flowed, incited by . . .
'hallowed' dialectical reason . . . as Comrade Bookchin knows" (*BB*, p.
46), further contending, "It's hard to say whether fascist irrationality or
marxist rationality killed more people. If [Bookchin is] going to hold any
and all mythic thinking responsible for its excesses, shouldn't he do the
same for rationality and dialectics?" (*BB*, p. 72-73)

Even if I were a comrade of David Watson – a prospect I find dis-
tasteful – I would find this identification of "dialectical reason" and
"marxist rationality" with Stalinism or even Leninism to be odious. As a
former Trotskyist, Watson should know – better than many of his young
anarchist readers – that Marx would have been the first to condemn
Stalinist totalitarianism. Instead, Watson panders to filthy prejudice. As
for the supposed link between dialectical reason and the Stalinist system,
a much stronger case could be made that mythopoesis fostered the
Stalinist cult of personality, the well-orchestrated "May Day" parades, the
rewriting of Bolshevik history, and the endless myths about the Great
Father of the People who stood atop Lenin's mausoleum – in short, all the
trappings that Russian fascism borrowed from the warehouse of
mythopoesis. To call Stalin a dialectician, let alone a philosopher, would
be like calling Hitler a biologist or a geneticist.

But nothing fazes Watson. If "myth and metaphor" are "needed" and
"probably inevitable" in politics (*BB*, p. 50), as Watson contends, then
whatever politics he has to offer is deeply troubled. Certainly, peasant
revolutionaries like John Ball and Wat Tyler, in the fourteenth century,
genuinely believed in and thus invoked "the idea of a renewed Golden
Age," while abolitionists and civil rights clerics took up "the biblical
metaphor of exodus" (*BB*, p. 50). Within the context of those very religious times, these uses of myth by religious people are understandable.
Yet it remains troubling that, no matter how much the rebellious peasants

believed in the Garden of Eden, their belief was still illusory; Ball could never have created a Garden of Eden on earth, least of all with four-teenth-century knowledge and technology. And no matter how much the abolitionists and civil rights clerics may have believed in the reality of the biblical exodus, they would have been unable to take American blacks to any such promised land. Even after the Civil War and the Emancipation Proclamation, as one former Confederate put it, "All the blacks got was 'freedom' and nothing else." With greater or lesser degrees of faith, these movements held out myths whose realization was nevertheless impossi-ble to achieve.

In modern times we know better than to accept the reality of super-stitions, and today the job of a revolutionary is not to cynically propagate myths for the consumption of the supposedly gullible masses, but to show that domination and exploitation are irrational and unjust. It is to offer precisely those dreaded "explanations," to form a worldly movement that can struggle to achieve a rational, ecological society in reality. One of the great dangers of myth in politics is its fictional nature; because myth is contrived, its use is therefore instrumental and manipulative, and its application demagogic.

Worse, as a betrayal of the highest ideal of social anarchism – name-ly, that people can manage their social affairs through rational discourse – the advocacy of myth in politics is implicitly undemocratic and authoritarian. When a myth is based on mystery, it provides a justifica-tion for demanding obedience to the inexplicable. Thus, medieval chil-iasts claimed that they were instruments of god or his earthly embodiment, only to manipulate their supporters in their own interest, demoralize them, and lead them to terrible defeats.

Watson's own case for mythopoesis rests squarely on the lure of mys-tery rather than reason; on animalistic adaptation rather than on activi-ty; on acceptance rather than on innovation; and on recovery rather than discovery – the long-hallowed theses of priests, despots, and authoritari-ans of all sorts. Astonishingly, the myths that Watson himself chooses to propagate can in no way be construed as liberatory, even by those who favor myth in politics, but rather inculcate irrationalism and passivity. Favorably quoting Joseph Epes Brown, he enjoins his readers to "humble themselves before the entire creation, before the smallest ant, realizing their own nothingness" (*BB*, p. 56). At a time when political and social passivity have sunk to appalling depths, does Watson really feel that such an injunction, applied to politics, would not be laden with extraordinary dangers?[36]

The subjectivity of aboriginal peoples, as I argued in *Re-Enchanting Humanity,* understandably makes it difficult for them to account for dreams, in which people fly, the dead reappear as living, and game animals acquire fantastic anthropomorphic powers, such as speech and the formation of institutions. It was a historic contribution of secular philosophy and science to dissolve the seeming objectivity of dreams and reveal them as pure subjectivity – an enlightenment that is by no means complete in the present era of reaction.

For Watson, however, such an enlightenment is problematic at best and obfuscatory at worst. Complaining that I "opt for the reductionism of modern science and economistic rationality" (*BB*, p. 59), he celebrates instead the most limiting features of primal subjectivity – shamanism, dreams, and ritual – thereby pandering to the trendy mysticism abroad today. He commends what he sees as the aboriginal way of perceiving reality, in which as "'everything that is perceived by the sense, thought of, felt, and dreamt of, exists'" (*BB*, p. 59). Here he is quoting the anthropologist Paul Radin, who was describing the way American Indian perceptions of reality include everything sensed, felt, and dreamed. Watson, however, turns this description into a prescription, indeed into a desirable epistemology in which dream and reality are essentially indistinguishable.

In order to provide "a larger idea of reality," Watson thereupon transports us not only through this dream world but into ineffable shamanistic knowledge; he aims to convince us that shamanism is a calling, that shamans are seers, poets, sages – and, by implication, that they have access to the special knowledge of reality that is denied to reason and science.[37]

Let me emphasize that Paul Radin (who I used as a source in *The Ecology of Freedom*) held a very skeptical attitude toward shamans, regarding them as the earliest politicians of aboriginal societies, shysters who manipulated clients for self-serving purposes (which is not to say that a number of them may not have had good intentions). He showed that the shamanic life, far from being a calling, was often well-organized and based on trickery handed down from father to son over generations. Shamans in consolidated tribes commonly formed a social elite, based on fear and reinforced by alliances with other elites, such as chiefs.

Here the reason Watson favors the absence of literacy among aborigines becomes somewhat less murky: precisely the use of spoken words by shamans made it all the easier for them to manipulate the community, claim exclusive access to knowledge, use the unrecorded word to instill fear in the community, and thereby manipulate it. Radin's "pragmatic" judgements of their impact were more than justified. "The dread of the practical consequences of the shaman's activities hangs over the ordinary individual," Radin wrote of such situations, referring to alliances between shamans and chiefs as "clearly a form of gangsterism."[38]

To discredit Radin, Watson accuses him of "excessive pragmatism" (*BB*, p. 60) and, to undermine his account of shamanism, warns that "Radin's own examples of manipulative shamans come mostly from communities influenced by encroaching money economies or from Africa" (*BB*, p. 62). The reader is then referred to pages 139-41 of Radin's *The World of Primitive Man* – which Watson should actually hope the reader will not consult, since these pages contain a discussion, not of an African people, but of the Yakuts, a *California* people, and no "encroaching money economy" is mentioned there at all.

Even when he gets his citations and page numbers straight, however, Watson's views are nothing if not preposterous. His own mythic view of aboriginals and especially shamans is nearly bereft of social and institutional awareness. He prefers to defend the vagaries of their subjectivity as though, like Athena, it sprang from the head of Zeus. Without telling us how, he merely asserts that shamanism is "a complex process, bound to be of great interest to an organic, holistic outlook" (*BB*, p. 64).[39]

Nothing arrests him in his leaps to defend the mystical – and even the religious. Thus while calling for "an abiding spirituality," he declaims that "we cannot reduce the experience of life, and of the fundamental, inescapable question of *why* we live, and *how* we live, to secular terms" (*BB*, p. 66). The reader may reasonably ask, Why not? The answer: because "an attempt to do so brings its revenge – if not in nihilism or alienation, then in a literalistic fundamentalist reaction" (*BB*, p. 66). It's not clear what a "literalistic fundamentalist reaction" would be – somehow the clear prose style on which Watson prides himself fails him on this crucial point – but what he *seems* to mean is that secularism breeds a backlash of religious fundamentalism. This is a compelling homeopathic argument: to avoid religion, get religion!

If any doubts remain that my own views and Watson's are unbridgeable, the chasm that separates us on the issue of aboriginal subjectivity should resolve them. At the close of his chapter on this subject in *BB,* he recounts a 1994 telephone conversation between us in which I queried him on his notion that wolves have a "point of view." (Watson charges that I "grilled" him, "aggressively" challenged him, "jabbed" him, "chortled," and "snorted," whereas, in fact, he himself was so hostile that I quietly suggested, more than once, that we just hang up and that he should merely send me the issue of *Fifth Estate* that I had called to request – which he never did.)

During the course of this conversation, I said that Watson's remarks on the "wolf's point of view" reminded me of Bill Devall's contention that redwood trees have consciousness. "Do you think the same is true of wolves?" I asked. In response, he simply reversed my question: "How do you know they don't?" The burden of proof, of course, belongs squarely with the person who claims that trees and wolves *do* have consciousness, especially if by consciousness we mean anything that resembles that of humans. In fact, neither trees nor wolves are *constituted* to have consciousness in any such sense, just as humans are not constituted to "navigate" like birds, as Robyn Eckersley once brightly pointed out. To assume that they do or even that they might is an example of "thinking" that is neither holistic, dialectical, nor even conventional, but is bereft of the least ability to place wolves in a graded evolutionary development or ecological context.

Actually, Watson gives his full answer to my query at the end of Chapter 3 of *BB,* where he trots out an entire team of experts, presumably of impeccable qualifications, to testify on behalf of the notion that wolves have a "point of view" and that trees have consciousness. The reader is first exposed to the testimony of Hans Peter Duerr, a New Age anthropologist of sorts who believes that "it is possible to communicate with snowy owls, provided . . . we dissolve the boundaries to our own 'animal

nature,' separating us from snowy owls" (quoted in *BB*, p. 55). Duerr tes-
tifies that scientific evidence is illegitimate, but he is hardly qualified to
speak on the subject, since his own flaky work could benefit from more
attention to scientific evidence; he apprises us that "the spirits leave the
island when the anthropologists arrive" (*BB*, p. 68) – a compelling argument only for those who believe in spirits.

Duerr is followed by Herakleitos, who remarks that "wisdom is
whole," thereby telling us nothing whatever about the question at hand.
For reasons even less clear, we are then given Vandana Shiva, who celebrates the fact that the women in the Chipko movement in India gained
spiritual strength by "embracing mountains and living waters" – a bold
challenge to anyone's dexterity. She is followed by Robert Bly, who waxes
poetic about a violet color inside badgers' heads and informs us that
when humans see trees, they emit "tree consciousness" to the trees, which
gives them (the trees) consciousness.

Following this overwhelmingly persuasive argument, we are exposed
– inevitably! – to a poem by the Taoist sage Chuang Tzu, whose conclusion is simply sentimental pap: namely, he knows the joy of fishes
through his own joy as he walks along the river! Finally, the whole exercise comes to merciful end with comments from Tatanga Mani, a Stoney
Indian, who declares: "Do you know that trees talk? Well they do. They
talk to each other and they'll talk to you if you'll listen" (*BB*, pp. 68-72).
The "explanation," I take it, is: a Native American says it, hence it must be
true. Is that the inference were are to draw here? Perhaps the snapping
and crackling of burning branches in pre-Columbian North America
was a conversation between Indian horticulturists and the trees they were
obliged to burn away in order to cultivate food and protect their communities from enemies.

Watson's team of experts, despite all their splendor and glory, fail to
convince me that trees have consciousness; on the contrary, they succeed
mainly in causing me – and perhaps other readers – to wonder about
Watson's own grip on reality. Watson's own inclinations to accept "nothingness," to listen to trees ("a future social ecology, if it is to endure as a
meaningful philosophical current, must *learn to listen*" to trees [*BB*, p.
72]), and to mistake dreams for reality are likely to make the thoughtful

reader wonder if eco-anarchism is not suffering from a profound mental crisis.

The "Dialectics" of Distortion

Confusions between truth and reality have consequences, and one of them becomes painfully obvious in the way Watson handles the matter of Francisco Goya's *Capricho* no. 43.

In *SALA* I took issue with *Fifth Estate*'s use of this etching, their translation of the caption, and the interpretation they gave to it on the cover of their Fall/Winter 1993 issue. The original *capricho* shows the artist asleep, his arm and head resting on his desk, while around him, as in a dream, hover monstrous figures of bats, owls, and lynxes. On one side of the desk, Goya inscribed the caption: *"El sueño de la razón produce monstruos."*

Now *sueño* has two meanings in Spanish: it may mean either "dream" or "sleep." Depending upon which translation one chooses, the caption has diametrically opposite meanings – and diametrically opposite evaluations of reason. If *sueño* is translated as "dream," then the caption means that reason produces monsters (when reason dreams), and therefore it is a pejorative statement about reason. But if *sueño* is translated as "sleep," then the caption means that monsters appear when reason is absent (asleep); the caption is therefore favorable to reason.

Fortunately, we have it from Goya's own commentary that he meant that the "sleep" of reason produces monsters. As he explained in another context, he meant: *"La fantasia abandonada de la razón, produce monstruos imposibles; unida con ella, es madre de las artes y origen de sus maravillas"* ("Fantasy abandoned by reason produces impossible monsters; united with reason, she is the mother of the arts and the source of their marvels").[40] Far from anathematizing reason, Goya intended the *capricho* to affirm its crucial importance.

Fifth Estate, however, translated *sueño* to mean "dream" – thereby giving the caption the antirational interpretation. To emphasize their point, the collective's artist drew in a computer atop the artist's desk, enlisting the *capricho* in support of periodical's anti-Enlightenment technophobia.

This choice of interpretation might have been forgiven as an understandable error (I've seen the same misunderstanding occur elsewhere), and once I pointed it out in *SALA* – providing them with the Goya quotation as evidence of their misinterpretation – Watson might have admitted to it and let the matter drop with a decent self-correction.

But no! *Fifth Estate* and Watson can do no wrong! Instead, raising his hackles, Watson duly informs us that they knew it all along – but the mistranslation was deliberate! "The *Fifth Estate* cooperative, aware of the original meaning," he declares, chose to "bring this notion into a *contemporary context,* with the dream of reason no longer the victim of monsters but a full-fledged *confectioner* of them" (*BB*, p. 198, emphasis added). That is to say, the collective made a *conscious* decision to change Goya's meaning into the very opposite of what he intended. Put in straightforward language: they chose to distort and lie.

In most arenas of responsible discourse, such behavior would be called immoral – but presumably not in the offices of *Fifth Estate.* Instead, Watson lectures me on the virtues of distortion: "An authentically [!] dialectical [!] perspective would not cling *mechanically* to meanings long superseded [!] by the unfolding of actuality itself" (*BB*, p. 198). Here we learn what "dialectics" really means in Watson's universe: it is a warrant for liars to falsify to their hearts' content, despite an author's patent intention, indeed, despite the truth. In conjunction with the Native American epistemology that mistakes dream for reality, this misuse of the *capricho* supports the Watsonian imperative that we are to accept lies and distortions as truth. Caught with his own hand in the cookie jar, this man screams out "thief!" against his captor. (Elsewhere in the book [*BB*, p. v], he has the nerve to accuse me of having "misused" Goya!)

Watson's handling of the Goya matter throws a glaring spotlight on his modus operandi in most of *BB.* Disdaining to "cling mechanically" to such mundane matters as my actual intentions in my actual writings, he puts his mendacious "dialectics" into practice by cynically and maliciously snipping out phrases and sentences from their context – often to reverse their meaning (as in the case of Goya) – and, employing a creative, indeed imaginative use of ellipses, he fabricates a fictional Bookchin, tailored to his own polemical needs. Thus, I become, as we have seen, a "technocrat," a promoter of "reified hyper-rationality and scientism," and one who "no longer seems to have anything good to say about early societies." My recreated texts, like his recreation of Goya's *capricho,* correspond to the new "actuality" generated by the monsters in Watson's fevered imagination. This procedure can be taken as yet another lesson in shamanism à la Watson: Watson's interpretations of reality are to be accepted as more real than the phenomena we witness and experience, including phenomena that contradict him. What Watson doth say, so be it!

Accordingly, *BB* becomes a work of fiction – an "artistic" calumny posing as political critique. Certainly, I would be the last to accuse Watson of failing to put theory into practice; indeed, using his creative cut-and-paste methodology, one could easily make Lenin into a fiery anarchist, Stalin into a bland pacifist, Bakunin into a crypto-capitalist – and perhaps even *Fifth Estate* into an organ for technocracy.

Thus, in this work of fiction, Watson "artistically" and "dialectically" writes that in my view "Nature ... is normally 'stingy'" (*BB*, p. 91), even though the view of "Nature's stinginess" is one that I have emphatically and repeatedly challenged in many of my works. Indeed, Watson is able to create the illusion that I regard first nature as "stingy" only because he replaces with ellipses the words where I actually imputed this view to "social theorists of the past century" (*EF,* p. 64). Interested readers may check this passage for themselves.

Nor should the reader be surprised to learn from Watson that I regard humanity as "a curse on natural evolution" and a "parasite." He is, once again, apparently counting on the probability that his readers will not refer back to my original text.

> Bookchin even occasionally sounds like the deep ecology misanthropes he attacks, for example suggesting that humanity is "still a curse on natural evolution, not its fulfillment. Until we become what we *should* be in be in the constellation of life, we would do well to live with a fear of what we *can* be." (*EF*: 238) Humanity is a "highly destructive parasite who threatens to destroy his host – the natural world – and eventually himself," he comments [*PSA*: 61]. Truer deep ecological words were never spoken. (*BB*, p. 18)

The distortion here is outrageous. The sentence that begins "Until we become ..." actually explains that this "curse on natural evolution" is not a matter of some inherent "human nature" but is *socially* conditioned – far different from the potentiality that a libertarian socialist society would actualize. Obviously, the aim of the book from which he quotes – subtitled *The Emergence and Dissolution of Hierarchy* – is to show that humanity is trapped in hierarchical society, not inherently doomed to be a "curse on natural evolution."

To conjoin this quotation with the second one – about the "parasite" – is an a gross manipulation of the trusting reader. The "parasite" quotation is taken from my 1964 essay "Ecology and Revolutionary Thought," in which, after a long account of the pollution of the planet, the passage Watson quotes appears:

> *Obviously, man could be described as* a highly destructive parasite who threatens to destroy his host – the natural world – and eventually himself. *In ecology, however, the word "parasite" is not an answer to a question, but raises a question itself.... What is the disruption that has turned man into a destructive parasite? What produces a form of parasitism that results not only in vast natural imbalances but also threatens the existence of humanity itself? ... The imbalances man has produced in the natural world are caused by the imbalances he has produced in the social world.* (PSA, pp. 61-62; italics added to indicate deleted words)

Certainly, neither *parasite* nor *curse* is a word I would use today, as I did in 1964 and 1982. But in both cases the context shows that I used these words as metaphors for a phenomenon that is socially conditioned. Knowing full well that I did not mean what he is saying I meant, Watson cynically pulled these phrases completely out of their context.[41]

The number of egregious falsifications that Watson makes over hundreds of pages in *BB* is prohibitively large to point out, let alone reply to individually. What these examples demonstrate is that Watson places no limits on the degree of calumny he is prepared to use. Most important, however, by using these tricks, he demonstrates his utter contempt for his readers: he lies to them, plays his shamanistic tricks on them, and violates their trust in him, which will ultimately vitiate their own desire for knowledge, understanding – and explanations.

If Watson distorts my writing, he distorts my political behavior even more grossly. Indeed, almost every paragraph of BB is either an insult or a lie. To accept Watson, one must believe that I do not hold a point of view: I invariably hold a "dogma" (BB, p. 9). I do not assert the validity of my ideas: I suffer from "megalomania" (BB, p. 19) or egomania (BB, p. 15). I am designated variously as "General Secretary" (Stalin?) and "Chairman" (Mao?) (BB, pp. 16, 40). If I use the word *must*, I obviously am an author-itarian, although Watson employs this word freely when he cares to.[42] If Janet Biehl defends my views, she is my "hagiographer" (BB, p. 37), while someone who objects to Watson's hatchet job, Daniel Coleman (whom I do not even know), must be my "sycophant."[43]

My work, it seems, must be deprecated in its entirety, including my widely acknowledged pioneering efforts in the development of a social ecology; so must my contributions to anarchist theory, including writ-ings that, Watson admits, "introduced" him "to anarchist ideas and a radi-cal critique of leninism" (BB, p. 10), as well as writings that he once praised as "poetic" (in a telephone conversation). All must now be depre-cated, and my role in the rise of political ecology must be minimized (in the bizarre account in BB, pp. 15-16). Social ecology, a label that had fall-en into disuse by the early 1960s and that I spent many years providing with a substantive meaning, fighting for it so that it gained an interna-tional reputation, is now somehow a concept that I usurped. Actually, in the late 1960s I visited Detroit and importuned members of the *Fifth Estate* crowd to concern themselves with ecological issues – but to no avail. In those days the Situationists who greatly influenced *Fifth Estate*'s erstwhile sage, Fredy Perlman, were mocking me as "Smokey the Bear" for my advocacy of ecological politics. Watson now tells me that my con-tributions to ecological politics are negligible at best and warped at worst – this from a man whose recognition of the importance of ecological politics apparently did not come until the mid- to late 1970s.[44]

Above all I have tried to create an ecological politics that is *activist* in its political and social outlook, one that could underpin a *revolutionary,* libertarian, anticapitalist movement that could take up the struggle to form a rational ecological society in which people may fulfill their potential for freedom and self-consciousness. As recently as 1990 Watson even appeared to share this militancy to a considerable extent when he wrote, "We must begin to talk openly and defiantly of . . . mass strike and revolutionary uprising" (*SIH*, p. 11).

But in *BB*, which appeared in 1996, Watson strikes a radically different tone. Although he wishes us to take up the prodigious task of all but eliminating technology and "civilization in bulk," he leaves the question of precisely how we are to do so enshrouded in dark mystery. His book contains no appeals to his readers to create the organizations necessary to build a new society, let alone hint at the social institutions that would constitute it. Rather, he tells them that what is needed is medieval technology, "epistemological luddism," irrationalism, and a subjectivity that omits distinctions between dream and reality. Readers should celebrate the fantasies of shamans, quasi-religious poets, and mystics, no matter how far they lead us from reality.

Pervading it all, he prescribes that they should "humble themselves before the entire creation, before the smallest ant, realizing their own nothingness" (*BB*, p. 56) – a prescription that echoes the self-obliterating apathy inculcated by religions and political despotisms everywhere. The book's title page, quoting Dogen, quintessentially expresses this passivity to the point of self-effacement. "To carry yourself forward and experience myriad things is delusion," declared the thirteenth-century Zen master piously. "But myriad things coming forth and experiencing themselves is awakening." Blessed are the meek, for they shall inherit the earth! This recipe for quietism has well served the ruling classes of the world: together with Watson's injunctions that we should "listen" to things that are not actually speaking and that are indeed incapable of speaking, the content of Dogen's quote vitiates the rebelliousness necessary for a movement to radically change society and replaces it with complete resignation.[45]

If Watson's anti-Enlightenment outlook were ever to prevail among a sizable number of anarchists, then anarchism would become a self-centered, fatuous, and regressive body of nonideas that deserves contempt, if not derision, for its lack of substance and social value. If this noble ideal were ever to be so degraded, then anarchism would indeed have to be rescued from the anarchists, who would be among its most insufferable opponents.

David Watson, One Year Later

Amusingly, scarcely a year after *BB* was published, Watson erupted with an article in *Fifth Estate,* subtitled "Farewell to All That," in which he significantly backtracked on many of the cherished positions that he so adamantly advanced in his book.[46]

On progress: Watson, who flatly refused to consider any alternative notion of progress when I advanced one, now writes: "Our alternative [!] notion of 'progress' might be that we've inevitably learned some things along history's way, things we didn't necessarily need to know before, but which are probably indispensable to us now" (*SF,* p. 19). Really! But hasn't the very idea of progress served as a "core mystification concealing what is *worst*" in civilization (*BB,* p. 9)? And what could we learn from the history of a "civilization" that is nothing but a forced labor camp?

On civilization: The author of "Civilization in Bulk" who once scolded people for being so wishy-washy as to put quotation marks around the word "civilization," now writes: "I believe the claim to oppose 'the totality' of civilization is empty theoretical bravado" (*SF,* p. 18). And: "Vernacular, communal and liberatory visions and practices persist, scattered throughout [!] civilization. . . . Such visions and practices are also, quite problematically, woven *into the sinews of civilization itself.* To 'oppose' civilization as a totality" – writes Watson, for whom the very word was recently abhorrent – ". . . could only imply somehow 'opposing' not only the repressive and dehumanizing aspect of civilization but also the valuable and painful historical experience that has nurtured new insight" (*SF,* p. 18). Really! Perhaps Watson, who once called civilization "a maladaption of the species, a false turn or a kind of fever threatening the planetary web of life" (*CIB,* p. 10), has come to accept my idea that civilization has a legacy of freedom after all. Perhaps he will even admit it in the next issue of *Fifth Estate.*

On a related matter, I should note that in *BB* Watson denounced me for my suggestions that the nation-state may have been a historically necessary development (a view held by no less a personage than Bakunin!) and that the concept of "socially necessary evil" may have merit. (I actually prefer to call it "socially unavoidable" evil). My point, I should explain, was that "the groundwork for making a civilizatory process possible . . . may have required what we would regard today as unacceptable institutions of social control but that at an earlier time may have been important in launching a rational social development" [PSE: xvi-xvii]" (*BB*, p. 90). Coming from me, Watson found this idea intolerable, fuming that it "capitulates to bourgeois and marxist notions of progress. . . . Bookchin never escapes his Marxism" (*BB*, p. 91).

I still hold to the belief, as I wrote in *The Ecology of Freedom*, that "to be expelled from the Garden of Eden can be regarded, as Hegel was to say, as an important condition for its return – but on a level that is informed with a sophistication that can resolve the paradoxes of paradise" (*EF*, p. 141; another quotation that Watson truncates, *BB*, p. 91, in order to make it sound brutal).

Thus it was with some hilarity that I read, in "Farewell to All That," that Watson now actually accepts a crude version even of this view: "However atrocious the process," he writes, "conquest and domination have always [!] been syncretic, dialectically unfolding into resistance" (*SF*, p. 18) – nebbich! Indeed, he goes much further than I do: I would hardly have used the word *always* in this connection. The inevitability it implies would have been anathema for the earlier Watson. I look forward to reading in future issues of *Fifth Estate* about the inevitable ("always") transformation of the "megamachine" into resistance and civilization into progress.

On primitivism: The Watson who, in *BB*, furiously denounced me for objecting to primitivism in politics, now acknowledges that some people at *Fifth Estate* – obviously including himself – "have growing doubts about pretenses to an anarcho-primitive perspective or movement" (*SF*, p. 18). He even tries to withdraw primitivism from the political realm altogether: "to speak of primitivism does not require a political primitivism" (*SF*, p. 18). This man who has been trying to create a "political primitivism" for over a decade now – and excoriating critics like me – now renounces the whole endeavor!

Our twisting and writhing "neoprimitivist" who, in *BB,* wanted a "future social ecology" to recognize that "firm ground, if any, *must* [!] be found" in a reorientation of life "around perennial, classic and aboriginal manifestations of wisdom" (*BB,* p. 154), now advises us that primitivism is "more and more a fool's paradise, the dogma of a gang, . . . however irrelevant and however sincere – potentially even a racket," and he wants "less and less to do with it" (*SF,* p. 19)! Having done more than just about anyone to promote primitivism for more than a decade, he now declares: "Self-proclaimed primitivists are . . . deluded in thinking they have a simple answer to the riddle of prehistory and history" (*SF,* p. 20).

This is truly uproarious! The ink on the pages of *BB* had scarcely had time to dry before Watson made a complete reversal. Only one thing could possibly surpass this about-face for sheer nerve – and sure enough, he does actually go on to blather: "my opinions have not really changed" (*SF,* p. 23). Ah! The closer he comes to my views, it would seem, the more he must deny it – anything to avoid confessing that he was utterly wrong as well as vicious in *BB.*

I have no doubt that Watson will reply to the present essay in *Fifth Estate.* Given his track record of malicious lies, massive distortions, and ad hominem deprecations, compounded with these recent extreme shifts in his own basic positions, I see no reason why I should waste any more time on this man. Finis – Watson! I await further "farewells" with minimal anticipation.

The World According to Clark/Cafard

The back cover of *BB* is prominently adorned with a euphoric blurb by one John Clark, a philosophy professor at Loyola University in New Orleans. "*Beyond Bookchin,*" Clark gushes, "is a brilliant, carefully argued critique. . . . Watson's thoughts on technology, culture, and spirituality make a major contribution to social theory." Clark's esteem for Watson's meanderings is apparently more than reciprocated, as Watson has opened the pages of *Fifth Estate* to Clark, who chooses to hide behind his pseudonym, Max Cafard, when he writes there. The summer 1997 issue thus contains, under the Max Cafard byline, what purports to be a review of my book *Re-Enchanting Humanity (RH),* titled "Bookchin Agonistes," but is actually another savage attack on me and my work.

So unrelenting is the attack, in fact, that it is difficult to believe that from the mid-1970s until early 1993, the author was a close associate of mine. As recently as 1984, Clark wrote the following passage in his essay collection *The Anarchist Moment*:

> I want to express my deep gratitude to Murray Bookchin for his invaluable contribution to the development of the ideas present- ed in these essays. His synthesis of critical and dialectical theory, teleological [!] philosophy, social ecology, and libertarian and utopian thought has carried on the great tradition of philosophy in this anti-philosophical age. It has been a great privilege to know him and his work.[47]

In 1984, it was widely assumed among my readers, opponents, and libertarian radicals generally that John Clark was my spokesman, a status he had apparently adopted with alacrity. Thus, it seemed perfectly natural in 1986, on my sixty-fifth birthday, that he would present me with a Festschrift that he edited in my honor.[48] As recently as 1992 he was selected to write the entry on my political contributions for *The Encyclopedia of the American Left,* in which he described me as "the fore- most contemporary anarchist theorist."[49]

Now, only a few years later, Clark explodes with "Bookchin Agonistes," in which he pillories me as, among other things, "a theoretical bum," "an enraged autodidact" (as if anarchists typically disdained auto- didacts!), a practitioner of "brain-dead dogmatism" characterized by "ineptitude in philosophical analysis," an "amateur philosopher" (Socrates, who detested the Sophists for professionalizing philosophy, would have expressed some sharp words about this one!), "an energetic undergraduate," and an all-around rogue. After reading this torrent of abuse, one can only wonder: How could Clark have so completely mis- judged me for almost two decades?[50]

Not only does Clark wholly repudiate me, but he even minimizes the portion of his own biography that he spent in association with me, writing that it was only in his "misguided youth" that he spent "on the fringes of the Bookchin cult" (*BA*, p. 23). Now, I am mindful that for many baby boomers the pursuit of eternal youth exceeds in zeal even Ponce de Leon's pursuit of the Fountain of Youth in the wilds of Florida several centuries ago. But such fancies have their limits. After all, is one really only a mere "misguided youth" at the age of 30, as Clark more or less was when he first sought me out? Was he really only a youth at 41, when he prepared the embarrassing Festschrift? Was he not an adult, at the age of 48, when he wrote the laudatory entry for *The Encyclopedia of the American Left*?

For reasons that I shall explain shortly, I am glad that Clark and I are finally publicly disassociated from each other; our ideas, indeed, our ways of thinking, are basically incompatible. I would have hoped that our disassociation could have occurred without the personal hostility, indeed vilification that Clark/Cafard exhibits in "Bookchin Agonistes." But since he has decided to infuse his criticism of me with personal insults, I see no reason why he should enjoy immunity to a discussion of his own work from my point of view. Throughout the many years of our association, after all, I restrained myself from publicly criticizing him in the areas in which we seriously differed, and it comes as a great relief to me that I am no longer obliged to place that limitation on myself.

Although Clark and I had a personal friendship that lasted almost two decades, he told me remarkably little about his own activities in social and political movements before I met him. Judging from the little he did leak about his past, however, I gather that he was never a socialist. He once told me that during the 1960s he had been a disciple of Barry Goldwater – that is, the reactionary senator from Arizona who, running for the U.S. presidency in 1964, frightened the wits out of most Americans by calling for an escalation of the war in Southeast Asia. That the incumbent, Lyndon B. Johnson, later did precisely what Goldwater had recommended does not alter the nature of the ideological clash of the 1964 campaign. Most intellectual Goldwaterites sat at the feet of Ayn Rand, William F. Buckley, and other right-wing notables, advocating a

reduction of the state in favor of laissez-faire capitalism, and individualism as an alternative to collectivism in social affairs. If Clark was a sup-
porter of Goldwater, he would have been such a right-wing antistatist
well into the 1960s.

It would seem, then, that he came to anarchism from the Right rather
than from the Left. Causes such as the workers' movement, collectivism,
socialist insurrection, and class struggle, not to speak of the revolutionary socialist and anarchist traditions, would have been completely alien
to him as a youth; they were certainly repugnant to the right-wing ideo-
logues of the mid-1960s, who afflicted leftists with conservatism, cultural
conventionality, and even red-baiting.

How deeply Clark participated in the ideological world of the
Goldwater Right, I cannot say. But it requires no psychological wizardry
to suggest that the awe of academic degrees and "scientific training" that
he displays in "Bookchin Agonistes" – indeed, his disparagement of the
validity of nonspecialists' criticisms of their work – is evidence of a conventional elitism that has nothing in common with the radical dimension
of anarchism.

In any case, 1964, the year Goldwater ran for president, was also a
year when the best and brightest Americans of Clark's generation were
journeying to Mississippi (in the famous Mississippi Summer), often
risking their lives to register the state's poorest and most subjugated
blacks for the franchise. Although Mississippi is separated from
Louisiana, Clark's home state, by only a river, nothing Clark ever told me
remotely suggests that he was part of this important civil rights movement. What did Clark, at the robust age of nineteen, do to help these
young people? Unless he tells us otherwise, I can only guess that he did
very little and instead was busy acquiring his college degree. So far as I
can judge, he seems to have been potted in the academy quite early in life
and thus experienced reality primarily from the shelter of undergraduate
and graduate campuses.

This brief excursion into Clark's background is not gratuitous; it
helps to explain how unlikely our association was, and with what for-
bearance I allowed it to continue for as long as it did. For the present, let
me note that, far from inhabiting the fringes of the "Bookchin cult"
(whatever that might be) or at least my circle of friends and comrades,

Clark barged eagerly into my life in the mid-1970s and positioned himself as close to the center as he could. So fawning was his adoration of me that I often found it unsavory.

Still, he did make contributions to social ecology by regularly assigning *The Ecology of Freedom* to his students at Loyola, and by writing a well-meaning but inept review of that book for *Telos*. In turn, I brought him into the Institute for Social Ecology as a visiting lecturer; urged (sometimes reluctant) students to attend his classes; gave him access to my unpublished manuscripts; and introduced him to an appreciable number of people whom he might never have known had I not said kind words about him. In effect, he gained some distinction for himself in great part through his acquaintance with me.

As I have said, despite the repugnance I felt for some of his ideas, I never wrote a line against Clark in public. But in our personal conversations I was quite vociferous in my objections to his Taoism – indeed, most of my arguments with him, dating almost from the beginning of our relationship, concerned Lao-tzu's *Tao Te Ching*. I consistently claimed that the book itself is inherently mystical, antihumanistic, and irrational – and therefore incompatible with social ecology. It was because of this disagreement that, as much as I wanted to, I was never able to quote from Clark in my own writings.

Like many professors of philosophy, Clark, I found, tends to reify ideas into mental constructs, bereft of roots in the time, place, or society in which they are developed. Academic philosophy, in its remote aeries, divests even ideas that have a direct bearing on social life of the social context that makes them relevant to the public sphere. Instead of preserving that relevance, it transforms them into abstractions, and assigns them to a transcendental world of their own, not unlike that of the Platonic domain of forms. Ideas are traced not in terms of the society in which they develop but from classroom to classroom, so to speak, and from professional journal to professional journal.

As a result of its social myopia, academic philosophy tends to be blind to the social and political *implications* of ideas. Even an avowed "dialectician" such as Clark (perhaps because of his skewed understanding of dialectics) appears to be incapable of seeing the *logic* of an idea:

where it will lead in social terms, how it will unfold, its likely consequences for the real world outside the campus.

By his own description in the following passage, for example, Clark's interpretation of Taoism is divorced from its context in Chinese history, and from the implications of its ideas for present-day societies:

> When each follows his or her own Tao, and recognizes and respects the Tao in all other beings, a harmonious system of self-realization will exist in nature. There is a kind of natural justice that prevails, so that the needs of each are fulfilled.... Order and justice are assured when each being follows its appropriate path of development.[51]

Here the mystically self-contained Tao, preoccupied with "self-realization," an ahistorical "natural justice," and an assurance that the "needs of each are fulfilled," could easily be seen as an affirmation of laissez-faire economics and their transposition into ordinary human behavior. "I engage in no activity and the people themselves become prosperous," says the governing Taoist ruler-sage [*Tao Te Ching*, chap. 57)][52] When Clark moved away from Goldwaterism and into social ecology, did he bring with him residual ideas of Adam Smith?

To my criticisms of Taoism, Clark long responded that I "confuse ancient Taoist philosophy (the *Tao Chia*) with the often superstitious and hierarchical Taoist religious sect (the *Tao Chio*)" (*BA*, p. 21). That is, he argued, the philosophy attached to the book itself must be separated from the Taoist religion that later developed. Certainly, as in the case of so many religions – not to speak of philosophical schools (the Church's codification of Aristotle's works, for example) – clerical Taoism represented a degeneration of philosophical Taoism. Taoism did become a theology, indeed a church, complete with a pantheon of deities and a complex hierarchy of priests. An entire array of superstitious practices, including alchemy, fortune-telling, astrology, communication with the dead, and quests for immortality, clustered around it. During certain periods of Chinese history, Taoism even became a state religion, teaching Chinese people the virtues, among other things, of loyalty to the emperor and making offerings to the gods.

As different as this highly organized religion may be from Clark's philosophical Taoism, it nonetheless takes the *Tao Te Ching* as a canonical document. Various elements of "the Way" clearly lend themselves to the creation of religion, to mystery and magic, particularly its vague mysticism, its pantheism (which is still a theism), and its focus on the Tao as "oneness." By Clark's account, however, we are to suppose that the *Tao Te Ching* can be understood apart from the religion that was built upon it. One might, with equal obtuseness, argue that Christianity can be understood as consisting of the Christian scriptures, apart from the oppressive institutions that were built upon them. Actually the *Tao Te Ching* can no more be separated from the Taoist religion than the Sermon on the Mount can be removed from Christianity. Only an ivory tower academic could abstract either the *Tao Te Ching* or the Bible from its social roots, its institutional consequences – and the present conditions that favor its development into an "eco-anarchist" ideology.

All religions by definition rest on faith rather than reason – that is, they appeal to the least critical faculties of their disciples and commonly reduce them to acquiescence to the ruling classes. Hence any religion may have reactionary social consequences. By no means did Lao-Tzu provide his followers with a theory that could be remotely called explanatory, still less rational. Instead, the *Tao Te Ching* is a deliberately cryptic, mystical behavioral guide that could readily be used as a tool for fostering passivity in a supine peasantry. Its message of quietism served the interests of Chinese ruling classes for thousands of years, while its allusions to ecological themes are incidental, except as part of the overall message that individual human beings should submit to the world at large.

In the 1980s and 1990s, as social and political disempowerment are rendering most of the public apathetic, and when quasi-religious and personalistic beliefs, among other things, are paralyzing the development of movements for social action, any doctrine of quietism – even one dressed in ecological garb – serves only to instill further forms of acquiescence. Coupled with egotism, it becomes a debilitating rationale for social withdrawal and self-absorption. It was for these reasons that I could never accept Clark's Taoism as part of social ecology.

Anarchism, Marxism, and the Future of the Left

That my association with Clark lasted as long as it did is testimony to my silent endurance of his Taoist claptrap and my distinctly nondogmatic public tolerance of views not in accordance with my own. But in the late 1980s, as this type of mystical quietism gained more and more influence in the ecology movement, I could no longer remain silent. In late 1986 David Foreman (a self-described deep ecologist and a cofounder of Earth First!), in an interview with Bill Devall (one of the high chieftains of deep ecology), had declared that hungry Ethiopian children should not be given any food relief and that nature should "be permitted to take its course." The "course" he advocated struck me as a brutal one, and anything but "natural." I objected with considerable heat to the cruel Malthusian demographics that Foreman's views expressed and to the mystical notion of a "course of nature" – ideas that, thanks to Devall's praise for Foreman, were associated with deep ecology.

In June 1987, for this and other reasons, I sharply criticized deep ecology at the national conference of the Greens at Amherst, Massachusetts, and in my article "Social Ecology versus 'Deep Ecology.'" My criticism visibly disturbed Clark for a variety reasons, some of which make me wonder why he had ever adopted me as his mentor in the first place. Most notably, my criticism seems to have placed him in a difficult professional position. He was still strongly identified publicly with me: but now, not only had I opened a critique of eco-mysticism that threatened to bring our disagreement over Taoism into the open, but I was distinguishing social ecology from deep ecology in a way that emphasized the fact that social ecology calls for nothing less than a social revolution. On the other hand, deep ecologists were growing in number; their ideas were consistent with Taoism; and many of them were already Clark's friends and professional contacts, including the poetic doyen of deep ecology, Gary Snyder (who broke off all relations with me after my criticism). In time, Clark saw that many environmental professors in American universities – his home ground – were beginning to adopt deep ecology as their ecological religion of choice.

Clark found the occasion to break with me in 1992, when the Institute for Social Ecology failed to invite him to return as a lecturer for its summer session of 1993. For reasons that had nothing whatever to do with my growing disagreements with him, the Institute's curriculum committee had decided, in late 1992 or early 1993, to drop him as a visiting lecturer. As Dan Chodorkoff, the Institute's executive director, later recounted the events for me: The school was no longer in a position to provide Clark with $500 for his travel expenses, because its budget was limited; moreover, it wished to correct a gender imbalance in its lecturers. Instead of funding Clark's visit, it chose to use its funds to bring a well-qualified woman lecturer from California. As Chodorkoff emphasized:

> there was a concern on the curriculum committee that the lecture series was dominated by male speakers, and given our concerns with diversity, the decision was made to try to bring more women into the program. The funds that we would have expended on John's visit were committed to bring in women lecturers.[53]

The curriculum committee also had another reason for not inviting Clark to return, one that Chodorkoff did not tell him at the time, in order to spare his feelings. As Chodorkoff later wrote to me:

> It was also true that John's lectures had not been well received by students the previous year. Student evaluations registered complaints about his presentations, and by his final lecture enrollment had dropped precipitously.
>
> Given these circumstances, despite the fact that John was a personal friend of mine, I accepted the curriculum committee's recommendation that John not be invited back to lecture.[54]

Clark's dis-invitation from the Institute in 1993 seems to have provided him with the occasion he needed in order to break with me. Judging from what others have told me since then, he held me responsible for his dis-invitation. Yet I never raised any obstacles to Clark's participation in the Institute's program. Indeed, although I have had serious differences with a number of other Institute instructors in the past, including an outright Wiccan, I never made any effort to remove them from the program. In fact, at an Institute faculty meeting in late 1992 that did touch on issues of curriculum, I urged the Institute that "John Clark should be teaching a course on the history of anarchism," as the minutes of the meeting put it.[55] But I do not sit on the curriculum committee, and therefore I am not involved in its decision-making processes.

After Clark's dis-invitation a few months later, however, his attitude toward me became hostile, culminating in the vituperation evident in "Bookchin Agonistes."

My purpose in writing *Re-Enchanting Humanity* (the book that "Bookchin Agonistes" ostensibly reviews) was to identify and condemn the rising tide of irrationalism, antihumanism, and anti-Enlightenment sentiment that is threatening to engulf contemporary Euro-American culture. More specifically, the book criticizes the theism, postmodernism, antiscientism, sociobiology, misanthropy, and mysticism that are currently so influential, both within the academy and without.

Early on in the book, I clearly define what I mean by *antihumanism*: namely, "a common deprecation of the remarkable features that make our species unique in the biosphere. Whether explicitly or implicitly, [the tendencies in question] deride humanity's ability for innovation, its technological prowess, its potentiality for progress, and, above all, its capacity for rationality. I have thus found it appropriate to call this ensemble of deprecatory attitudes *antihumanism*" (*RH*, p. 4).

The tendencies I discuss do not always embody *all* the traits of antihumanism that I identify, but as an ensemble they do, and they all share the most important feature of antihumanism: that it "places little or no emphasis on social concerns" but instead offers a message that is "primarily one of spiritual hygiene, personal withdrawal, and a general disdain for humanistic attributes such as reason and innovation" (*RH*, p. 4). Where humanism places its emphasis on the power of reason and its ability to confront and solve many of the problems human beings face, antihumanism places its emphasis on powers other than human abilities: notably, "the powers of God," "supernatural forces," indefinable "cosmic forces," "intuition," and "Nature" (*RH*, p. 13).

Although these tendencies and the problems they pose are the central subject of my book, in his "book review" Clark/Cafard deftly ignores them. Nowhere does he inform the reader of the purpose of the book, or explain what I mean by humanism and antihumanism; nor does he address even the "dumbing down" of the culture at large – a related theme that he, as a professor, might be expected to be concerned with. On the contrary, my considerable discussions of primitivism and civilization; of the emergence of deep ecology over the past two decades and its contradictions; the genetic determinism of E. O. Wilson's sociobiology; the crude atomism of Richard Dawkins's social "mimes"; the explicit misanthropy of James Lovelock's "Gaia hypothesis," which arrogantly derogates social problems as trivial beside the splendors of "Gaia"; the railing impotence of technophobia as a social critique; postmodernism as an ideological reaction to 1968; and the antirationalism of Paul Feyerabend's fashionable antiscientism – all of this and more is totally ignored.

Instead of making even a remote attempt to explain my contentions to the reader, Clark/Cafard actually comes to the defense of some of the antihumanists whom I criticized. He denounces me for taking on the sociobiologists E. O. Wilson and Richard Dawkins, saying derisively that I criticized them for "failing to recognize differences between *homo sapiens* and other species." If that had actually been my critique, it would certainly have been laughable and wrong, but that was not my critique at all. I criticized the two sociobiologists for their crude reductionism, which is antihumanistic by any definition. Wilson and Dawkins, I wrote, display "little appreciation of any evolutionary tendency that imparts value to subjectivity, intelligence, creativity and ethics, apart from the service they perform to the well-being of genes." Instead, for them, species "are primarily the media for genetic evolution" (*RH*, p. 37). Would Clark deny that this reductionism is the essence of sociobiology – or, as it is more commonly called today, evolutionary psychology?

Having defended sociobiologists, Clark/Cafard then rides to the aid of various prominent mystics – E. F. Schumacher, William Irwin Thompson, Thomas Berry, and Matthew Fox – to rescue them from my charge of antihumanism, still not telling his readers what I mean by antihumanism. Nor does he explore the very real prospect that antihumanism can easily lead to misanthropy. The Reverend Berry, he reproaches me, is after all an "amiable" man. But as my colleague Chaia Heller recently pointed out in a conversation with Clark, what is at issue here is not whether people are "amiable" or "nice," but whether their ideas are right or wrong.[56]

The good reverend, indeed, is anything but "amiable" in *The Dream of the Earth,* when he writes like a sociobiologist, enjoining us to look "beyond our cultural coding to our genetic coding, to ask for guidance"; like an antirationalist when he intones that the "very rational process that we exalt as the only true way to understanding is . . . itself a mythic imaginative dream experience. The difficulty of our times is our inability to awaken out of this cultural pathology"; like an intuitionist mystic, when he urges us to undertake a "a descent into our prerational, our instinctive resources"; and like an outright misanthrope when he denounces human beings as "the most pernicious mode of earthly being. . . the termination, not the fulfillment, of the Earth process. If there were a parliament of creatures, its first decision might well be to vote the humans out of the community, too deadly a presence to tolerate any further. We are an affliction of the world, its demonic presence. We are the violation of earth's most sacred aspects."[57]

The eco-mysticism that abounds among deep ecologists – who accept biocentrism and seek "ecological consciousness" and mystical experiences of "self-in-Self" – is of a piece with the deep ecology literature that generally deprecates human activity in the biosphere, as though its ill-effects had no social basis. Although Clark may gently criticize misanthropic views in their most limited and specific forms, he typically – indeed, very typically – refuses to generalize from them or ferret out their *sources* in deep ecology's most fundamental tenet: biocentrism, or the idea that "all organisms and entities in the ecosphere, as parts of the interrelated whole, are equal in intrinsic worth," as George Sessions and Bill Devall defined the concept.[58]

Instead, Clark excoriates me for supposedly misunderstanding biocentrism in at least two ways. In his first objection, he says:

> If one contends that a human being and a river, for instance, are both part of a larger "self," this *in no way* implies that the river possesses *any* capacity for "empathy," any more than it implies that the human being thereby possesses the capacity to be a home for fish. Rather, it *only* implies that the larger whole of which they are both a part (called the "larger self" in this view)

has both these capacities in some sense (*BA*, p. 22 emphasis added).

In what "sense" it has them, I must leave to Clark to explain. In any case, the notion that the natural world is a "larger self" that is capable of "empathy" is a patently anthropomorphic form of pantheism that abounds in nature mysticism. But this is not what I was getting at in the relevant passage in *Re-Enchanting Humanity*:

> If the self must merge – or *dissolve*, as I claim – according to deep ecologists, into rain forests, ecosystems, mountains, rivers "and so on," these phenomena must share in the intellectuality, imagination, foresight, communicative abilities, and empathy that human beings possess, that is, if "biocentric equality" is to have any meaning (*RH*, p. 100).

Contrary to Clark, I was decidedly not arguing that deep ecologists say rivers have a "capacity for empathy." I was arguing that if the notion of "biocentric equality" is to have any internal consistency as an ethical concept, then it must view all other life-forms and other entities as *equipped with the same capacities for moral action with which human beings are equipped* – which they patently are not! If this point seems too trite to expend energy on making, then the fault lies with the deep ecologists for overlooking such a basic and obvious point in their own thinking, necessitating that their critics undertake the tiresome task of making it.

Clark's second objection is equally absurd:

> Secondly, the concept of "biocentric equality" has no implication of "equality of qualities" among those beings to whom (or to which) the equality is attributed. Indeed, this concept, like most concepts of moral equality, are significant precisely because they attribute such equality to beings that are in other important ways *unequal*. Deep ecologists and other ecophilosophers who employ concepts such as "equal intrinsic value" or "equal inherent worth" clearly [!] mean that certain beings [!] deserve equal

consideration or equal treatment [!], not that they possess certain characteristics to an equal degree (*BA,* p. 22).

As readers of *Re-Enchanting Humanity* know, I emphasized the qualitative differences between human and animals there *precisely* because deep ecologists such as Bill Devall, George Sessions, and Warwick Fox, among others, have argued that "there is no bifurcation in reality between the human and the nonhuman realms" (quoted in *RH,* p. 101). It was the biocentrist Robyn Eckersley, after all, who wrote that "*our* special capabilities (e.g., a highly developed consciousness, language and tool-making capability) are simply one [!] form of excellence alongside the myriad others (e.g., the navigational skills of birds, the sonar capability and playfulness of dolphins, and the intense sociality of ants) rather than *the* form of excellence thrown up by evolution" (quoted in *RH,* p. 100). Guided by this "egalitarian" precept of shared qualitative "excellence" (which is not moral but largely anatomical), we might well *lose* our ability to distinguish birds from people in terms of their qualities and capabilities.

If there are other deep ecologists who share Eckersley's enthusiasm for the "navigational skills of birds" and, like me, do see qualitative differences between human beings and nonhuman life-forms, I for one have not heard them criticize her. Yet I emphatically reject the biocentric notion that all life-forms "deserve equal consideration or equal treatment," as Clark puts it[59] – primarily because only *one* of those life-forms is capable of doing the "considering" and "treating." The natural world is *intrinsically* neither moral nor immoral, valuable nor valueless; inasmuch as it does not know anything, it can make no attributions of worth.

If I criticize a concept of "equality of qualities" in *Re-Enchanting Humanity* and many other places, I do so to support my critique of the ethical concept of "equal intrinsic worth." Only human beings can attribute worth to other creatures and entities; no animal can be regarded as an ethical agent without attributing to it the most egregious anthropomorphic attributes. Where I cite differences in qualities between humans and nonhuman animals, it is precisely to correct this patent absurdity and to substantiate my case that animals are by no means of "equal intrinsic value" to humans. It is only human beings who are in a position to remedy their societies' relations with the rest of the natural world and consciously address the ecological crisis, or, for that matter, even be aware that such a crisis exists.

I submit that at least one reason Clark/Cafard neglects to inform his readers of the purpose and message of my book is the fact that his own muddled ideas are very much part of the antihumanist and mystical trends that my book denounces. Indeed, had I chosen to, I could easily have used his own writings as a case study of those same regressive trends.

For one thing, irrationalism significantly pervades Clark's Taoist beliefs. Lao-Tzu, Clark has written approvingly, launched "an attack on knowledge and wisdom in the name of simplicity" and counseled people to "'abandon sageliness and discard wisdom'" (*AM*, p. 178) Clark's rationalization for this prescription – that it was artificial knowledge, not wisdom, that Lao-Tzu despised – hardly passes muster, since from its very first line the *Tao Te Ching* is anti-intellectual: "The Tao (Way) that can be told of is not the eternal Tao; The name that can be named is not the eternal name."[60]

Now, something that cannot be named is something that is ineffable and cannot be discussed. And something that cannot be discussed is something that cannot be thought about rationally. Thus it is not a rational but is an emotional or creative process – or a private mystical experience. In the case of the *Tao Te Ching*, it is a private mystical experience that is in question. "Tao is eternal and has no name" (chap. 32), we read; and: "The thing that is called Tao is eluding and vague" (chap. 21). Knowledge and wisdom – rationality – are, in the *Tao*, only sources of problems: "When knowledge and wisdom appeared, there emerged great hypocrisy" (chap. 18). Consequently, Lao-Tzu advises, "discard wisdom" (chap. 19); "Abandon learning and there will be no sorrow" (chap. 20). If this is not irrationalism, a form of antihumanism that deprecates what is unique about human beings – their ability to generalize, foresee, and create – I don't know what is.

Moreover, the *Tao Te Ching* is patently a mystical work. As Max Weber put it, "With Lao-Tzu, *Tao* was brought into relationship with the typical god-seeking of the mystic. *Tao* . . . is the divine All-One of which we can partake – as in all contemplative mysticism – by rendering one's self

absolutely void of worldly interests and passionate desires, until release
from all activity is attained." For Lao-Tzu, Weber observed, "the supreme
good was a psychic state, a *unio mystica*."[61]

How sound is Weber's interpretation? Clark, for one, might reject it,
since in his review he objects to my statement that mysticism "generally
celebrates its very imperviousness to rational analysis. Explicitly *antirational*, it makes its strongest appeal to the authority of belief over
thought" (*BA*, p. 21). As against my interpretation, Clark claims that the
mystical outlook "often clashes with systems of belief" and "typically
privileges direct experience over any sort of authority" (*BA*, p. 21). But
does "experience" here mean empirical observation, personal "experience," or – most likely – mystical "experience"? In *Re-Enchanting
Humanity* I was definitely not discussing the relationship of mystics to the
hierarchs of orthodox belief systems. To the contrary, I was addressing
the social consequences of mysticism and its relationship with reason. If
mysticism privileges "direct experience," that phrase means something
very different in mysticism from what it means in science. By Clark's
account, however, one might almost think that mystics are rational
empiricists – even that they are not concerned with *mystical* experiences.

What is the relationship between faith and reason in the mystical
outlook? To cite *The Encyclopedia of Philosophy*'s unequivocal summary:
There is none. The mystical vision, Ronald W. Hepburn writes, "must be
a unifying vision, a sense that somehow all things are one and share a
holy, divine, and single life, or that one's individual being merges into a
'Universal Self,' to be identified with God or the mystical One. Mystical
experience then typically involves the intense and joyous realization of
oneness with, or in, the divine, the sense that the divine One is comprehensive, all-embracing, in its being." Since all is "one," reason can play no
role whatever; "oneness" is ineffable, and "no logically coherent account of
[the] mystical vision seems attainable."[62] Not even Clark's pedantry can
successfully separate mysticism from irrationalism. Moreover, as a deprecation of reason, mysticism is antihumanistic, for all the reasons I have
give above.

Clark's Taoism is antihumanistic, in fact, not only by my definition
but by his own admission. Says Lao-Tzu, "The sage is not humane. He
regards all people as straw dogs" – that is, as worthless. Clark, who objects

to my calling other mystics antihumanists, has no problem with antihumanism when it comes from Lao-Tzu; to the contrary, he says, "the *Lao Tzu* is predicated on anti-humanism *(in fact, this is one of its great strengths)."* Indeed, "it is only with a rejection of humanism that the greatest possible compassion can arise," since "to act 'humanely'... implies, at best, remaining within the biased perspective of our own species." What is the alternative to that humanistic bias? "To transcend this 'humane' outlook means . . . to be 'impartial, to have no favorites' [i.e., no favorite species] . . . to respect all beings and value their various goods" (*AM*, p. 175, emphasis added). If this is not an affirmation of biocentrism – and its attendant antihumanism – I fail to understand what is. Little wonder that Clark is blind to the arguments I raised in *Re-Enchanting Humanity*. He displays all the classic symptoms of the very pathology I denounced.

Even though the *Tao Te Ching* patently presupposes the existence of government, some writers have tried to present Taoism as a proto-anarchist philosophy. Clark too has tried to represent Taoism as anarchist, in his case by using clerical casuistry. We are advised, for example, that unlike most rulers, Lao-Tzu's ruler-sage "exercises . . . non-dominating authority" and "imposes nothing on others, and refuses to legitimate his or her authority through the external supports of either law or tradition" (*AM*, p. 185). Only a few lines later, however, we learn that the ruler-sage commands a veritable apparatus, inasmuch as "he can apply his understanding of the *Tao* to government" (*AM*, p. 186). The meaning of this statement would be clear enough if it appeared in Plato's *Republic* or Aristotle's *Politics*, not to speak of Machiavelli's *Prince*, but for Clark, Lao-Tzu is garbed in a golden robe that renders him immune to criticism – including the charge of statism.

Indeed, the reader who takes Lao-Tzu at his word is condemned by Clark as guilty of "a rather extreme literal-mindedness" (*AM*, p. 186), indeed as petty-minded for believing that "'ruling' must always mean holding political office." Now this is really cute! Despite all appearances, what Lao-Tzu means seems to be what *Clark* tells us he means. Clark's juvenile claim to have the true understanding of a basically metaphorical text replicates the ages-old priestly manipulation of holy books generally, while the notion of the "ruler who does not rule" is an ineffable paradox typical of mysticism but not of any worldly institutional arrangement.

If we were to apply this ineffable mystical paradox – that rulers do not necessarily rule – to present-day politics, we could easily justify every kind of political hypocrisy. We could make a case, for example, that anarchists could support certain kinds of candidates for state office and still remain anarchists in good standing. If to rule is really not to rule, after all, then why should anarchists abstain from statist politics? Why be so "literal-minded" even about a presidential candidate? Actually, Clark himself (who declined to support the Left Greens in their early-1990s effort to create a left-libertarian Green movement) is now placidly marching in step with the highly parliamentary U.S. Greens: in 1996 his Delta Greens endorsed Ralph Nader's candidacy for the U.S. presidency on the Green ticket, even conducting a local fund-raising campaign on Nader's behalf.[63] In Taoist politics, to be sure, only the literal-minded would find something to reproach about an anarchist endorsing Nader. Insofar as Taoism smuggles statism into anarchism, however, it constitutes a superlative justification for this increasingly common development: It allows us to be on-again, off-again anarchists and suggest that the presidency is not an executive office in a centralized bourgeois state but merely a metaphor or – who knows? – perhaps even a worldly illusion.

Like Plato's *Republic*, the *Tao Te Ching* can easily be read as a guide for the enlightened ruler-sage, who sits at the pinnacle of a vast administrative machine, at least in Chinese history, where rulers were often based on vast, far-flung bureaucracies. What does the *Tao Te Ching* instruct the ruler to actually do? Not much – a point that has presumably given Taoism its anarchist flavor. But alas, it is only a flavor. Not only does the book have authoritarian underpinnings, but some of "Master Lao's" positive instructions to the ruler-sage are anything but benign. Indeed, they smack of crass, cynical manipulation: "Discard wisdom; then the people will benefit a hundredfold. Abandon humanity and discard righteousness; then the people will return to filial piety and deep love" (chap. 19). The true ruler-sage is one who keeps the people's "hearts vacuous, fills their bellies, weakens their ambitions, and strengthens their bones. He always causes his people to be without knowledge or desire" (chap. 3). He "treats them all as infants" (chap. 49); he should not "seek to enlighten the people but to make them ignorant" (chap. 65). If this is anarchism, then I am obliged to ask, what is tyranny?

Least of all does the *Tao Te Ching* advise the people to stand up and overthrow the tyranny of an unjust ruler. On the contrary, it urges them to surrender to situations that they presumably cannot change. In this regard, Clark's celebration of Taoist quietism – notably, its rejection of "forms of self-assertive and aggressive action" – is as disturbing as it is revealing. He marvels at the concept of "'non-action' *(wu-wei)*, activity which is in accord with one's own Tao and with those of all others" (*AM*, p. 179). *Wu-wei* is, among other things, a rejection of the very assertiveness and militancy that any revolutionary movement direly needs.

Historically, whether they follow *wu-wei* or some other precept, mystics have seldom exhibited any active participation in worldly affairs. Generally they tend, as a matter of doctrine, to intervene as little as possible in affairs of the mundane world, the better to preserve and retain the purity of their mystical state of being. In the Middle Ages and Renaissance, to be sure, many subversives presented their doctrines in mystical form, as Thomas Münzer did during the German Reformation. But that occurred in an era when nearly all political and intellectual discourse was conducted within a religious framework. Münzer was in fact a furious activist and a decidedly strong believer in armed struggle. Not so with our Taoists, whose concept of *wu-wei* instructs them, in general, not to rock the boat, not to struggle, or in good American mystical jargon: to go with the flow (although in the absence of rational analysis, it is difficult indeed to determine what the flow *is,* still less *where* it is flowing).

Indeed, in Clark's Taoism struggle is by its very nature futile: "Even if we 'win,'" he warns, paraphrasing Lao-Tzu, "we are defeated, since we have conformed to the alien values of those whom we have vanquished" (*AM*, p. 179). An extraordinary statement, coming from an alleged anarchist! Make no effort to change the social order, lest you yourself replicate its worst features! But without resistance and struggle, a social revolutionary movement would subside into quiescence. No wonder, in "Bookchin Agonistes," that Clark portrays me as "pugilistic." By the stan-

dards of Taoism, anyone possessed of any spirit of resistance to the social
order would be pugilistic, or worse.

That mysticism in a political movement tends to have a depoliticizing effect is illustrated very clearly by Clark's own recent statement: "We
need a spiritual revolution more than a political platform."[64] This
remark's unmistakable disdain for an active, programmatic politics, in
favor of an inward focus, can be regarded as a sure recipe for the triumph
of the present social order over any potential resistance.

The same can be said of Clark's recommendations that art should
become a substitute for politics. "Let the next Gathering of the Greens
conduct all its business in poetry," he has declaimed.[65] What a lovely
thought! Perhaps when a meeting nears the point where it might actually
decide to do something political, the participants should pause to contemplate the Tao and read poems to one another (as, I am told, Clark did
at a social ecology conference in Scotland several years ago). The myth of
artistic vanguardism, I should note, died with Dada and surrealism some
two generations ago and with the cultural "insurrections" of the 1960s,
when oppositional art was adopted by advertising agencies and fashion
designers to satisfy the "naughty" tastes of the middle classes.

Clark's advice against struggle ("Even if we 'win,' we are defeated") is
in full accord with Taoist philosophy generally, which holds, as Arthur C.
Danto points out in his book on Asian moral philosophies, that "if we
struggle we are lost already. . . .

> We ought not to try to impose our will upon the world; this is
> going against the grain, hence a formula for frustration, dishar-
> mony, and unhappiness. . . . The absence of struggle emerges as
> the sign of being rightly in the world. . . . What the Tao Te Ching
> is urging, finally, is the loss of the self. If there is an injunction, it
> is to find the way the world wants to go and then to take that way
> oneself.[66]

In political terms, this avoidance of "going against the grain" essentially
means accepting the existing social and political order, indeed accom-

modating oneself to it; in short, "The Way" that the Tao promises is a path to social and political submission.

In tandem with his penchant for capitulation, the Lao-Tzu of New Orleans places a high premium on the cultivation of childlike personal qualities: "just as in nature the softest and weakest thing, water, can overcome the hardest obstacle, so softness and weakness are the most effective qualities in personal development" (*AM*, p. 181). Clark's Taoism thus catapults us back to the regressive belief that truth lies not in rational discovery but in the divine recovery of a lost infantile stage when all was innocence – and ignorance.

Clark's arguments, like those of many anarcho-Taoists, advise us to return to the wisdom of the mythic (which, I submit, is really the fearfully superstitious) and to the chthonic world of the mysteries (which is really where men and women live on the lotus plant, in blissful ignorance of the world around them). The *Tao Te Ching* casts this ignorance as a secret knowledge that produces peace of mind, when in fact it is a case of mindlessness yielding passivity – a state of mindlessness that plays directly into the hands of the ruling classes.

The Taoist maxim of "non-action" is also very useful to those who would pursue a professional career as, let's say, a philosophy professor. It provides a superb rationale for bringing one's self into blissful conformity with the very real "larger self" composed of one's academic peers and a state of mind that, by accepting the prevailing Selfhood, is conducive to academic advancement. Let us be frank about the fact that deep ecology is not a dissident ecological outlook; it is becoming widely accepted by the academic environmental studies establishment. Not surprisingly, in "Bookchin Agonistes," Clark falls in with the notion that I would be buried in the oblivion of obscurity if I had not assailed deep ecology – a particularly odious way of circumventing criticism, and one that contradicts the history of the ecology movement.[67] And this criticism, let it be emphasized, comes from an "anarchist," who should be celebrating his marginality in an era of cultural counterrevolution, where success is often an indicator of capitulation to the status quo.

One aspect of Clark that becomes evident, from the nature of his insults, is his pedestrian, indeed solid bourgeois reverence for academic credentials. This vacuous pedant accuses me of being an "autodidact," "an amateur," and an "undergraduate" – waving his Ph.D. in my face! – as though, with qualifications invented by the bourgeoisie, his elitist peers have bestowed a superior status upon him. By the same token, he defends Dawkins and Wilson against me, who have, among other things, a "scientific background" (*BA*, pp. 20-21) – no less! That settles everything. In *Re-Enchanting Humanity* I was criticizing the regressive *social* consequences of their scientific ideas, not casting aspersions on their scientific methodology. But for Clark, apparently, even on such grounds, one must have a "scientific background" in order to "reply coherently" to scientists, who are apparently immune to criticism from all but their fellow scientists.

This little professor is a blooming elitist! Indeed, in the spring of 1994, when Paula Emery, a member of the curriculum committee of the Institute for Social Ecology, visited Clark in New Orleans, she raised the troubling subject of his dis-invitation and tried to explain the decision to him. By her account, he flew into a rage – and called her a "peon"! As Emery later wrote to me: in Clark's eyes, "because I am young, because I am female, because I am not Murray Bookchin or Dan Chodorkoff, or some Man with a Name in the Ecology Movement, I am a peon."[68] Having known Paula for many years as a person of great integrity and objectivity, I have no reason whatever to doubt her account.

I must now assume that social thinkers must be equipped with Ph.D.'s before their ideas may gain credence with Clark. By this criterion, a wide range of social thinkers, including Lewis Mumford,[69] would be sent to perdition, not to speak of Darwin, Faraday, and many others who laid the basis for modern science. And if "peons" too are to be excluded from the realm of social action, then we must discard the Zapatistas – both of the Mexican Revolution and of the recent Chiapas uprising.

The remainder of Clark/Cafard's criticisms of me in "Bookchin Agonistes" are too mean-spirited and trivial to be dignified with a reply. Mainly calculated to produce chortles among the deep ecology crowd and validate, by sheer malice, Clark's return to the fold of his peers, they reveal the extreme pettiness of Doctor Professor Clark and demonstrate that not even a Ph.D. can make a philosopher out of a pedestrian thinker.[70]

There is one issue, however, that I find so offensive and so outrageously false that I feel obliged to examine it in some detail. It involves the Parisian events of 1968. On other occasions I have noted that I witnessed street struggles in Paris between the French police (the CRS) and radical protesters in mid-July 1968. The facts are that I flew into the French capital on July 13 – the general strike during May and June had paralyzed Air France, making earlier travel to Paris impossible. When, at length, I managed to get a reservation, it was for a July 13 flight. Accompanying me on this trip were my two children and my ex-wife, Beatrice.

Now Clark/Cafard worms his way into the matter, sneering:

> If we read carefully, we . . . discover that [Bookchin's] first-hand experience of May '68 came, unfortunately, in the month of July. He reveals that he made a "lengthy" visit to Paris "in mid-July [sic] 1968, when street-fighting occurred throughout the capital on the evening before Bastille day" (p. 202). Bookchin is obviously trying to convey the impression that he was in the midst of things during the historic "events" of 1968. But as one history summarizes the events after the June 23 elections, "France closes down for the summer holidays" (*BA*, p. 23).

By no means does one have to look "carefully." as Clark puts it, at anything I wrote about my experiences on July 13; I dated them very explicitly. Had I been guided by less moral standards, I could have lied quite brazenly and dated my Parisian trip to, say, May 12 – and no one would have been aware of the falsehood.

In fact, when my family and I arrived in Paris on July 13, the situation on the Left Bank was so volatile that we had difficulty getting through the CRS cordons to reach our *pension*: the major streets were filled with zigzagging buses of mobile CRS, dressed in full riot gear. Knots of protesters clustered almost everywhere, scowling and hurling ironic gibes at the CRS men and the Parisian flics.

Exhausted by my transatlantic journey, I was resting in the *pension* that afternoon when Bea and my daughter, Debbie, rushed in and told me that furious fighting was taking place along the Boulevard St.-Michel. The CRS, they said, had been wildly shooting off tear gas canisters at all and sundry; in fact, Bea, Debbie, and my son Joe had had to turn to solicitous demonstrators for protection. I quickly accompanied Bea back to the Boulevard, but the fighting had essentially subsided. A few scattered CRS forays dispersed the remaining demonstrators, and at times we were obliged to take refuge in shops along the Boulevard.

Later, in the evening, I attended a neighborhood party that continued until midnight. After the festivities ended, Bea and I followed a group of young men – probably students who had decided not to go on their summer vacation (it *does* happen, you know!) as Clark's "history" prescribes – carrying a red flag and singing the "Internationale" and marching to the Boulevard St.-Michel. No sooner did we reach the Boulevard than we saw large numbers of CRS men racing up and down the avenue, alternately attacking and withdrawing from the crowds that filled the Boulevard. Caught up among a group of Africans, who seemed to be special targets of the racist CRS men, Bea and I were attacked with especial fury and had to scatter up toward the Pantheon, where we finally escaped our pursuers.

Alas for Clark/Cafard, I have more than my own memory to verify these events. Quite to the contrary of his unnamed "friends" who depict a placid Paris: not only was there street fighting in Paris on July 13, but it was featured on the front page of *The New York Times* the next morning. I had thought that the *Times* would bury its story on the back pages of the paper, but the fact is that the story was prominently featured on the front page under the disconcerting headline "De Gaulle Insists on Public Order." The May-June revolt was not dead, even in mid-July. John L. Hess, who reported on the fighting he saw at the Place de la Bastille, noted:

> As if to underscore [De Gaulle's] warning, riot policemen clashed tonight with several hundred youths carrying black and red flags and snake-dancing through the Place de la Bastille during celebrations on the eve of Bastille Day. Several youths were

slightly injured. Using tear gas, the police cleared the square of thousands of intermingled celebrators and demonstrators, some of whom threw paving stones.[71]

Since Clark observed so very little in Paris during his own visit to that charming city in "late July," I am obliged to wonder what his own motives were in traveling to the French capital. Was it to stroll through the Louvre? Or to dine along the Champs Elysées? Or to improve his French?

The Future of Anarchism

Will anarchism in the twenty-first century be a *revolutionary* tendency within the broad realm of socialism – the *most* revolutionary tendency, as Kropotkin hoped – or will it be devitalized by technophobic primitivism and Taoist quietism? Will it be a coherent theory capable of providing a future social upsurge with a viable direction? Or will it consist of a pastiche of unfinished, reactionary ideas, of the kind that the Watsons and Clarks serve up? Will it become a well-organized movement, composed of responsible and committed supporters? Or will it dissolve into personalistic, gossipy encounter groups and a juvenile clutter of "personal insurrections" that consist of offensive behavior, fruitless riots, and outré styles of dress and demeanor – as well as, in some cases, sociopathic "actions" and barefaced criminality, masked with claims that one is an anarchist and is therefore free to do whatever one chooses?

It was these questions that impelled me to write *Social Anarchism or Lifestyle Anarchism*. The response I received from the anarchist press in the United States – notably, *Anarchy* (which published Bob Black's diatribe) and *Fifth Estate* (which produced Watson's *Beyond Bookchin* and Clark's "Bookchin Agonistes") – as well as *Capitalism Nature Socialism*, (which published Joel Kovel's "Negating Bookchin," a psychologistic attempt to explain my disagreements with Marxism primarily as a personal competition with Marx for recognition.) – are remarkably lacking in social perspective and thereby bear out the validity of the argument I made in *SALA*.

Anarchism, Marxism, and the Future of the Left

At the peril of becoming mundane, allow me to point out that capitalism is a system of incredible dynamism that is not only becoming global but is penetrating every pore of society. Its commodity relationships are percolating from the economic realm ever farther into the private domains of the kitchen and bedroom – as well as into the community domains of neighborhood, city, and region. Capitalism is coming closer to being an all-embracing social system than ever before in its history. It is doing so not because of some abstract technological imperative or domineering sensibility (although both surely facilitate the process) but above all because the deep-seated imperatives of capital accumulation that are generated by marketplace competition drive it unrelentingly to extend and maximize its worldwide outreach for resources and profits.

This system cannot be ended without conflict: indeed, the bourgeoisie will categorically not give up its privileges and control over social life without a ruthless struggle. What can be said with certainty is that it will not be overthrown by adopting a quietistic mysticism, or by mindless denunciations of "civilization in bulk" and technology. Nor will it be overthrown by the creation of Temporary Autonomous Zones, or by "closing" down a government or commercial center for a few hours or even a day, or by routine tussles with the police, or by having a street festival with black flags draped from lampposts. It will not be overthrown by Hakim Bey-esque "happenings," or by Clark's poetic effusions on "surregionalism."

Those who wish to overthrow this vast system will require the most careful strategic judgment, the most profound theoretical understanding, and the most dedicated and persistent organized revolutionary groups to even shake the deeply entrenched bourgeois social order. They will need nothing less than a revolutionary libertarian socialist *movement*, a well-organized and institutionalized endeavor led by knowledgeable and resolute people who will foment mass resistance and revolution, advance a coherent program, and unite their groups in a visible and identifiable confederation.

In 1919, amid the collapse of the German Reich at the end of the First World War and the establishment of a Social Democratic government, various German leftists in Berlin and elsewhere attempted to drive

German politics, which were then still in disarray, further to the left and complete the November 1918 Revolution in order to create a communist social order. It was a time when history held its breath – when, indeed, the future of the entire century hung in the balance. The German Revolution of 1918-19 was a disastrous failure. But its lessons are in many respects more instructive for anarchists and revolutionary socialists than even those of the Spanish Revolution, which was probably doomed once major European powers began to participate in its civil war in the autumn of 1936 and the international working class pathetically failed to come to its aid.

The events that characterize the German Revolution are an often-confusing welter, but in January 1919 serious revolutionaries faced a brief but decisive period. The counter-revolutionary Social Democratic government under Ebert, Scheidemann, and Noske tried to remove the radical Independent Social Democratic police chief, Emil Eichhorn, from his post in Berlin. In response, the city's leftist organizations – the IndependentsSocial Democrats, the *pre*-Leninist Communists around Rosa Luxemburg and Karl Liebknecht, and the Revolutionary Shop Stewards – distributed leaflets denouncing the move and calling for a protest rally. On Sunday, January 5, 1919, to everyone's astonishment, 200,000 workers came into the streets and squares of Berlin, from "the statue of Roland to the statue of Victory . . . right into the Tiergarten," as *Die Rote Fahne* (The Red Flag), the Communist Party's organ, reported in a retrospective account a year later. They were armed with rifles, and with light and heavy machine guns, ready to fight for the retention of Eichhorn and, very probably, to replace the counterrevolutionary Social Democrats with a "Workers' and Soldiers' Council Republic."

They are correctly described as potentially the greatest proletarian army history had ever seen, and they were in a belligerent, indeed revolutionary mood. They waited expectantly in the squares and streets for their leaders – who had called the mobilization – to give them the signal to move. None was forthcoming. Throughout the entire day, while this huge proletarian army waited for tactical guidance, the indecisive leaders debated among themselves. Finally evening approached, and the masses of armed proletarians drifted home, hungry and disappointed.

The next day, a Monday, another appeal to take to the streets was distributed among the workers, and the same numerically huge mass of armed workers reappeared, once again ready for an uprising. Their demonstration was comparable in its potential revolutionary force to the one that had assembled on the previous day – but the leaders still behaved indecisively, still debating their course of action without coming to any definitive decision. By nightfall, after waiting throughout the day in a cold fog and steady rain, the crowd dispersed again, never to return.

At the time of these two mass mobilizations, in early January, the counterrevolution still lacked the effective military force it needed to suppress an uprising. With these few days of grace, however, it managed to muster sufficient forces to gain control of Berlin and put down the so-called *Spartakus* (Communist) uprising that led to the murders of Rosa Luxemburg and Karl Liebknecht.

Had the leaders been unified and decisive; had they given the signal to unseat the government, the workers might well have succeeded in taking over Berlin. Would the capital have remained isolated from Germany as a whole, or would successful uprisings have followed in key cities throughout Germany as well? We will never know: with the failure of the Independents, Spartakus, and the Revolutionary Shop Stewards to unseat the Social Democratic government, the validity of these various speculations were never tested. What is clear, however, is that a revolutionary possibility of historic proportions was squandered for lack of organization and decisiveness. In the estimation of many historians, the German Revolution came to an end on January 6, 1919, when the last of the two working-class mobilizations melted away – and for the rest of the century, the world as well as Germany had to live with the grim consequences of this failure.

The events of January 1919 in Germany, remote as they are, haunt me because I cannot help but wonder what today's anarchists would have done in a similar situation. Would they have had an organization ready and able to play a significant role in moving great masses of workers in a revolution against the Majority Social Democratic government? Would they have been able to mobilize forces strong enough to defeat the Free Corps, the paramilitary units that the Majority Social Democrats, especially Noske, were organizing against them, while the disorganized and indecisive revolutionary leaders bickered, delayed, and acted late and irresolutely?

In the great revolutions of history, the first demand that the masses made of their leaders was *responsibility* – not least the potentially insurrectionary Germans, who demanded order and purposiveness as evidence of a movement's seriousness. Had today's lifestyle anarchists been on the scene in 1919, I can only suppose that their position – or lack of one – would have helped to seal the doom of the German Revolution by excluding decisive organized action. As I wrote in *SALA*, many of them expressly shun organization of any type as authoritarian – or ipso facto as a Bolshevik-Leninist-Stalinist party. In the absence of a program, a politics, and a responsible organization – not to speak of a theory or even a sense of purpose beyond the "self-realization" of their writers – lifestylers, it can be stated as a matter of certainty, would have impeded rather than facilitated the unseating of a basically bourgeois state machine.

Indeed, for all I know, they might even have opposed the CNT and the FAI in Spain in 1936. Given their mysticism and irrationalism, they would turn either to introspection of one kind or another, or to reckless acts of personal rebellion and mindless adventurism. As for Clark, when he is not trying to replace left-libertarian politics with poetry and mysticism, he approaches, in practice, a social-democratic gradualist. To ordinary people, however dissatisfied they may be, no protest is more frivolous than the sight of a spindly kid throwing a stone at a cop (as in the cover art on Black's *Anarchy After Leftism*) – the image, par excellence, of irresponsible, juvenile bravado.

What makes the limited outlooks of lifestylers so damaging, especially in a time of reaction, is that they indirectly make the prevailing disempowerment into a virtue. Whether it is the quietism of some or the adventuristic episodes of others, their ineffectuality *promotes* disempowerment. Perhaps most important at a time when the lessons of the revolutionary tradition must be preserved and carefully analyzed, they undermine the socialist core of anarchism and offer essentially fragmentary impressions and actions as substitutes for serious reflection and responsible discussion. They lower the level of theoretical reflection: Watson's denunciations of civilization are no substitute for an analysis of capitalist social relations, any more than Clark's use of poetry and pop Asian theology is a substitute for rational insight and revolutionary social action.

For the present, the most precious arenas we have in which to cultivate an effective opposition are the minds of libertarian social revolutionaries who are eager to find alternatives to the prevailing social order and ways to change it. Either an anarchist is committed to a social war against class rule and hierarchy, offering a message based on revolutionary socialism or libertarian communism; or anarchism has been reduced to another of the many chic fads that constitute so much of the culture of modern capitalism.

As we enter the twenty-first century, anarchists should ask themselves whether a serious revolutionary opposition ought really to discard critical reason and knowledge in favor of mystical intuition, a cosmic reductionism, self-realization in the form of personal riots, the creation of Temporary Autonomous Zones, and the joys of throwing bricks at cops. Unfortunately, at least among many American anarchists, a refusal to reason out a libertarian socialistic standpoint is becoming widespread, and the thinking of those who might best form such a movement is being fogged by mysticism, antirationalism, primitivism, and technophobia. Far from being agents to advance society's insight into its grave plight, these anarchists are symptomatic of the social regression that marks the present period.

At the end of my life, it is my firm commitment to convey the revolutionary tradition and its lessons to young people. Unless they study its events and learn from its advances and its errors, they will float mindlessly into the barbarism that capitalism is bringing to the world. The danger of social amnesia is very real: indeed, the *idea* of revolution itself is waning from the collective mind of radicals today, and if it disappears, then the capitulation of the Left to capitalism will finally be complete – for it is only revolution that will ultimately change this society, not aesthetics, technophobia, antirationalism, and the like.

Those who advocate making changes in lifestyle at the expense of building a revolutionary movement are no less part of that definitive capitulation than the depoliticizing tendencies that are abroad today. Years ago it could be validly argued that lifestyle and politics go together;

that changes in lifestyle do not necessarily entail the surrender of revolutionism. In the 1960s I myself made the need for a convergence between the counterculture and the New Left the focus of most of my activities. But today – and especially today! – lifestyle anarchism is growing *at the expense of rational theory and serious organization,* not in tandem with it.

Revolution must be cultivated by means of systematic propaganda, step-by-step measures, careful planning, and rationally formulated programs that are flexible enough to meet changing social needs: in short, it must be cultivated by a responsible, dedicated, and accountable movement that is serious and organized along libertarian lines. It is the height of self-deception to suppose we can substitute personal "militancy" for organization, or personal "insurrection" for a consistent revolutionary practice.

March 2, 1998

Notes

1. Murray Bookchin, *Social Anarchism or Lifestyle Anarchism* (San Francisco and Edinburgh: A.K. Press, 1995); hereinafter *SALA*.

2. Thomas Frank, "Why Johnny Can't Dissent," in Thomas Frank and Matt Weiland, eds., *Commodify Your Dissent* (New York and London: W.W. Norton, 1997), pp. 34-35.

3. Kingsley Widmer, "How Broad and Deep Is Anarchism?" *Social Anarchism,* no. 24 (1997), pp. 77-83; emphases added. The name of this journal should not be confused with the title of my *SALA* booklet.

4. Bob Black, *Anarchy After Leftism* (Columbia, MO: C.A.L. Press, 1997); hereinafter *AAL*.

5. The use of the epithet acquired an international reach when the Oxford Green Anarchists wrote an unsavory letter to the anarchist-communist periodical *Organise!,* lacing into its editors for printing a cordial review of *SALA* and denouncing me as "Dean Bookchin." See "Letters," *Organise!* issue 45 (Spring 1997), p. 17.

6. For more on Black's activities, the reader may care to consult Chaz Bufe's "Listen, Anarchist!" (Tucson, AZ: Match, 1987; still available from See Sharp Press, A.K. Press and Freedom Press); Fred Woodworth's "I Go Time Traveling," *Match,* no. 91 (Winter 1996-97), esp. pp. 18-21; and Michael Pollan's "Opium, Made Easy: One Gardener's Encounter with the War on Drugs," *Harper's* (April 1997), especially pp. 42-45.

7. David Watson, *Beyond Bookchin: Preface for a Future Social Ecology* (Brooklyn: Autonomedia, 1996); hereinafter *BB*. Other works in this

section are cited according to the following key:

By Murray Bookchin:

EF   *The Ecology of Freedom*
SALA   *Social Anarchism or Lifestyle Anarchism*
TMC   *The Modern Crisis*

(For publication information about these volumes, please see the bibliographical listing at the end of this book.)

By David Watson:
(under the pseudonym "George Bradford" unless otherwise indicated)

ATM   "Against the Megamachine," *Fifth Estate*, vol. 15, no. 5 (July 1981); pseudonym "P. Solis."
BPA   "Bhopal and the Prospects for Anarchy," *Fifth Estate*, vol. 20, no. 1 (Spring 1985).
CIB   "Civilization in Bulk," *Fifth Estate*, vol. 26, no. 1 (Spring 1991).
HDDE   *How Deep Is Deep Ecology?* (Ojai, CA: Times Change Press, 1989).
MCGV   "Media: Capital's Global Village," *Fifth Estate*, vol. 19, no. 3 (Fall 1984).
NST   "Notes on Soft Tech," *Fifth Estate*, vol. 18, no. 1 (Spring 1983); unsigned.
SDT   "A System of Domination: Technology," *Fifth Estate*, vol. 18, no. 4 (Winter 1984).
SIH   "Stopping the Industrial Hydra: Revolution Against the Megamachine," *Fifth Estate*, vol. 24, no. 3 (Winter 1990).
TOC   "The Triumph of Capital," *Fifth Estate*, vol. 27, no. 1 (Spring 1992).

8.   As I did in *The Ecology of Freedom*.

9. If my views on medicine are "quite conventional" (*BB*, p. 114), they could stem from the fact that modern medicine is what is keeping me alive. To be sure, many alternative therapies are also very helpful. But I wonder if Watson makes the same kind of antimedical argument to his elderly family members and friends who, in all likelihood, depend as I do on antihypertensives and other medications for their continued existence.

10. Lewis Mumford, *The Myth of the Machine: Technics and Human Development* (New York: Harcourt, Brace & World, 1966), pp. 186-87.

11. Lewis Mumford, *The Pentagon of Power* (New York: Harcourt Brace Jovanovich, 1964), p. 356.

12. Ibid., p. 404, emphasis added.

13. Ibid., p. 373.

14. I do not advocate the use of all technologies – I would exclude, for example, clearly malignant ones like nuclear power. Perhaps the most outrageous piece of fraud Watson commits is to claim that I make a "fervent advocacy of pesticides" (*BB*, p. 139). This insinuation is scandalous – I pioneered criticism, from a left perspective, precisely of fertilizers and petrochemical pesticides. My 1952 article "The Problem of Chemicals in Food" (not to speak of my 1962 book *Our Synthetic Environment*) objected strenuously to the chemicalization of the environment, and my position has not changed since then.

15. A nervous Watson tells us that "the word *ultimately* must be stressed here" (*BB*, p. 163); presumably this caveat is intended to mitigate the sentence's determinism by bringing it into the short term, but how this makes a difference escapes me.

16. Mumford, *Pentagon*, p. 404, emphasis added.

17. Ibid., p. 349, 362. Just after speaking of modern technology's "poten-

tial benefits," Mumford refers to its "inherent defects." How something "inherently defective" can also have "potential benefits" is a paradox whose resolution escapes me; the fact remains that Mumford did see potential benefits in modern technology.

18. Richard B. Lee and Irven DeVore, "Problems in the Study of Hunters and Gatherers," in Richard B. Lee and Irven DeVore, *Man the Hunter* (Chicago: Aldine-Atherton, 1968), p. 6.

19. Marshall Sahlins, "Notes on the Original Affluent Society," in Lee and Devore, *Man the Hunter,* pp. 85-86.

20. In *BB* Watson ignores this introduction completely and gleefully quotes me against myself, juxtaposing writings from my excessively primitivistic works with my current writings on aboriginal society, as if he were revealing a highly compromising contradiction.

   It is no secret that the ideas of politically engaged writers change and develop. In fact, any theorist who is politically engaged will necessarily undergo such shifts. Had I written about social theory from the ivory tower of academia, my ideas might have remained entirely consistent over forty years – and entirely irrelevant. Certainly my core ideas have not changed, but even as I retained my adherence to them, I continually had to respond to changing political circumstances, to new issues that arose in movements, and to new movements for that matter.

   Watson shows that he understands this phenomenon when it comes to Lewis Mumford's ideas on technology, which evolved over several decades. He brims over with understanding for Mumford's shifts (*BB*, pp. 198-203) and, when his ideas stray too far from his own, grants him all sorts of extenuating circumstances. ("Though he many not have completely thought through the processes and period he long studied, he evolved along with them" [*BB*, p. 202].) But with typical malice, no such latitude is given to me: Watson treats the multitude of books and articles I wrote over a span of thirty-one years, from 1964 to 1995, as if they were a single book written at one time. (Indeed, on page 161 [n. 164], Watson specifically rules out making allowances for my intellectual evolution. The reason? I once objected, in a way he dislikes, to someone taking my ideas out of the context of their time. Thus, when he finds discrepancies now, he freely takes me to task for contradicting myself. Using this technique, one could set about making Mumford or any politically engaged theorist look entirely ridiculous.

21. Mumford, let it be noted, would have regarded Watson's claim that aboriginal society was this kind of libertarian paradise as nonsense. "Wherever we find archaic man," he wrote, "we find no lawless creature, free to do what he pleases, when he pleases, how he pleases: we find rather one who at every moment of his life must walk warily and circumspectly, guided by the custom of his own kind, doing reverence to superhuman powers." *See Myth of the Machine*, p. 68.

22. Roger Lewin, "Past Perspectives," *Science*, vol. 240 (May 27, 1988), p. 1147.

23. Thomas N. Headland, "Paradise Revised," *Science* (Sept.-Oct. 1990), pp. 46, 48.

24. Richard B. Lee, *The !Kung San: Men, Women, and Work in a Foraging Society* (Cambridge and New York: Cambridge University Press, 1979), p. 308.

25. Ibid., pp. 308.

26. Richard Lee, *Subsistence Ecology of !Kung Bushmen,* Ph.D. diss. (University of California, Berkeley, 1965), p. 94; quoted in Edwin N. Wilmsen, *Land Filled with Flies: A Political Economy of the Kalahari* (Chicago and London: University of Chicago Press, 1989), p. 304.

27. Richard Lee, "!Kung Bushmen Subsistence: An Input-Output Analysis," in A. Vayda, ed., *Environment and Cultural Behavior* (Garden City, NY: Natural History Press, 1969), pp. 47-79; and Lee, *!Kung San*, p. 278, table 9.12.

28. Quoted in Roger Lewin, "New Views Emerge on Hunters and Gatherers," *Science,* vol. 240 (May 27, 1988), p. 1146. This article describes the changes in the study of the !Kung; its thesis is that "a very simple but persuasive model of hunter-gatherer life dominated anthropological thought for two decades, but is now being replaced as challenges come from several directions."

29. It is worth noting that Mumford, who Watson likes to suggest was something of a primitivist, observed:

> The fragility of [a paleolithic foraging] economy is obvious: the gifts of nature are too uncertain, the margin is too narrow, the balance too delicate. Hence primitive cultures, in order to be sure of continuity, tend to be restrictive and parsimonious, unready to welcome innovations or take risks, even reluctant to profit by the existence of their neighbors. . . . In so far as the power complex has overcome that species of fossilization, we owe it a debt. Plenitude on such a solitary, meager, unadventurous basis too easily sinks into torpid penury and stupefication. . . . It is not to go back toward such a primitive plenitude, but *forward to a more generous regimen, far more generous than the most affluent society now affords,* that the coming generations must lay their plans. (Mumford, *Pentagon of Power,* pp. 401-402, emphasis added)

30. To my contention in *SALA* that most tribal spirituality as we know it today has been influenced by Christianity, Watson raises no objection; instead, he dismisses its significance. "That the Ghost Dance was influenced by Christianity doesn't mean it wasn't authentically native" (*BB,* pp. 235), he counters. True, many Indian people today follow these religious admixtures and even Christianity itself. But that's not the point: presumably the effects of Christianity – the religion par excellence of European colonialism and imperialism – have vitiated the force of "ancient perennial wisdom" in resisting oppression. If the "ancient wisdom" of the primitive is necessary for a

"future social ecology," I am obliged to wonder if it will also contain the sacraments of baptism and the eucharist?

31. John E. Yellen, "The Transformation of the Kalahari !Kung," *Scientific American* (April 1990), pp. 102B-102D.

32. Lee, *!Kung San,* p. 458.

33. Yellen, "Transformation," p. 102D.

34. It is worth noting that Mumford would have been shocked by this hypostasization of irrationality and impulse. "So dangerously infantile are man's untutored and undisciplined impulses that even the most stable cultures have not been able to prevent life-threatening explosions of irrationality – 'going berserk,' 'running amok,' practicing systematic torture and human sacrifice or, with pseudo-rational religious support, embarking on the insensate slaughter and destruction of war" (*Pentagon of Power,* p. 369). I would add that "ordinary men" made up the German police battalions that slaughtered Jews in Poland during World War II, while ordinary Japanese conscripts engaged in the rape of Nanking during the occupation of China in the 1930s.

35. Not surprisingly, Watson rejects the idea that reason or other learned behavior is to be valued more highly that instinct, intuition, and the extrarational. He suggests that we do not "benefit intellectually, ethically, socially, or practically by privileging the learned behavior of human society over innate behavior" (*BB,* p. 31) and agrees that between "learned behavior" and "instinct," "one kind of behavior is not really higher and another lower" (quoting the mystic Paul Shepard, *BB,* p. 31). It is worth noting, again, that Mumford would have disagreed with him profoundly, indeed furiously. "While most of the 'emotional' responses to color, sound, odor, form, tactile values, predate man's rich cortical development," he noted, "they underlie and enrich his *higher* modes of thought" (*Myth of the Machine,* p. 39). The later chapters of *The Pentagon of Power* are pervaded with

contempt for the mysticism of the 1960s youth culture and the atavistic behavior, as he also told me, of the Living Theater.

36. Even the qualification Watson gives – "it is possible to be both unimportant and uniquely important" (*BB,* p. 56) – is reminiscent of the doublethink promoted by National Socialist ideology, in which the will of individual Germans came to be identified with the will of the Führer. See J. P. Stern, *Hitler: The Führer and the People* (Berkeley and Los Angeles: University of California Press, 1975), chaps. 7 and 8.

37. Anyone who doubts Watson's extrasensory ability to penetrate unknown realms should consider his account of my meeting with Mumford at the University of Pennsylvania, which I mentioned in *SALA.* Although Watson was not there, he somehow knows that I spent a only "few minutes chatting with Mumford" (*BB,* p. 198). Since he would have no other way of knowing this, I am convinced he must have used shamanic dreaming. In fact, Mumford and I had a very fruitful discussion, in which I challenged him on many things. (Although he certainly had my admiration, he was not my guru.) We spoke probably for an hour or so – I didn't clock the conversation. Nor was my relationship with Mumford limited to this encounter. Sadly, Watson's shamanic wisdom failed to guide him to the acknowledgements section of my book *Our Synthetic Environment* (published in 1962), where I thanked Mumford "for reading my discussion of urban life," the book's chapter on cities. Back in the mid-1950s, in fact, Mumford sent me an encouraging response to my leaflet "Stop the Bomb," and in the early 1970s, when I applied for a grant from the Rabinowitz Foundation, he, Marcuse, and René Dubos provided me with letters of commendation. But it is not my association with Mumford that is at issue here.

38. Paul Radin, *The World of Primitive Man* (New York: Grove Press, 1953), p. 140.

39. Watson's chosen guru, Mumford, was more dubious about shamans and aboriginal subjectivity. He warned that "the taboo-ridden savage

. . . is often childishly over-confident about the powers of his shaman or magicians to control formidable natural forces." See *Pentagon of Power*, p. 359.

40. Quoted in Jose Lopez-Rey, *Goya's Caprichos: Beauty, Reason and Caricature*, vol. 1 (Princeton, N.J.: Princeton University Press, 1953), pp. 80-81. See also F. D. Klingender, *Goya in the Democratic Tradition* (New York: Schocken, 1968), p. 92. It is worth noting that by "arts," it is not at all clear that Goya was referring only to the visual and performing arts – to painting, poetry, and music; in its eighteenth-century usage, the word *arts* would also have encompassed the mechanical arts and technics – which makes *Fifth Estate's* inclusion of the computer an even more arrant distortion.

41. Oddly, in another recent discussion of social ecology, Michael Zimmerman uses the very same two quotations to cast me in a negative light. Although he is a philosophy professor and therefore presumably a more scrupulous scholar than Watson, Zimmerman, like Watson, removes both phrases from their context, even truncating the "parasite" quotation in exactly the same way that Watson did.

> While rightly condemning such remarks, Bookchin himself recently restated a view he advanced years ago, that "man could be described as a highly destructive parasite who threatens to destroy his host – the natural world – and eventually himself." . . . Bookchin himself has described humans as "a curse on natural evolution."

Michael Zimmerman, *Contesting Earth's Future: Radical Ecology and Postmodernity* (Berkeley and Los Angeles: University of California Press, 1994), p. 171. That both Zimmerman and Watson juxtapose the identical quotations causes me to wonder whether they were both influenced by their mutual friend, John Clark.

42. By Watson's account, I demand that my readers "must" agree with everything I write, "must accept the whole program as a unitary

whole," and so on – indeed, in one such extended paraphrase he uses the word "must" no fewer than six times on a single page (*BB,* p. 15), as though whenever I assert a point of view, I place my readers under a stringent requirement to agree with me – or else!

Yet Watson himself insists that "social ecology *must* discover a post-Enlightenment politics" (*BB,* p. 51), and that "A future social ecology, if it is to endure as a meaningful philosophical current, *must* learn to listen" to trees (*BB,* p. 72). And: "A future social ecology . . . would recognize that . . . firm ground, if any, *must* be found" in a reorientation of life "around perennial, classic and aboriginal manifestations of wisdom" (*BB,* p. 154; emphasis added).

43. Daniel A. Coleman wrote a review of *Beyond Bookchin* that was published in *Z* magazine, April 1997, pp. 55-57. He was called my "sycophant" in an unsigned note in *Fifth Estate* (Fall 1997), p. 34.

44. "To sense and comprehend after action is not worthy of being called comprehension. Deep knowledge is to be aware of disturbance before disturbance, to be aware of danger before danger, to be aware of destruction before destruction, to be aware of calamity before calamity." Watson quotes this passage from Sun Tzu's *The Art of War* against me, at a point when he thinks my foresight has failed (*BB,* p. 162). It could well be applied to his own belated recognition of the importance of ecological politics.

45. What makes Watson's book interesting is that he follows the logic of lifestyle anarchism to its preposterous end – and for this reason alone, it is well that serious revolutionaries should read it.

46. David Watson, "Swamp Fever, Primitivism, and the 'Ideological Vortex': Farewell to All That," *Fifth Estate* (Fall 1997); hereinafter *SF.*

47. John Clark, *The Anarchist Moment* (Montreal: Black Rose Books, 1984), p. 11. The title for this book was suggested by me and effusively accepted by the author, with warm expressions of gratitude.

48. John Clark, ed., *Renewing the Earth: The Promise of Social Ecology: A Celebration of the Work of Murray Bookchin* (London: Green Print, 1990). This book includes many misbegotten essays that I do not hold in high regard and whose inclusion I vigorously protested to Clark.

49. Mary Jo Buhle, Paul Buhle, and Dan Georgakas, eds., *Encyclopedia of the American Left* (Urbana and Chicago: University of Illinois Press, 1992), p. 102.

50. Max Cafard (pseud. for John Clark): "Bookchin Agonistes: How Murray Bookchin's Attempts to 'Re-Enchant Humanity' Become a Pugilistic Bacchanal," *Fifth Estate,* vol. 32, no. 1 (Summer 1997), pp. 20-23; hereinafter *BA.*

51. Clark, *Anarchist Moment,* pp. 173, 175; hereinafter *AM.*

52. Whether Clark ever understood what I was writing for years about postscarcity and its implications for freedom, his Taoism explicitly advises a community to reject even labor-saving technologies: "though there should be among the people contrivances requiring ten times, a hundred times less labour, he would not use them" (quoted in *AM,* p. 178).

53. Daniel Chodorkoff, executive director of the Institute for Social Ecology, letter to Murray Bookchin, Feb. 12, 1997.

54. Ibid.

55. "1992 Annual Meeting/Summer Program Evaluation," Institute for Social Ecology, Oct. 3, 1992, p. 9; minutes taken by Paula Emery; Janet Biehl files.

56. Chaia Heller, ISE faculty member, personal conversation with Murray Bookchin, 1997.

57. Thomas Berry, *The Dream of the Earth* (San Francisco: Sierra Club Books, 1988), pp. 194, 205, 207, 209.

58. Bill Devall and George Sessions, *Deep Ecology: Living As If Nature Mattered* (Layton, UT: Gibbs M. Smith, 1985), p. 67.

59. In the quoted passage, to be sure, he says "certain beings," not "all life-forms," but he is not consistent with biocentrism here. Once again, the definition by Sessions and Devall: "*all organisms and entities in the ecosphere*, as parts of the interrelated whole, are equal in intrinsic worth," ibid., emphasis added.

60. Wing-Tsit Chan, trans. and comp., *A Source Book in Chinese Philosophy* (Princeton, NJ: Princeton University Press, 1963), p. 139. All quotations from the *Tao Te Ching* herein are taken from this source.

61. Max Weber, *The Religion of China: Confucianism and Taoism*, trans. Hans H. Gerth (New York: Free Press, 1951), pp. 181-82.

62. "Mysticism, Nature and Assessment of," *The Encyclopedia of Philosophy*, vol. 5 (New York: Macmillan and the Free Press, 1967), pp. 429, 430.

63. "Nader Campaign Targets Corporate Abuse of Power and the One-Party State," *Delta Greens Quarterly*, no. 43 (Summer 1996), pp. 1-2. The Nader fund-raising advertisement ("From the grassroots ... Important!") is on page 3 of this issue, which was co-edited by Clark.

64. John Clark, "The Spirit of Hope," *Delta Greens Quarterly*, no. 39 (Summer 1995), p. 2.

65. Max Cafard (pseud. for John Clark), "The Surre(gion)alist Manifesto," *Fifth Estate*, vol. 28, no. 1 (Spring 1993), p. 18.

66. Arthur C. Danto, *Mysticism and Morality: Oriental Thought and Moral Philosophy* (New York: Basic Books, 1972), pp. 107, 110.

67. It is particularly obnoxious that this pompous academic now derides me for not being au courant about academic theories of justice – specifically Rawls's neo-Kantian notions. As Clark should know, my views on the subject of justice are drawn from sources that long antedate Rawls's work. Indeed, I was at pains in *The Ecology of Freedom*, to emphasize that they were guided by Marx and Engels (*EF*, pp. 87, 149), both of whom elucidated their ideas about a century before Rawls's tedious *Theory of Justice* appeared on the shelves of college bookshops.

68. Paula Emery, former ISE administrator (1987-93) and assistant director (1989-93), letter to Murray Bookchin, Feb. 11, 1997.

69. According to his biographer, Mumford took occasional courses at various New York academic institutions on subjects that interested him. But "although he eventually accumulated enough credits to graduate, he never took a degree, and he saw no need for it." Donald L. Miller, *Lewis Mumford: A Life* (Pittsburgh: University of Pittsburgh Press, 1989), p. 73.

70. Although Clark/Cafard laments his space limitations, he devotes much of "Bookchin Agonistes" to mere grammatical errors.

71. John L. Hess, "De Gaulle Insists on Public Order," *New York Times*, July 14, 1968, p. 1.

Part III

The Future of the Left

Reflections on Marx and Marxism

Interviewer: Janet Biehl

You have long been an outspoken critic of Marxism, at least from "Listen, Marxist" in 1969 and continuing through various essays in the 1970s and 1980s, including "Marxism as Bourgeois Sociology." Recently, however, your comments on Marx have reflected a more appreciative attitude. In this interview I'd like to examine to what extent this new attitude is a shift in emphasis and to what extent it represents a change in your view of Marx.

While you were writing on Marxism in the 1970s, the so-called "socialist" countries and movements – especially the Soviet bloc – still existed but they had long ceased to stand for human freedom. At the same time in Western Europe, social democracy and Euro-Communism were openly complicit with the rationalized order of bourgeois capitalism. Citing this historic development, you wrote in 1979 that "Marx's work, perhaps the most remarkable project to demystify bourgeois social relations, has itself become the most subtle mystification of capitalism in our era" and "the most sophisticated ideology of state capitalism." Do you still agree with this assessment?

First of all, I'd like to examine the context further. "Listen, Marxist" was written in 1969, when Progressive Labor was attempting, in the name of Marxism, to penetrate SDS, not with a view to building it or providing it with guidance but with a view to taking over SDS and draining it of its members and recruiting them into PL. From my own experience as a Communist in the 1930s, I recognized that PL was engaged in a typical Stalinist-type operation, known as "fraction work." Yet at the same time the opponents of PL within SDS – both RYM 1 and RYM 2 – were themselves becoming Maoists of one kind or another and designating themselves as Marxists, even though they seemed to know very little about Marxism.

These groups were exercising a great influence on large numbers of inexperienced radical youth who had entered into SDS by June 1969. The *Anarchos* Group, to which I belonged, was trying to work out an independent libertarian revolutionary position, only to find ourselves fighting the vulgar Marxism of both sides, particularly of PL but also of the two RYM groups.

"Listen, Marxist" was written to arrest their influence. It tried to demystify the notion of proletarian hegemony, the idea – which seemed valid thirty years earlier – that the industrial proletariat would be the leading class in any social revolution or any struggle for socialism. This view was no longer true in the 1960s. Although in Marx's day, and in my youth, the industrial proletariat might easily have been regarded as the hegemonic class in the struggle for socialism, today the proletariat no longer regards itself as an oppositional class to bourgeois society. While it would be impossible to make any revolution without the support of workers in industrial manufacturing, the proletariat can no longer be *singled out* as the leading class to initiate and drive a revolution to its end, as Marx once supposed. It has largely been economically integrated into the bourgeois industrial order, to an extent that none of us, before World War II, could have imagined.

In the meantime ecological destruction emerged as a major problem, threatening to destroy the biosphere itself. As a political issue, ecology cut across class lines, as did the oppression of women and people of color, and as did the imbalance between cities and the countryside. Under those circumstances the idea that the struggle between wage labor (the proletariat that works in factories) and capital (the bourgeoisie that owns these factories) was the central issue of our era appeared no longer to be all-encompassing, and the issue of proletarian hegemony had to be dropped. I thought and still think we have to explore these and other transclass issues, which is what I argued in "Listen, Marxist!" – which categorically does *not* mean that I reject class struggle.

It's notable that in "Listen, Marxist!" I often use Marx against the Marxists, invoking some of the best elements in Marx's ideas and quoting appreciatively from *The Eighteenth Brumaire of Louis Napoleon,* one of his most brilliant historical and analytical studies. So "Listen, Marxist!" is less an anti-Marx pamphlet than an *anti-Marxist* pamphlet. It was part of my desperate attempt to prevent SDS from being colonized by parasitic Marxist, especially Maoist groups. Unfortunately, as it turned out, these groups did destroy SDS and brought the life of the New Left to an end.

A decade later, in writings such as "Marxism as Bourgeois Sociology" in 1979, I was addressing a different problem. I was trying to encourage an ecological outlook in the Left – that is to say, an ecological philosophy and sensibility – and help it build a movement that advanced the preservation of the natural world as an ethical activity on the part of human beings. The ecological politics I advanced was one that not only saw the natural world as the fundament of human life but considered human beings as the stewards, the ethical custodians of a natural world whose evolution human thought could potentially render self-conscious. I was trying to distinguish this outlook from one that wants to preserve forests and lakes merely because they are resources needed to enrich capitalism. I feel that a rational society would also be an ecological society that would bring mind to the service of biological evolution as well as meet human material and cultural needs. Or as the young Marx put it: *harmonize* the natural world in the course of fulfilling humanity's own rich potentialities for self-consciousness and rationality. This view should be sharply distinguished from deep ecology's commitment to biocentrism, in which the notion of "intrinsic worth" – itself a construction of the human mind and anything but "intrinsic" – relegates human beings to the same moral status as bears, wolves, or for that matter roaches.

In those days, the late 1970s and early 1980s, I found that some Marxists were attempting to incorporate ecology into their politics by making Marx into an ecologist, attributing to him some kind of concern for preserving the natural world. When I considered what Marx's attitude might have been toward ecological issues, in the light of what I knew about his thinking, it became very clear to me that he regarded the natural world as an ensemble of forces that humanity had to master to satisfy its productive needs. Apart from his youthful writings, he had a very limited view of environmental issues: a concern for soil fertility and clean air for the sake of good nutrition and public health. I agreed with these issues. But I also felt that Marx did not assign any *ethical* responsibility to humanity as a rational steward of the natural world, as potentially evolution rendered self-conscious and rationally purposive.

In "Marxism as Bourgeois Sociology," then, I was trying to counter the attempts by Marxists to portray Marx as an ecologist, in the sense that I have described ecological consciousness. My criticisms in that essay – such as calling Marx's work a "subtle mystification of capitalism" and "the most sophisticated ideology of state capitalism" – may seem harsh, but I was obliged to demonstrate that when it came to the despoliation of the biosphere, Marxism agreed with capitalism on that issue.

Admittedly I was one-sided, because the essay was highly polemical. Indeed, if I were to rewrite that essay today, I would still make this criticism but put it in its historical context. Considering the historical circumstances a hundred and fifty years ago, when he did his most important political writing, I would say that it's at least understandable that Marx was not imbued with an ecological outlook.

In the mid-nineteenth century, when Marx was calling for the reduction of first nature to a mere ensemble of objects or raw materials, first nature still seemed to be the "master" of humanity. Disease was still commonly treated by bloodletting, and the germ theory of disease was only being accepted in a few medical works. Families had to produce a large number of children because so few survived to adulthood. Marx himself lost most of his children before his own death, including his only son Edgar. To be in one's mid-sixties was to be quite elderly. Famine was still a reality: if crops failed in a single season, not only would food prices soar but entire communities would starve. Much of North America was still relatively unsettled. Electricity was still a marginal phenomenon: Marx's son-in-law Paul Lafargue, I believe, once described a scene in which the two men were both watching a toy electric train running along tracks. Marx suddenly exclaimed, "See! This is the basis of communism!" Thus when Marx prescribed that nature had to be fully commanded by humanity, he was writing at a time when such a project made sense, indeed seemed necessary, not only to him but to the whole society except for a few romantics.

But there was also another, perhaps even more significant sense in which I called Marx's work a "mystification of capitalism" and an "ideology of state capitalism." Marx had developed the notion that the development of capitalism out of European feudalism was unavoidable,and that this development was an indispensable precondition for the emergence of socialism. Specifically, he thought that industrially undeveloped countries would have to go through a *bourgeois* phase of development before they could hope to place socialism on their revolutionary agenda – a view that, in retrospect, was one of his greatest errors: it provided the rationale for the regressive role played by the German Social Democrats in their 1918 revolution and the Russian Mensheviks in 1917.

In the years after his death, the Marxists completely rigidified this view. Marx, in fact, had been ambiguous, at times. Even as he held, for example, that a bourgeois phase was a precondition for socialism, he allowed for the possibility of exceptions, as in the case of Russia, where the *obschina* – the Russian peasant system of communally reallocating land according to family needs every few years – could be a direct pathway to socialism or even communism without a preceding bourgeois stage. Yet so far did Marxists casat Marx's views favoring a "bourgeois democratic stage" in stone that Lenin's first major economic work, as well as some of the most important theoretical works of Plekhanov, the so-called father of Russian Marxism, ignored any alternatives to a preceding bourgeois stage and insisted that a capitalist development was indispensable before socialism could become a realistic issue in the Russian revolutionary agenda.

The German Social Democrats were even worse, in this respect. In 1893 Marxism had become the official doctrine of the Social Democratic Party of Germany, the largest workers' party in Europe. At the end of the First World War a major theoretical issue separated the SPD's left wing, led by Rosa Luxemburg and Karl Liebknecht, from the rest of the party: Should Germany have a socialist revolution – that is, use insurrectionary methods and, in 1918, establish a council government? Or should it have a bourgeois democratic parliament – that is, remove the Kaiser and what remained of feudalism in Germany and after establishing a parliamentary system, raise the issue of a socialist society? Liebknecht and Luxemburg felt that Germany was ready for a socialist society then and there.

During the period 1918 to 1923, the period of real revolutionary possibilities in Germany, this argument turned into a war to the death. The right and the center of the SPD – which were opposed to a revolution – used Marx's stages theory of historical development as an apologia for the perpetuation of capitalism. I'm not speaking about capitalist parties here; I'm speaking about socialist parties influenced by Eduard Bernstein and, more equivocally, by Karl Kautsky and Rudolf Hilferding, the major German Marxist theorists of the interwar era. They argued that Germany had yet to develop the necessary capitalist preconditions for socialism, at least culturally and institutionally, and they used Marxist theories to defend capitalism as an indispensable economic stage that would create the material and political preconditions for socialism. Politically, their idea was to bring Germany from a quasi-feudal system, led by Prussian Junkers and by the Kaiser, through a representative democracy in a parliamentary government, and only then, later, into socialism. A constituent assembly, they argued, should therefore be established to create a bourgeois republic that would hopefully foster a peaceful evolution into socialism. This indispensable political phase would create a democracy that would make it possible to develop the working class and bring socialist institutions to Germany. How wrong they proved to be is clearly shown by the later recourse of the German bourgeoisie to fascism – a lesson whose implications are still not grasped by Marxists today.

I thought I had every reason in the world to regard these ideas, attributed to Marx, as apologias for capitalism. And these ideas were not questions of pure theory – they had been put into practice and led to bloodshed in two uprisings. In the so-called "Spartakus uprising" of January 1919, leaders of the newly formed German Communist Party (led primarily by Karl Liebknecht and Wilhelm Pieck) tried to overthrow the Social Democratic government, led by Ebert, Scheidemann, and Noske. Between this insurrection and the following one in March 1919, nearly the entire Luxemburg leadership of the KPD was killed off, especially with the death of Leo Jogiches – and they were murdered with the blessings of socialists, who professed to be seeking a socialist society through a capitalist route and who invoked Marx's writings as a justification. It is for these reasons, most significantly, that I viewed Marxism –

and Marx's own ideas, to a great extent – as inadvertent apologias for capitalism and even, in the case of the Social Democrats, as playing a counterrevolutionary role.

I still think that when I say Marx was not an ecologist, even in the sense of genuine stewardship, I'm far more accurate than the eco-Marxists who, even today, are still going through Marx's works and trying to snip out statements here and there that they can piece together to simulate an ecological viewpoint. But if we try to transcend polemical emphases and to go beyond the bitter and even bloody conflicts over various interpretations of Marx's ideas, I would say that Marx was far more flexible than the theory I depicted in "Marxism as Bourgeois Sociology." I should have presented my criticisms of him in their historical context. There is a great deal to be learned from Marx, and we cannot dismiss *him* as a bourgeois sociologist. Unfortunately, Marx's ideas were very ill used when they fell into the hands of Marxists, and he has been held responsible for ideas that he doubtless would greatly modify or reject if he were alive today.

You've often criticized Marxism for its economism. In the preface to Capital, *you've pointed out, Marx reduces people to "personification[s] of economic categories, the bearer[s] of particular class interest." Elsewhere you say that Marx "objectifies the proletariat and removes it as a true subject," such that "the revolt of the proletariat ... becomes a function of inexorable economic laws and 'imperative need.'" Would you modify this criticism in any way today?*

I would say yes and no. *The Holy Family,* one of the earliest Marx-Engels works, written years before *The Communist Manifesto,* certainly seems to see the proletariat as a mere instrument of history, and workers as social forces rather than as human beings. Marx's later works describe workers as real living beings who are being grossly exploited; in volume one and also volume three of *Capital,* Marx conceives of the proletariat as people who are burdened by crushing material problems. They suffer incredibly and are obliged, as human beings, to revolt against the system that is oppressing and exploiting them inhumanely. At some point Marxists –

most recently the old Stalinist types who mutated into Maoists and Castroists – began to deal with the proletariat not as people who happen to be workers but as a nonhuman social force, lacking will and an understanding of their condition. They invoked those works of Marx and Engels that seem to regard the proletariat merely as an instrument of history. In fact, a sizable Marxist literature emerged over the generations that argued that Marx was practically a mechanist in his treatment of social development – I refer to the work of Althusser, as an example, with his rigid and schematic and seemingly structural outlook.

But on the other hand, another interpretation of Marx, based on the *Economic and Philosophical Manuscripts of 1844,* emphasizes his humanistic side. Herbert Marcuse, with considerable justification, pointed out that, in his early manuscripts, Marx was very humanistic and very mindful of, indeed empathetic with the suffering of the proletariat. So one can find many different Marxes.

The later Marx, near his death in 1883, was actually amazingly flexible. In his ethnological notebooks (which contain words and phrases from a multitude of languages), he was immensely sympathetic to preliterate people and respected their seeming innocence, drawing particularly from Lewis Morgan and the evolutionary school of anthropology. Between 1878 and 1883, I would say that he was far more flexible than any of the Marxists who spoke in his name after he died.

Anarchism, Marxism, and the Future of the Left

Your concepts of hierarchy and domination bear a certain correspondence to the Marxian concepts of class and exploitation. Hierarchy and class are both unequal social arrangements: hierarchical rankings are based on status, power, and physical force, while class rankings are based on wealth. Domination and exploitation, for their part, are the acts of oppression that constitute the foundations of hierarchy and class, with domination being an act of mastery or rule, and exploitation being the act of appropriation of the economic surpluses produced by human labor. Did you and do you intend for your concepts of hierarchy and domination to replace class and exploitation in social analysis, or to encompass and broaden them? It would seem that they overlap to a great extent, since the domination of women, for example, also involves (in a very broad, non-Marxist sense) the exploitation of their labor and their bodies.

That is an extremely important question, and I must say absolutely and categorically, as I have in the past, that I do not and never did intend the concept of hierarchy to replace the concept of class in social analysis and theory. Class society is very real, and it has existed for thousands of years in different forms. "Asiatic" class society (in Marx's language) and slave society, feudal society and capitalist society, every one of these societies was or is a class society, beyond any shadow of a doubt. The class struggle also always exists in one form or another, sometimes consciously and sometimes unconsciously, sometimes in a mystified form and sometimes in a clear and secular form.

There is also no doubt in my mind that economic exploitation – the appropriation of labor, the exploitation of labor-power, and under capitalism the sale of labor-power as a commodity – are very real and have produced great social crises, uprisings, civil wars, and ongoing conflicts in history. I've never surrendered the idea that classes and class struggles exist, or that hierarchy supplants these divisions and conflicts.

What, then, did I intend to emphasize with the concept of hierarchy? In *The Ecology of Freedom* and other works I tried to *enlarge* and *broaden* existing concepts of social oppression. I tried to indicate that hierarchies preceded the emergence of classes, indeed that hierarchy was one of the major sources of class society. Social classes emerged out of hierarchies, as well as out of the division of labor, as Marx claimed. The chiefdom of a simple tribal society, for example, was a potential hierarchy, usually an emerging one. The chief, who was almost invariably male, at first appeared as the ablest and/or wisest individual in the tribe, an *adviser* rather than a leader, who by degrees became a dominating figure. The social conditions that fed into this shift involved the increasing complexity of society – in technology, territorial expansion, and wars of conquest.

I also tried to indicate that hierarchies persisted throughout all class society. Gerontocracy, for example – the domination of the young by the elderly – was one of the oldest forms of hierarchy, and gerontoncracies were retained all through the course of civilization. The ancient world, particularly classical Greece and Rome, placed an enormously high premium on elders, as did China. The elders were given enormous authority and power – not simply exploitative powers but powers of domination – that persisted for thousands of years even as class societies developed in the West and East and underwent transformation.

But by no means did all domineering status groups – groups organized in hierarchies – accrue wealth the way exploitative groups did. In fact, if I may give an example from literature, in Plato's ideal society in *The Republic* – the system where the philosopher-kings rule – the hierarchs are the most materially deprived of all the strata in society. Their children are taken away from them, they are subjected to grueling training, hunger, suffering – tests to determine whether they will be warriors or rulers. Their life is stripped down to bare material essentials. Even when one finally proves that one is entitled to play a dominating role, the only advantage one accrues is the respect of the community – while other strata of the population are permitted to enjoy whatever wealth they have and live sybaritic lives if they can afford to. Domination is thus not necessarily congruent with the good life in a material sense. I don't think many people would have wanted to be in the ruling stratum that Plato described in *The Republic*.

I also wanted to show in the book that even if classes were abolished, oppression might well remain in existence in the form of hierarchical domination. This concept arose out of my attempt to understand societies like "Soviet" Russia, where classes had *ostensibly* been abolished yet hierarchy still remained. (I regarded the "Soviet Union" as a state capitalist society, where key strata of the hierarchy were classes.) Engels had made a spirited defense of hierarchy, explicitly declaring that it would be necessary in order to operate even a single factory. In other "socialistic" societies – Cuba, Nicaragua, Vietnam – that were not as brutal as Stalin's, class had ostensibly been abolished yet hierarchies still existed and were recognized as such.

A second reason I took up the question of hierarchy was the rise of new transclass issues that were not anchored strictly speaking in class rule and economic exploitation. Ecological problems, while clearly produced by capitalist growth, have existed for a long time and cannot be anchored simply in a specific class society. Women's oppression also transcends specific class boundaries. Wealthy women have been oppressed and degraded to an outrageous extent in patricentric societies, whether ancient, feudal, or capitalist. And they have been oppressed even when classes were supposedly abolished. In the so-called "Soviet Union," the moment women became the majority of physicians, the very status of the medical profession began to decline, often to the level of wage work. Male physicians enjoyed the most privileged positions in hospitals – they were heads of departments and chief surgeons – while women doctors were little more than caretakers of sick people, even though they had medical degrees.

So hierarchy became a medium by which I could raise these transclass issues – the human oppressions that had to be eliminated even after classes were abolished. This effort became very important in the utopian visions in the 1960s and 1970s, when people were discussing new ways of living, new sensibilities, and new types of social relationships. To address the transclass issues on which the "new social movements" that had emerged out of the 1960s were based, I found the concepts of hierarchy and domination to be absolutely necessary.

In a broader sense I was trying to *expand the meaning of freedom*, the extent to which a revolution has to go to finally completely emancipate human beings. Bourgeois republicans in their day had established principles of political liberty and emancipated slaves and serfs. Marx had tried to expand the meaning of freedom beyond political liberty to include economic freedom. There is a long history of an ever-expanding horizon of freedom, and I tried to contribute to it in the 1960s by advancing the notion of a nonhierarchical society. This notion has now been accepted as conventional wisdom, even on the part of my critics.

In 1892 (in Socialism: Utopian and Scientific*) Engels defined historical materialism as:*

> *that view of the course of history which seeks the ultimate cause and the great moving power of all important historic events in the economic development of society, in the changes in the modes of production and exchange, in the consequent division of society into distinct classes, and in the struggle of these classes against one another.*

You share with Marx a view of history as developmental, and its processes as moving dialectically through time. But in "History, Civilization, and Progress" your terms are not at all economic:

> *History . . . is the rational content and continuity of events (with due regard for qualitative "leaps") that are grounded in humanity's potentialities for freedom, self-consciousness, and cooperation, in the self-formative development of increasingly libertarian forms of consociation. It is the rational "infrastructure," so to speak, that coheres human actions and institutions over the past and the present in the direction of an emancipatory society and emancipated individuals. That is to say, History is precisely what is rational in human development.1*

In many respects your History seems far more idealistic than historical materialism. To what extent does it represent a return to the Hegelian idealist view that Marx sought to overturn?

In "History, Civilization, and Progress," I was not concerned with the *specific* forces that generate a historical development. I was concerned essentially with *meta*history, with what historical development is *as such*, as distinguished from mere chronicles. I was concerned with the actualization of historical potentialities, and with the goals that historical development should actualize when it is rational. Like Hegel and Marx, I believe that the all-encompassing actualization of humanity's potentialities lies in the achievement of a rational society and a rational life – that is, in freedom and self-consciousness – not simply in a full stomach and the absence of toil. The ancient Athenians, although they weren't as historically oriented as we are today, also believed that the actualization of humanity's potentialities, or at least that of the Greek male citizens, lay in the *polis,* that is, in a free, self-conscious community. So if I omitted economics from my discussion in "History, Civilization, and Progress," it is *only* because I was not trying to analyze or account for any of the forces that make for historical development. I was defending the ideals of the Enlightenment against the postmodernist disintegration of history into mere events – or Castoriadian "imaginaries," for that matter.

Now let's turn to Engels's statement, which is indeed concerned with the specific forces that motivate historical development. Engels brought into sharp relief one of the great insights of Marx's work, albeit that was also one of its failings. Marx correctly saw that the *preconditions* for freedom and self-consciousness are material: that human beings have to enjoy freedom from toil if they are to be able to think, create, and become self-conscious as well as manage their own society. I know that as a young man, when I came home after working in a foundry all day, I was incapable of doing much more than eat, listen to the radio, and then pass out. Many of my fellow workers would jokingly declare that they were too exhausted to sleep with their wives – and that does happen when you work under extremely burdensome conditions. Engels, like Marx, was dealing with the preconditions for freedom, or what might be called the "necessary" conditions for freedom.

Now at various times these preconditions for freedom, which are the *necessary* conditions for freedom, have been confused with the *sufficient* conditions for freedom. Without advances in the material condition of life and the diminution of the work week, human beings cannot be free – except under very rare conditions, such as during revolutions and for limited periods of time; even then, they must still leave the barricades and return to work to satisfy their needs and those of their families. They have to eat, if you please. In May 1937 in Barcelona, the workers had to conquer the Stalinist counterrevolution then and there. But they delayed, and after four days they had to leave the streets to obtain food – and they thereby surrendered whatever advantages they had gained. Thereafter the counterrevolution smashed them and essentially put an end to the anarchist experiment in Catalonia and other parts of Republican Spain. Similar stories can be found throughout history.

If these material preconditions are necessary, however, they are often not the *sufficient* conditions for revolution and social development. An immense variety of cultural factors also come into play, either enhancing or impeding social development. What I'm saying is that the sufficient conditions for social change are more than strictly economic and involve issues such as organization, politics, democratic institutions, ethics, and yes, traditions, intellectual expression, hopes and aspirations for a better life. They involve the ability to discard religion, and nationalistic and ethnic prejudices. All this has to be addressed as well before material imperatives can drive people to revolution and consolidate the gains they make.

Now in Marxism there is a great deal of confusion between the necessary conditions and the sufficient conditions of social development. Marx wrote that the relations of production have to be transformed in order for a society to be transformed. I regard this as quite sound. In addition to this basic structure he wrote about the superstructure – the legal, the religious, the ideological, and so on. Unfortunately he treated the superstructure *too dismissively*. In fact, unless we address the superstructure of, say, ancient Rome, it would be impossible for us to explain why Roman slave society did not develop into capitalism during the Empire. After all, by the time of Domitian and the later emperors like Constantine, enormous material resources had accrued in the ancient world – and some people had wealth that could have been invested in capitalist production. But Rome did not develop capitalism, for reasons that were largely traditional or superstructural: Romans viewed trade as a socially debasing activity, and the Roman bourgeoisie was dominated by the values of landed nobles. That is to say, the values generated by land ownership and the prestige of being a landowner kept a capitalistic bourgeoisie from developing, since the nascent capitalists wanted to become landed magnates. Often they did not reinvest their profits in their various productive enterprises. They did not bring money back into an enterprise or readily introduce machines – instead they bought estates and titles and tried to intermarry with the nobility.

Thus capital, in ancient Greece and Rome and in the Middle Ages, was dissipated into the acquisition of landholdings, which were often far less profitable but far more prestigious. The desire for this prestige was a cultural factor – a superstructural factor – that greatly inhibited the economic development of these societies.

It was primarily in England, but also to some degree in northern Italy and the Lowlands, that an industrial bourgeoisie finally began to think less in terms of acquiring estates and more in terms of expanding its productive enterprises. This breakthrough was one of historic proportions. And it might very well not have happened, because alternatives to the explosive industrial development of England after about 1760 might very well have emerged. Artisans and the yeomanry could have become more enlightened and agriculturally more productive; small enterprises, capitalistic to be sure, might have decided to engage in quality production rather than mass production. But when textile manufacturers brought in their new spinning and weaving machines, they threw commodities upon the world market that were so inexpensive that artisans' products could not withstand the competition of cheap factory-made commodities.

Today, now that capitalism has become so pervasive, the economic has indeed become even more important than it was in Engels's day. The commodification of the world today is going on at a dizzying pace, together with enormous technological advances – all of which have brought economics more to the foreground than in the past. Capitalism, which was once primarily an *economy*, has now become a *society*, in the sense that the family is becoming little more than a unit of consumption, cities or at least suburbs are becoming shopping malls, and everything is being verbalized in businessese, from "the bottom line" to "the balance sheet." We're using a language and concepts borrowed from finance, not from ethics or morality. Ironically, Engels's remark, which at best explains the preconditions rather than the conditions for historical development, may be more appropriate today than it was at any time in the past.

But Marx and Engels were correct in pointing out that the full actualization of human potentialities for self-consciousness and freedom requires a sufficient development in the material conditions of life. The anthropologist Marshall Sahlins and his followers would have us believe that in foraging societies – societies that, by today's standards, exist in conditions of extreme scarcity – people live leisurely lives because first nature provides food in abundance and, above all, because the socially defined needs of the society's members are much more limited.

But I find this view unconvincing and naive. However cooperative and caring a preliterate community may be, at least within its own kinship group, and however much "free time" it has, is it really actualizing the human potentiality for knowledge of and activity in the world? Most tribal societies were actually quite uncertain as to where they were going to gain the means of life, and their consciousness was shrouded in myth and magic. Their "historical records" consist mainly of genealogies committed to memory by elders; myths and an ensemble of mystical beliefs; and notions of cause and effect that were most often wrong.

Even if preliterate people did have a lot of free time, which is questionable, what did they do with it? Based on what we know today about human potentialities, they were quite undeveloped. When one looks at the potentialities that we now know that human beings possess, the wondrous life that has been imputed to, say, the San "Bushmen" was far from attractive. I would not want to live in a society like that one, and I do not know any anarcho-primitivist who would really want to do so either, except maybe a Ted Kaczynski, whose behavior verges on the pathological (and whose politics I do not respect). Even the San "Bushmen" do not seem to want to follow the old ways – especially since the 1970s they have been abandoning them rapidly.

I would like to add one more point about history. The accusation has been made that I think that there has been nothing but progress at all times in history. This is a despicable caricature. I maintained, not only in "History, Civilization, and Progress" but in *The Ecology of Freedom,* that there are two sides to the history of humanity, its overall development, both rational and irrational; a legacy of domination and a legacy of freedom. The legacy of freedom is the history of ever-expanding struggles for emancipation, while the legacy of domination is the chronicle of domination and all its brutalities. The two have interacted, competed, and to some extent been stimulated by each other for better or worse, in a genuine dialectic. In *The Ecology of Freedom* I tried to show in great detail how the two interact with each other. Despite the faults I now find in that book, some of which I pointed out in the introduction to the revised edition in 1992, I take great pride in the book's emphasis on the two interacting forces of freedom and domination.

I would also like to recall a very important Hegelian conept about evil: What we often regard as good at one time is considered evil at another time, under new conditions. For example, Bakunin described the state as a, "historically necessary evil," which I take to mean that humanity was forced to use the state to arrive at a level of self-conscious-fulfillment. Here an evil became a means for humanity to extricate itself from animality, and it seems to have been unavoidable. This is not to say--as Marxists might believe--that the state was , "inevitable." I would rephrase Bakunin's--and for that matter Marx's--statement to read that the state was a "historically unavoidable evil," one that we now can completely eliminate. It was an evil, yes, but one that may have been impossible to avoid. In retrospect, the difficulty of achieving the steps that led humanity out of mere animality tends to be underestimated or overlooked altogether. .

Today, when we realize that warfare may exterminate humanity as well as tear down the natural world, feminists, pacifists, and other radicals sometimes look back to tribal society and derogate the warrior as the historical origin of a militaristic society. I find this somewhat arrogant. These societies lived in entirely different times and circumstances, under living conditions that were very uncertain and dangerous: tribes were chronically fighting with each other, pastoral communities were invading agricultural communities, the world was in a state of continual upheaval.

At that point in history the warrior was a necessary and very important person. Young men were needed by the community for its protection and they had to be so trained. Chiefs were necessary to marshal military forces against marauders. Even before Europeans came to the American continent, the Hopi had to defend themselves against the Navajo. Every agricultural community has displaced a foraging community – and foraging communities often kill off most of the animal life in their territory, which obliges them to go to war with still other foraging communities that do have game. Let me emphasize that I am not trying to praise war-riors and patriarchy. I am saying that we cannot always view history through the lens of our current values; historical events and phenomena must be understood as a development in the context of their own time as well.

In your earlier writings, you criticized a belief in progress that identified "'progress' with increasing control of external and internal nature," with "an industrial 'paradigm' of mastery and discipline." You've also condemned the "Promethean drama in which 'man' heroically defies and willfully asserts him-self against a brutally hostile and unyielding natural world." But recently you have been more accepting of certain concepts of progress, saying that progress appears "in the overall improvement, however ambiguous, of humanity's material conditions of life."[2] Is your view in any way becoming more favorable toward attempts to "control internal and external nature"?

Once again I must say that in an earlier period, in order to inculcate respect for the natural world and validate an ecological approach against the prevailing technocratic and bourgeois approaches, I had to empha-size and even overemphasize the need for a "humble" attitude toward the natural world. Ideas evolve under changing circumstances and contexts, and in ideological conflicts, the programmatic issues of a given political agenda may sometimes lead to overstatement – a one-sidedness often comes with factional and political disputes. In general the development of political ideas does not move in a straight line, especially when the theorist propounding them is engaged in *living political movements* rather then shut up in an academic cloister, or viewing events as a bystander, or barely out of diapers. Looking back on the lines you quoted, I would now want to modify them, to put them in a proper perspective and advance a more complete and rounded view because of the new conditions that have emerged.

On the identification of progress with "increasing control of external and internal nature": Under modern capitalist conditions, the produc-tive imperative of growth for the sake of growth, technological innova-tion, and productivity has indeed been turned into a system that is a huge monster to which many people surrender themselves and their beliefs. In recent years progress has been identified almost exclusively with support for this monster, including control over natural forces. Under such conditions, I found it necessary to criticize *this* notion of progress. Today such criticisms have become commonplace.

Unfortunately, the critique of this specific notion of progress – especially of progress conceived overwhelmingly as technological development – has become outrageously one-sided and has led to its complete opposite: a deprecation of the notion of progress as such. Instead of merely opposing the view that technological innovation is *always* progressive, it's common today for people in the ecology movement and lifestyle anarchists to reject the idea that progress of *any* kind is either possible or desirable, including the invention of immensely useful machines. Against those who make this blanket rejection, then, it has become necessary to defend technological innovation and the use of machines and the importance of science.

I am encountering idiocies in the ecology movement and among lifestyle anarchists that urge humanity to return to medieval systems of agriculture and even to foraging. Today, even as deep ecology exercises a great deal of influence in academic environmental studies departments and Euro-Americans are turning to semimystical vagaries of the most self-indulgent and juvenile kind, the level of material distress in other parts of the world is becoming enormous. To recognize the important role that technological development can play in bettering the material conditions of human life is a necessity. Technics cannot be written out of any concept of progress.

But let me emphasize that in saying this, I don't identify progress exclusively with technological development. In fact, I insist that unless technological development has an ethical thrust and is designed to address ecological as well as social problems, it will be used to deepen such problems, especially under a system of capitalist relations. I argue for a balanced approach to technics, not the one-sided myth – so widely propagated in the 1930s and 1950s – that technological advances in themselves guarantee improvements in human life.

The negative interpretation of the Prometheus metaphor, so popular today, gained currency when Marcuse contrasted the Promethean mentality (toward which he was *not*, as I recall, entirely deprecatory) with the passive-receptive Orphic mentality (toward which his attitude was more favorable). It gained favor among the few people who read *Eros and Civilization* in the late 1950s and early 1960s, then percolated into the counterculture, which gave it a ridiculous twist. It has been too many years since I read Marcuse's book to be in a position to comment on it with assurance. But I would like to point out that Prometheus, in mythical terms, gave us fire, and if only for that reason he remains a hero. And while Orpheus's outlook on the world has very inviting, laid-back aspects, I fear that many people who should be in an engaged and combative struggle against the existing social order – in effect, Promethean – are becoming increasingly passive-receptive, egocentric, and too indifferent to social issues to try to improve any human condition other than their own.

The Orphic approach has become a passport for entry into the dreamlike world of the *Odyssey*'s lotus eaters, where one lives in blissful forgetfulness and an eternal, blissful present, with neither memory nor responsibility. I consider this passivity to be an integral part of the ideological counterrevolution that is sweeping the world today, including an often unthinking acceptance of capitalism. I would like to see a more Promethean sense of *defiance,* indeed *rebellion,* for among Prometheus' greatest traits was his defiance of the Olympian deities. He was a rebel and in my opinion a revolutionary. Thus I feel far more sympathetic to that image today than I did when I wrote those lines.

When you say that human beings are biologically constituted to intervene in the processes of first nature, to what extent are you agreeing with Marx's view that first nature must be "conquered"? More broadly: How, in your view, should human society treat first nature? To what extent should it try to gain technological control over natural processes in order to further humanity's material interests?

Let me answer this complex question by discussing what I believe is humanity's place – at least potentially – in first nature, which I define as natural evolution. A red thread runs through first nature, or natural evolution, and that red thread is the development of ever greater subjectivity and behavioral flexibility in life-forms. By subjectivity, I do not mean rationality alone; I meant what Denis Diderot, more than two centuries ago, called sensitivity and reactivity, which undergoes a graded development toward intelligence and rationality. Human beings constitute the culmination of this evolutionary process of subjectivity and potentially, at least, may one day come to be nature rendered self-conscious.

Two hundred years ago the German idealist philosopher Johann Fichte in his *Vocation of Man* (1800), essentially wrote that human beings are nature rendered self-conscious; later in the nineteenth century Elisée Reclus followed him in a similar statement; but neither of these affirmations is satisfactory. For one thing, neither man told us, as far as I know, what he meant by "nature" in those phrases. Second, while I would like to believe that human beings will one day *actualize* their potentiality to do so, it is absurd to say that they are "nature rendered self-conscious" today. At present they're not even society rendered self-conscious: in fact, society seems to be moving along without any conscious human guidance at all. Thus, although human beings are potentially first nature rendered self-conscious, they have yet to actualize that potentiality – and it is a decidedly open question whether they will do so.

What would it mean to actualize that potentiality? First let me say that the potentiality to be "nature rendered self-conscious" would not be actualized by a society that merely preserved and expanded wilderness areas. Indeed, by failing to intervene in first nature we would be so immersed in the natural world that we would disappear in the unconscious evolution of life-forms, rather than raise ourselves to the level of self-conscious activity. In any case, it is self-deceptive to ignore the fact that capitalism is now transforming the planet to such an extent that the notion of wilderness is becoming meaningless. Even sub-Saharan Africa has ceased to be the wild "dark continent." Vast tracts of land have been deforested, and many so-called wildlife areas have been converted into ranches, either for breeding purposes or as tourist recreation centers. Apart from the bloody warfare between the Tutsi and the Hutu, much of tropical Africa is becoming a theme park. Tibet, too, is no longer the land of mystery it once was, except insofar as Beijing has closed it off to Western travelers.

Some people in the ecology movement react to these developments with horror. They demand that human beings withdraw from these areas, so that they may be restored to their pristine condition. I would say that the idea that we have to suddenly cease intervening in the natural world is preposterous, indeed that many ecosystems – including those inhabited by wildlife – would collapse if humans did not intervene in them to keep them "wild." Bison and grizzly bears would have long migrated out of Yellowstone Park, for example, if attempts were not made by park employees to keep them there – and they would wander into more settled areas, where they would be killed. Global warming may well proceed no matter what restrictions we place on the use of fossil fuels today – it seems to have gone into its own kind of uncontrollable development. If capitalism does persist as a social order for much longer, then science will be obliged to enter into a race with capital accumulation and globalization to remedy the enormous problems emerging in the world's ecology before the growth imperatives of the capitalist market succeed in pulling down the existing biosphere.

What, then, would it mean to actualize our potentiality to become "nature rendered self-conscious"? It would mean creating a society that can live in a complementary relationship with first nature. It would mean creating a free, rational, ecological society – agriculturally, industrially, in our lifeways and sensibilities – to bring our potentially rich ethical equipment to bear in our dealings with first nature, that is, with the evolution of nonhuman life. We would learn to intervene in first nature for ethical, aesthetic, and humane, as well as material reasons, so as to render inhospitable areas more amenable to a great variety of life-forms, designing our communities and technologies to foster the well-being of nonhuman as well as human beings.

Allow me to be more precise, lest we drift off into hazy metaphors. First of all, I do not mean that we should try to "conquer" first nature, or seek the "conquest of nature" that Marx favored. I often come across such phrases in the literature of ecological politics: the "conquest of nature," "domination of nature," "exploitation of nature," and so on, and they're used as if everyone knows what they mean. In fact, these phrases are merely anthropomorphisms that do nothing but obscure the ecological issues we face. It's impossible to conquer, dominate, or exploit nature.

Conquest, domination, and exploitation are *entirely* social phenomena, which some people inflict on other people. These concepts can be applied to the nonhuman natural world only in a metaphorical sense, to denote the intensive use of the natural world for harmful (as well as useful) ends. They have no real meaning when we are talking about the relationship between human beings and first nature.

Thus human beings cannot conquer, dominate, or control first nature. But there is something that they can do: they can try to *control the forces of first nature.* That there really are forces of nature should be obvious. Gravity is one of them, despite Abbie Hoffman's and Jerry Rubin's lunatic attempts to levitate the Pentagon in the late 1960s, during the great demonstrations that swept hundreds of thousands of people to Washington to protest the Vietnam War. But gravity can be controlled, in the sense that we have learned how to make use of it, and we have done this remarkably well with various aircraft. The same, in principle, can be said about other natural forces. Human beings are able to control and use many natural forces – because biological evolution has equipped us to innovate, to change our environments rather than merely to adapt to them the way other animals do. Human beings, in effect, have themselves become a force of nature in their own right, a fairly conscious force if not always a wise one.

Many people in the ecology movement who talk about the "conquest of nature" or the "domination of nature" use these phrases as inherently objectionable. They want us to resist a sensibility that seeks to "conquer nature" and develop a sensibility oriented toward "oneness" with nature, usually wilderness. The notion that we could or should "control the forces of nature" raises their hackles. The word "control" in particular smacks of an unacceptable authoritarian project.

I don't know how long capitalism can continue to prevail on this planet. I don't know how long it will take for the capitalist economy to irreparably damage the biosphere. But let me say quite plainly that in the thirty or forty years in which I have been raising ecological issues, technological development has occurred so rapidly that the question of whether we should control natural forces is actually becoming moot. We already do control the basic natural forces of the planet – or at least the bourgeoisie does, due to advances in science. Nowadays when we debate the question of whether or not human beings should control first nature, what we're really talking about is *our attitude toward a situation that already exists*.

In fact, Marx's prescriptive approach toward the humanity-nature relationship has now become merely a descriptive one: humanity's control over the forces of nature describes an existing situation. We – by which I mean the ruling classes – have crossed a historic threshold and have gained a vast degree of control over the forces of first nature. We know both the atomic "secrets" of matter and the genetic "secrets" of life; in this decade the human genome is well on its way to being mapped. This society is already able to manipulate these two basic forces – matter-energy on the one hand and life on the other. Science and industry can already transform matter into energy and energy into matter. And people who engage in bioengineering are on the threshold of making enormous innovations in agriculture and medicine that will affect all spheres of life. They are even beginning to introduce human genes into animal chromosomes and are cloning mammals.

Unfortunately, the knowledge of how to control natural forces is, at present, in the hands of the bourgeoisie and its scientific servants, who use it to serve the interests of capital. The searing question we face is: How would people use this knowledge in a free, rational, ecological society? In fact, in a rational society we *must* control the forces of nature, if for no other reason than to create, restore, and maintain ecological areas for nonhuman life-forms. First nature has already been remade to such an extent that a free, rational, ecological society would have to engage in widespread ecological restoration, and this cannot be done without the use of science, technics, and our active intervention in the biosphere. We could even use genetic engineering, for example, in such a way as to restore "wild" areas. Ironic as it may seem, in a rational society we would have to exercise control over natural forces *precisely in order to restore first nature*.

So objections to the prescription that humanity should control the forces of nature are now moot. Control already exists – but in the service of profit and social control. The question we face today is not "*Should we use our knowledge of the forces of nature?*" but *"How are we going to use our knowledge of the forces of nature?"* To answer these questions, we need an ethics that can guide the application of our knowledge of first nature, and a rational society that will prevent the damage that capitalism is now inflicting on the natural world.

You've often said that Marxism has not produced an ethical socialism. What would you regard as a proper ethics for socialism?

Let me first examine certain views that Marx actually held. He eschewed making ethical prescriptions for a socialist society. He felt that socialism and communism would have to be devised by future generations, based on the concrete problems they faced. Accordingly, he believed that there was no point in trying to establish anything more than basic objective criteria for a socialist society. But he did not always honor that goal. In *The Communist Manifesto,* for example, written in 1847-48, moral indignation emerges throughout the work. Marx fully recognized the inhumanity of capitalism, a recognition that was reinforced by the data that was being published about the industrial revolution in England. In 1844 Engels had visited England, especially a number of the industrial towns, and written vivid descriptions of the poverty of the English working class, notably the extent to which women and children as well as men were overworked in the factories that were spreading over parts of the British Isles. One senses in the writings of both men an intense indignation at the consequences of the Industrial Revolution. Yet they never idealized preindustrial society, however much they admired tribal mores, nor did they idealize life in the Middle Ages or in the periods immediately preceding the emergence of industrial capitalism.

Second, when Marx does discuss communism, he adds a very strong ethical dimension to a cooperative society. He distinguishes between bourgeois right, the legal system that existed under capitalism, and the ethical system that would exist under communism. Under communism, he contends, distribution should be based on need rather than work (an idea by no means original with him, it appears in the writings of Robert Owen and Louis Blanc). An individual who has to support several children, in a communist society, would get a greater return for his or her work than one who has only himself or herself to support, despite the fact that they do the same amount of work with the same skills. This is an *ethical* arrangement, not simply an economic one. It's an attitude that people under communism would be expected to have, toward labor and the distribution of its fruits.

With Hegel and the rationalist classical philosophers, Marx shared the idea that freedom and self-consciousness are the actualization of human potentialities. Under communism, he believed, people would enter into their real history; he considered the history that preceded communism to be the "prehistory of humanity." Freedom and self-consciousness would thus be the actualization of the communist maxim and of human potentialities as such.

Unfortunately, Marx never presented such ethical views systematically. He eschewed ethical interpretations of communism when he was called upon to make them. His failure to provide a system of ethics is a major lacuna in his writings – a lacuna that, needless to say, served men like Stalin very well. Many Stalinists in the interwar period and even after World War II justified Stalin's cruelties, to the extent that they acknowledged them, on the grounds that he was building the material preconditions for socialism in Russia. Only after these preconditions were achieved, they argued, would it be possible for the Russian people and Communists generally to indulge in ethical vagaries, as they tended to think of them.

The anarchists, for their part, or at least the *social* anarchists, called for an ethical society and advanced an idea of freedom that was very expansive. But socialism requires a dialectic of ethics, that is, an ethics that is a product of history and a rational interpretation of social development, not a series of absolutes that are divined like the commandments of a deity. Like expanding ideas of freedom, ethical ideas are conditioned by existing social contexts and new possibilities, as well as being grounded in history. For my part, I think the history of ethics can be phased into three general categories, or normative modes.

The earliest normative mode was simply custom: behavior that is *unreflective,* that is practiced unthinkingly as though it were an instinctive rather than a learned heritage. Custom prescribes how one does certain things in a certain way but offers no rationale for doing it that way except that that is how things have "always been done." In tribal society, for example, the individual is expected to defend his or her blood relations unthinkingly and to privilege them over friends and allies who are not blood relations. That form of normative behavior is handed down culturally, from time immemorial, but it was regarded very much like an unquestionable instinct. The incest taboo, to take another example, is very widespread among many peoples, yet there is no innate biological aversion to incest in human beings – it is really prescribed by custom. So, too, is early mutual aid. Custom, which is typical of tribal society, is thus the most primal, least rational, and most socially conditioned system in the unfolding dialectic of normative modes.

Morality, the next normative mode, is a definite *code* of behavior, but one that is seen as dictated by a deity or other suprahuman force. The best-known example is the Ten Commandments that Moses is said to have brought down from Mount Sinai. The Decalogue prescribes that a person must follow a certain kind of behavior not because things have always been done that way but because a deity has *commanded* as much. Society typically developed from custom into morality when hierarchy emerged, certainly when religious hierarchies began to demand certain forms of behavior in the name of a god or goddess. The individual who follows moral prescriptions is given canons of right and wrong through priests, who convey the dictates of the deity. In contrast to custom, which the individual absorbs almost from birth, moral prescriptions are always debatable and priests typically have to cajole people into following them, with the threat that if they violate or ignore them, they will be the targets of the deity's wrath.

It should not be surprising that, after the long development from custom through morality, the most advanced normative mode is that of ethics itself. Ethics is based on reason: its distinguishing feature is that prescriptions of right and wrong have to be *justified* by rational activity, not simply by tradition or blind and fearful acceptance. In an ecological society it is ethics that would guide human behavior, elaborated through rational discourse, logic, and the evaluations of experience.

Murray Bookchin

What are the aspects of Marxism that you would consider to be valuable today for constructing social theory and building a new revolutionary left social movement? How would you integrate them with the four tenets of anarchism that you value, to wit: "a confederation of decentralized municipalities; an unwavering opposition to statism; a belief in direct democracy; and a vision of a libertarian communist society"?3

First, I'll address what lives in Marx's writings that are relevant to a libertarian communist social analysis and theory of revolutionary change. Most fundamentally, I definitely accept Marx's basic project of formulating a coherent socialism that integrates philosophy, history, economics, and politics. I especially would affirm this project at a time when fragmentation is so very pervasive, when postmodernism compels us in the name of relativism and pluralism to deal only with episodes and events, rather than produce generalizations out of them. As a result, in postmodernism nothing seems to hang together intellectually, and ideas are dissolved into goulash. Although I do not accept Marx's claim that socialism can be a "science," I find his demand for a coherent socialism to be immensely refreshing. His demand for coherence is as living today as it was a century ago, and perhaps even more significant today because of the confusion caused by postmodernism. I think it should be a guiding principle for all revolutionaries in the twenty-first century.

Another aspect of Marx that I appreciate is that fact that he was a brilliant dialectician. To be sure, as I have said elsewhere, Marx and Engels's dialectic (and it was Engels who tried to systematize it) is often too mechanical, too pat, as it were, and I would infuse it with a more organic and naturalistic approach, as I tried to do in *The Philosophy of Social Ecology*. But in its searching range and in its dialectical logic, I would say that as a social dialectic, volume one of *Capital*, taken as a whole, is comparable only to Hegel's *Logic*, which is the greatest masterpiece in philosophy.

Also of extreme importance is the vitality of Marx's political economy. I refer not only to the way he developed it dialectically, especially in volume one of *Capital* and in a number of other works. As a study of the capitalist economy as a whole, it has absolutely no equal today. Marx's economic studies are central to *any* socialist analysis. His theory of commodification, of capitalist accumulation, on a worldwide scale, anticipated the essential features of capitalism today. The same can be said for his grasp of historical development, which, despite its flaws, contains insights unequaled by subsequent works on political economy. Finally, I have a great respect for Marx's attempt to infuse theory with practice – the famous eleventh thesis on Feuerbach, in which he says, "Philosophers have only interpreted the world, in various ways; the point is to change it" – and to do that in as systematic, as knowledgeable, and yet as flexible a manner as possible.

Let me now turn to Marx's political ideas. As a means for the transition from capitalism to socialism, Marx relied greatly on the state. He thought a centralized state would be necessary as a successor to the bourgeois state, and that a workers' party should govern the new state in the interests of society as a whole. Marx called this state, as we know only too well, the "dictatorship of the proletariat." Actually he himself used that phrase very sparingly; it was Lenin who used it repeatedly, and of course the Stalinists who made it equivalent to a totalitarian state. But what Marx seems to have had in mind was a republican system modeled in many respects on the Jacobin republic of 1793 and 1794, although without Robespierre's Terror.

Examining Marx's ideas in the context of his era, I can understand why he advocated centralization and the formation of nation-states as indispensable for the development of the material bases for socialism. At that time nation-states were still being formed in Europe; the United States was engaged in a bloody, four-year civil war over whether it would be in fact a nation-state; Germany did not become a nation-state till 1871. The only clearly defined nation-states that existed in Europe during most of Marx's lifetime were in England and France. Especially to someone focused on Germany, I can see how the formation of a nation-state might be regarded as a political advance over the numerous small duchies, principalities, and the like, in which German-speaking people in Central Europe lived. In saying I understand Marx's view, let me assure you, I'm not saying that I agree with it. I believe that the formation of nation-states was very dispensable indeed, as I explain in volume one of *The Third Revolution,* my trilogy on the popular movements in the great European revolutions, and in *From Urbanization to Cities.*

Murray Bookchin

Marx did not believe that socialism could be achieved entirely by means of a parliamentary republic – he thought that, in most of Europe, a proletarian insurrection would also be necessary. But he did place a great deal of emphasis on parliamentary struggles, and in 1872, in a talk he gave at The Hague, he cited the possibility that in England, the United States, and possibly the Netherlands (later Engels added France), a workers' party could somehow legislate socialism into existence. That perspective was naive, and it proved to be a fatal mistake for Germany, where the Social Democrats actually accepted it – routinely concealing their parliamentary reformism with radical rhetoric. Their abhorrence of revolutionary means became so strong that it persisted into the German Revolution of 1918-19, under the Ebert-Scheidemann-Noske triumvirate.

Not only do I disagree with Marxists who think parliamentary methods are a desideratum, I oppose the electoral party system as such. A party is a bureaucratic apparatus structured from the top down – as opposed to a libertarian confederation, which is structured from the bottom up – and is nothing more than a state that is waiting for an opportunity to acquire power. When it does take power, it acquires the tyrannical features of the very state machinery it has come to control, irrespective of whether that state is a dictatorship or a monarchy or a republic.

So I would decidedly reject Marx's emphasis on parliamentary methods to achieve socialism. Instead, I favor communalism (or libertarian municipalism) based on direct democracy, community self-management, and confederal coordination, through democratic institutions and a public political culture. People in towns and city neighborhoods, in my view, would establish direct-democratic popular assemblies in which they could make their own local decisions, then form confederations that could constitute a dual power against the centralized state. I've explicated these ideas in several articles and books, and you have done a wonderful job of articulating them in your recent book *The Politics of Social Ecology: Libertarian Municipalism*.

The political legacy that Marx left behind, however, was very unfinished. Although he advocated a centralized state led by a workers' party, for a time during the early 1870s, during the Paris Commune of 1871, he seemed to shift his support to a communalist position, and he seemed to favor federalism (the word that the anarchists used for confederalism, as I think it should be called and as the Spanish anarchists called it). He also proved to be quite flexible about the *obschina* in Russia, with its redistributions of land. He wrote, not once but several times, that if a successful proletarian revolution occurred in Western Europe, the *obschina* might make it possible for the Russian peasantry to bypass the capitalist stage of development. Although he later abandoned his communalist views of 1871 and reverted to a republican position, he retained his hopes for the *obschina* until his death.

This ambiguous political legacy that Marx left behind fostered several tendencies in Marxist movements, especially in Germany and Russia. On the one hand, his statism and parliamentarism allowed the German Social Democrats to call for the legislation of socialism through parliamentary means. On the other hand, based on Marx's communalist period, Lenin could call for a "commune-state" based on soviets, which were to approximate direct democracy through councils; these soviets did emerge in 1905 and in 1917, and by early 1918 they gave rise to an elaborate structure, at *every* level of society: in neighborhoods, boroughs, cities, regions, and the army.

In 1918 and 1919 in Germany, the two tendencies in Marx's legacy – statist and communalist – came into open, even bloody conflict. Workers' and soldiers councils had sprung up in Russia (1917) and Germany (1918-19), where the official or "majority" Social Democrats continually worked to undermine them. In Germany they were definitively eliminated with the appearance of the Weimar republic. As for Russia, once the Bolsheviks came into power, they drastically subordinated the soviets to their party, and the soviet system as a whole languished as a mere adornment to a party-state rather than as a political reality. Marx's mixed political legacy was thus consolidated by different Marxists into dogmatic systems of one kind or another, *all* of which were highly centralized. In Germany, the Majority Social Democrats Ebert, Scheidemann, and Noske at the end of the First World War, and in Russia, Lenin and most of the Bolshevik leadership especially after 1918, moved in increasingly authoritarian directions. Stalin, of course, gave Marxism an odious name.

Murray Bookchin

Those four features of social anarchism that you cited are the points, I think, that represent decisive advances over Marx's political legacy. I strongly favor confederation over a state and a party; Marx was at best confused about the issue and at worst inclined toward a state. I strongly favor direct democracy, which seemed to be of no interest whatever to Marx. Indeed, if any socialistic movement was interested in direct democracy, it was above all the social anarchists who advocated it in some kind and degree. I strongly favor libertarian communism, although libertarian communism is ultimately communism itself, because in the last analysis Marx's own communism, after several stages of development, would have been libertarian – although it is far from clear how a socialist state would miraculously "wither away." History has shown that states, however limited their power, have a remarkable ability to enlarge themselves and create functions to perpetuate their existence.

Do you favor, in any sense, a revolutionary vanguard?

I'm not at all clear about why this word *vanguard* has become as disreputable as it is today. In fact, before the 1960s, the word *vanguard* was commonly used in the anarchist movement, appearing both in the titles of anarchist periodicals and in general anarchist discussion. As early as 1877, Kropotkin co-edited a periodical called *L'Avant-Garde*, which is simply the French word for *vanguard*. On the European continent the word was used repeatedly among anarchists, and in the United States during the 1930s and 1940s, the only anarchist periodical that I ever encountered was called *Vanguard*. It's only since the 1960s that the word has been identified with a Bolshevik type of organization and given a noxious odor. Perhaps the word *avant-garde* would be more palatable, since we commonly apply it to innovative artists and literati without feeling in the least that we are being totalitarian or authoritarian.

In recent years I have been doing a careful study of revolutions over the past three centuries, and this research has thoroughly persuaded me that any movement for social change must always be on guard against the authoritarianism that is latent in any form of leadership. Merely overthrowing one political structure, as anarchists have long pointed out, does not eliminate the seeds for a new tyranny; it is always possible that a new organization may emerge out of a revolution that would prevent the masses from reconstituting a libertarian society out of the ruins of the old. While I agree with Marxists that a vanguard is necessary, for example, I disagree that a highly centralized party rightfully constitutes the necessary vanguard.

Why then am I trying to rescue the concept, if not the word itself? For one thing, to stand completely against vanguards ignores the problem raised by spontaneity, namely the belief that in a revolutionary situation, the people without any guidance will be able to produce a new society without an organized leadership. The anarchists who argued for a spontaneous movement of the masses to *carry out* – not merely *initiate* – a revolution have not addressed this problem satisfactorily.

The fact is that vanguards come into existence *whether one likes it or not*. Some people are always going to be more advanced in their political understanding than others. There's no point in deceiving ourselves that the playing field is level in this respect – it simply isn't. There are always some people who have more experience, or have thought out their ideas more completely, or are more knowledgeable than others. Those who know less *invariably* turn to those who know more. I've seen this time and again – in strikes, street fighting, union struggles, civil rights demonstrations, sit-ins, and other crowd actions. The main problem of political organization is how to *institutionalize* the relations between those who know more and those who know less, and to do so in such as way that the more knowledgeable leaders – and leaders *do exist* even in confederal movements! – do not turn into bureaucrats or authoritarians.

Although major revolutions often do start out spontaneously, nucleating elements are also always present even at the outset, often as militants, who constitute the more respected, active, aggressive, and socially conscious of the revolutionaries. They play a distinct nucleating role in bringing together a crowd of people, who are commonly far more formed and organized than historians often suggest. These militants form the raw material for a vanguard, to use this word in its positive sense. At least at the beginning of a revolution, then, when the masses begin to challenge the ruling classes, a vanguard is already playing a role, whether one likes it or not. It's naive to think a revolution and certainly the transition to a new social order can be brought about by sheer instinct and enthusiasm; at the very least, spontaneity has to be *informed,* as I've put it, by these militants.

The real problem with vanguards arises *after* the ruling classes have been defeated. Such defeats are usually momentary; the ruling classes invariably rally their forces and try again, usually in a more organized and more centralized way than the revolutionary masses, to regain their power. In some cases, social democratic types like Ebert in 1919 will say, "Enough, we don't have to go any further, the revolution should end here." A contest may develop among the revolutionaries over how far the revolution should go, what steps should be taken to complete it, and what kind of organized movement they should form to effect those steps. At that phase of a revolutionary development, the masses decidedly *need* an organization to push the revolution forward, to drive it to its conclusion. At this point the need for the militants to form a distinct organization, a more structured type of vanguard, becomes acute. Long before such a turning point in the revolutionary process, they often develop a well-structured organization anyway; now is the time where it becomes crucial.

As a libertarian communist, I would call for a vanguard organization that is confederal in structure. It would consist of interlinked affinity groups that would play a leading role in democratic popular assemblies in towns, neighborhoods, and cities. I agree with the criticism that Lenin's kind of vanguardism institutionalized centralization, even mystified centralization to the point that the top party organization became omnipotent, not only to eliminate the old social order but to harness the masses themselves to a party bureaucracy. In fact, the centralized party became an end in itself.

I don't oppose centralization under any and all circumstances. But a libertarian revolutionary organization would centralize *as much as is clearly necessary and for only as long as is necessary. Its leadership would always be answerable to – and subject to recall by – its membership.* I think that a confederal organization should radically democratize decision-making as much as possible. Nevertheless a certain amount of centralization may sometimes be necessary for a limited period of time. The point is that a libertarian organization should prevent centralization from becoming institutionalized, and keep centralized bodies from being frozen into permanent organizational entities. It should abolish them *as soon as they have performed the functions for which they were established.*

Serious left libertarians – social anarchists and libertarian socialists – should not, in my view, reject all organizational forms and methods in the abstract, or else they may well forfeit the opportunity to play a socially transformational role. We have a responsibility to look back through history and examine the crucial moments and situations in revolutionary history, and all too often we find movements during revolutions when dogmatic shibboleths paralyzed leaders and organizations and prevented them from carrying through their revolutionary efforts. During the Great French Revolution, the failure of the *enragés* to effectively organize themselves in 1793, especially in the June 2 insurrection of that year, made it possible for the Jacobins to take control of the Revolution and essentially destroy the popular movement and all hopes for the creation of a sectional grassroots democracy. In February 1848 the failure of the militants to create an effective organization made it possible for Lamartine and his crowd to steal the popular revolution from the masses, as did the hapless behavior of the Central Committee of the National Guard in the Paris Commune of 1871. In November 1917 the Bolsheviks simply took the power into their own hands for want of any organized left-libertarian movement in Russia, while Luxemburg and Liebknecht's Spartakus League – most of whose members were actually syndicalists and anarchists! – was all but destroyed because it failed to split off from the German Social Democratic Party ten years before and create an independent organization.

My study of these revolutions while writing *The Third Revolution* has caused me to feel an unbearable frustration with the anti-organizational kinds of militants who think that basic social change will occur because of a mystical popular will or some "instinct" for revolution that exists in the people. This idea is nonsense. Anarchists should learn from serious Marxists, as Marxists should learn from serious anarchists, that we desperately need to strike a rational balance between theoretical insight and popular spontaneity, between organization and impulse. Each without the other is a guarantee of failure – irrespective of what anyone has said in the past.

Notes

1. Murray Bookchin, "History, Civilization, and Progress," in *The Philosophy of Social Ecology*.

2. Murray Bookchin, *The Ecology of Freedom*, p. 272; *The Modern Crisis*, p. 50; "History, Civilization, and Progress," in *The Philosophy of Social Ecology*, p. 169.

3. *Social Anarchism or Lifestyle Anarchism*, p. 60.

The Left: Past, Present, and Future

Interviewer: Doug Morris

You have been using the term Left, and I think many people are unclear about it. What do you mean by it? What about its origin, its history, its present and future?

The word *Left* emerged from the events and ideologies of the French Revolution of 1789 to 1794, in which the Left consisted of the most radical deputies in the National Assembly. The most radical deputies of the Assembly sat on the left side of the speaker's tribune, facing the deputies and, in time, were known as *les gauchistes*. To be sure, the makeup of that Left was ever shifting, with some people moving toward the Center and some in the Center moving toward the Right. But the most radical members of the Assembly sat on the left side. During the Convention the revolutionary Parisian deputies occupied the upper benches, thereby acquiring the name "the Mountain."

This is the standard account of the origin of the word *Left*. But in my view the real Left in the French Revolution consisted of other groups that were far more radical and were not well-represented in the various legislatures created by the Revolution. This Left had evolved out of the extreme radical democracy that existed in the Paris of 1792-93, a popular democracy that, as the revolution continued, grew ever more sophisticated, knowledgeable, and politically conscious.

I am speaking not of the Jacobins, who are the Left in most standard accounts of the Revolution, but of the so-called *enragés*, the insurrectionary activists among the poorest of the *sans-culottes*. They were the true progenitors of the popular radical democratism of the French Revolution, having inherited many of their egalitarian ideas from the American Revolution and even from the English Revolution of the 1640s. For these extreme radical Parisian democrats, freedom generally meant popular control over political life from below, by the masses organized in neighborhood assemblies or sections.

In the nineteenth century the Left gradually evolved toward socialistic notions that embraced not only political but economic equality. This Left believed that a free society had to reconstitute the political and economic establishment along collectivistic lines and, in its most radical forms, had to distribute the social output of goods along communist lines. By communism, of course, I do not refer to anything that remotely relates to the society that prevailed in Russia after 1917. *Communistic ideas,* according to their earliest modern advocates of the late 1820s and 1830s, as expressed by Owen, Cabet, and Blanc, meant sharing the resources of the planet in such a way that individuals should be provided with all the means of life that they needed to sustain themselves and their families.

A striking example of communism is the family card system, instituted by certain anarchosyndicalist collectives in Spain during the Revolution of 1936-37. In such collectives workers were issued a card denoting the number of dependent people in their families, and they were provided with the means of life for all of them, irrespective of the amount of work they contributed. If a worker had, say, six children and was working alongside another who had only one, they were supplied with what they needed to support their respective families, even if both possessed the same skills and worked the same number of hours.

In other words, the family card system organized the distribution of goods according to the maxim "from each according to ability, to each according to need." That is true communism. So far as I know, the Bolsheviks never officially instituted this system of work and distribution in 1917, let alone in any system that Stalin established. Quite to the contrary: Stalin distorted the communist maxim to create an absurd new definition: "from each according to ability, to each according to work." This rather circular maxim was a perversion of the communist ideal.

Anarchism, Marxism, and the Future of the Left

Actually, what existed in Russia was state capitalism, as Lenin and other Bolsheviks fully acknowledged. The various plans to build up the Russian economy were merely statist endeavors to engage in what Marx would have called the "primitive accumulation" of industrial resources at the expense of the peasantry, who were overworked in collective farms or dispatched to slave labor camps. The industrial working class, like the peasantry, was also ruthlessly exploited.

But I'm getting ahead of myself. In the nineteenth century, the Left added economic democracy to the largely political dimension of the Jacobins, based on collectivism or workers' control of industry and then ultimately on communism, in which remuneration would be based on needs rather than work.

Despite all the attention that many lifestyle anarchists and eco-primitivists give to the Luddites, the nineteenth-century Left was generally very eager to see the advance of technological development. Be they Marxists or anarchists, socialists or communists, they all wanted to develop the productive forces in such a way that it would be possible finally to resolve the "social question" – that is, to end exploitation and domination. They fully understood that without material sufficiency, it would be impossible for people to be truly free, even to be able to participate in a political democracy. After all, a hard day's work is not conducive to democracy.

So, if people were to *truly* participate in democratic political life, if they were to be *fully* involved in social affairs and social commitments, they had to be as free as possible from the demands of daily toil. But this freedom raised a serious problem: It could not be obtained for society as a whole unless the technological means existed to liberate them. And it raised another problem as well: If the productive forces did not produce enough material goods to sustain society, then some would always try to enjoy a more comfortable and secure life – and exercise power – by expropriating the labor of others, indeed the great mass of society. The nineteenth-century Left thus regarded it as essential that the forces of production – technology – be developed at least to meet the basic needs of all; in short, to provide humanity with the free time to create an authentically democratic society.

It also recognized that civilization, allowing for its malignant and demonic record of oppression, destruction, and war, had also achieved a great deal of progress. It recognized that great advances had been made, amid the muck and dirt of blood, evil, crime, and warfare; even if progress was intertwined with demonic elements such as exploitation, domination, and brutality, the Left was committed to creating the material preconditions for human freedom. Indeed, what justified the existence of the Left was the very need to separate the desirable from the demonic – a responsibility that has been abjured by anticivilizationists and primitivists.

Significantly, the Left also emphasized the need to overcome traditional local barriers, such as ethnicity, custom, and language. The Spanish anarchists even hoped that everyone would learn to speak a single language, Esperanto, so that all people could communicate easily with each other. Indeed, whatever historical Left we are speaking about, be it socialist or anarchist, it was overwhelmingly committed to internationalism. Leftists believed that the working class had no country, and they held out the ideal of a universal human interest that superseded cultural differences, not to speak of national differences.

This is not to say that the Left failed to recognize or appreciate cultural distinctions. But leftists did not tend to think of "cultural identity" as an integral part of their revolutionary politics, or of the need to define people in terms of their ethnicity, gender, nationality, or culture. They were concerned with humanity as a whole, and they recognized that a people's cultural identity – its folklore, traditions, language, poetry, music – was secondary to their affinity as a common species.

One has only to read the speeches of Rosa Luxemburg on nationalism in the first two decades of this century to see what I mean. She was opposed to nationalism in any form and inveighed against it repeatedly. And later, in the 1930s, all leftists were internationalists. If they were devoted to the Soviet Union, it was because the Soviet Union was supposed to be the *workers'* fatherland – the one area of the world that had been emancipated by a proletarian revolution – although Stalin manipulated this sentiment to bring their ideals into the service of Russian nationalism.

Anarchism, Marxism, and the Future of the Left

This internationalist mentality has since faded away. Regrettably, Lenin already paved the way when he exploited the national question in order to help the Bolsheviks gain power. Another very serious blow came in the 1960s, when many members of the New Left departed, psychologically and politically, for the third world and began to speak as though they were authentic representatives of oppressed nationalities. Finally, the identity politics that we have at present is, in my view, so much zoological garbage. As I've pointed out, the New Left initially emphasized alienation, but by the late 1960s it was disastrously misguided by Maoism and black identity politics. Today so-called radicals babble endlessly about their cultural identity and its impact on their self-esteem rather than discuss the need for class and social solidarity.

Do you think the Left has died?

A number of so-called leftist periodicals today have been discussing the death of the Left, or to what extent a Left exists at all. They have been talking about whether the word *socialism* should be dropped completely. *Dissent* had a debate on these questions, as did *The Nation* and *The Village Voice*. What astonishes me is that, especially since the fall of the Berlin wall, many self-styled leftists believe that the Left is dead. If we could bring all these people together, we would have enough of them to form a sizable left-wing movement.

Even more appalling is that so many people who called themselves leftists – not only socialists but also anarchists – really rested their leftist views on the existence of the so-called "actually existing socialism" behind the Iron Curtain, as though Russia under Stalin and his successors had ever been even remotely socialist. They seem to assume that Stalin personified the Bolshevik revolution, even though he was actually its worst enemy and slaughtered most of the old revolutionaries.

Apart from my youth in the Third Period, never, since I became socially conscious as a mature person, have I regarded the Soviet Union as socialist. In the late 1930s and early 1940s, the anti-Stalinist Left, the people with whom I was associated, already realized that the Soviet Union was by no means a "soviet union" in the literal sense of either word. It was clearly neither soviet nor a union. Many of us initially became Trotskyists after our break with the Stalinists, but we remained on the Left, designating ourselves as socialists or communists with a small "c." We knew that there was nothing socialist or communist about what existed in Russia.

One of the most important questions that occupied our attention was defining the actual nature of the phenomenon called the Soviet Union. Some said it was a totalitarian despotism held together by secret police and concentration camps. Others, like Trotskyists, called it a "degenerated worker's state." Still others maintained that it was a bureaucratic collectivist society, by which they meant a society that was neither socialist nor capitalist but one in which bureaucrats collectively ran everything for their own benefit at the expense of the masses. Finally, others thought it was a "fascist" country draped in a red flag. Hardly any of us thought the Soviet Union was socialist. Least of all would we have used the word *communist* to refer to Stalinist Russia or even Leninist Russia; indeed, Lenin made repeated attempts to distinguish Russia from socialism and saw the October Revolution primarily as an attempt to initiate revolution in Western Europe, especially Germany, which he thought was the main country that was prepared economically and culturally to build a socialist society.

For my part, as for many others, the dissociation between socialism and the Soviet Union is at least a half century old and certainly nothing new. So I'm astonished to find in the current issue of *Dissent* a debate called "The Crimes of Communism: What Did You Know, and When Did You Know It?" It's kicked off by Eugene Genovese, whose article poses the question in the title, and it's followed by replies from old-time Stalinists who have since been reconstructed into liberals, such as Mitchell Cohen and Eric Foner.[1]

Frankly, I am annoyed by the very title "The Crimes of Communism." Communism never committed crimes in Russia, because communism never existed in Russia. There was an entity called the Communist Party, run by a monstrous totalitarian despot named Stalin. But there was never any communism in the empire he ruled. As for the question "What did you know and when did you know it?" it has a typical social-democratic ambience, one that pervades the thinking of many fading "leftists" today.

Remarkably, several of the people who responded to the question declared that they discovered the "crimes of Communism" when Khrushchev denounced Stalin in 1956. But as early as the 1930s Stalin was sending millions of people to gulags, and a sizable leftist literature describing his crimes already existed during the 1940s. Could they really have been oblivious to the crimes Stalin committed between 1936 and 1938, when he executed almost all the people who had led the Bolshevik uprising? Indeed, whatever one might think of Trotsky, he produced a small library of pamphlets and articles publicly describing in detail the crimes that Stalin was committing at that time. How is it that they had to wait until 1956 to find out about the crimes of "Communism"?

Unfortunately far too many of the people who declare the Left to be dead now and are trying to disband it are themselves former leftists who "discovered" the "crimes of Communism" in the 1950s and later. They seem to be eager to return to the existing system and bourgeois respectability. After the 1960s many New Lefties wept into their teacups and sighed, "We're so disillusioned. We tried to change the system, but now we know we can't. It's time to become a stockbroker, or a lawyer, or a professor." Far too many of them have become postmodernist professors. Some of these men and women, in their younger days, were the ones who poisoned the New Left with Maoism and whom we on the libertarian wing of socialism had to fight bitterly to preserve the very integrity of the Left. When I hear them talk about how disillusioned they are, and justify their capitulation to the *existing* system as disillusioned radicals, I feel a deep nausea. These people committed a double crime. If the Left is dead, they clearly helped kill it by remaining Stalinists for too long and making it difficult to create a new Left.

Other former radicals say, "I'm still a socialist, but I don't believe it's possible to achieve socialism in my lifetime." The thinking here seems to be that, before one can commit oneself to socialism, one must be clear that it can be achieved in one's own lifetime, or else it is not worth fighting for. I am reminded of the many authentic revolutionaries who died fighting for a socialist society with no hope of ever seeing it themselves – and all I can think of these former radicals is that they are spoiled brats.

Yet more than ever today, we need an organized Left. It's entirely deceptive to say, as some do, that any movements that arise should be "beyond" Left and Right. People who want a movement that is "neither left nor right but forward" are ignoring the fact that in the United States and in the rest of the world today, a veritable counterrevolution is under way. Even apart from extreme reactionaries, right-wingers exist in every sphere of life. In the United States the political spectrum ranges from a "left" that consists of Republican moderates (who are for capitalism, a modest degree of social regulation, and abortion) and Democratic conservatives (who hold similar views) and to an explicit "right" that consists of Christian fundamentalists (they are against abortion and seem to want some kind of morally autocratic political system). British politics spans a similar spectrum, as do many countries on the Continent. We are plagued by a "neoliberal" capitalist Right, a Christian Right, and an outright Fascist Right.

Yes, there is a Right today. It is visible, and it appropriately refers to itself as the Right. But where is the Left? I do not mean simply a queasy liberal opposition, I mean a decidedly *revolutionary* Left, however small it may be, one that is determined not only to oppose the Right at every turn but to offer basic social alternatives to it.

The absence of a Left today has allowed right-wing movements to use quasi-leftist approaches, even left-libertarian approaches with considerable success. In Italy the Northern League has invoked regionalism, even decentralism to win a substantial following. It shrewdly invokes Proudhon – his ideas of federalism – for the very cynical purpose of establishing various regional states that are likely to be authoritarian. I find it tragic that many left-libertarians, both socialists and anarchists, have failed to regroup and formulate a program based on grassroots democracy and confederalism. Rather, they allow the Right to invoke some of their own traditional ideas for basically authoritarian ends.

Anarchism, Marxism, and the Future of the Left

In these very conservative and counterrevolutionary times, what can socially conscious revolutionary people do to recreate a Left?

I would like to answer that question by returning to the perspective, if I may, that arose within the revolutionary Left during the Second World War. When we were talking about the postwar period [in Chapter 2], I said that after the war, many non-Stalinist Marxists were discussing the problem of what to do if capitalism failed to end in a proletarian revolution and instead emerged from the war intact. We thought it was imperative to thoroughly reevaluate our traditional theories, and we held many discussions on how they would have to be changed.

The most important conclusion that emerged from our discussions was drawn from a maxim in Rosa Luxemburg's "Junius Pamphlet" of 1916. If capitalism continued to develop unimpeded, Luxemburg wrote, if it followed its internal logic and expanded over the entire planet, wreaking havoc and causing misery and exploitation everywhere, then it would fundamentally undermine social life as we know it. The complete degradation, possibly even the destruction, of social life would be inevitable. In other words, if the continued existence of capitalism did not end in socialism, Luxemburg wrote, then social life as such would end in barbarism.

We thought about these ideas and decided that the choice that confronted us was, now more than ever, between "socialism or barbarism." In 1945, when the war did not end in proletarian revolutions, we began to explore the nature of the barbarism that would doubtless ensue in the absence of socialism. We were not certain what it would look like, or what its structure would be. We only knew that in the absence of a proletarian revolution, it would inevitably come.

Our only model was German fascism: the barbaric outcome of the capitalist development, we thought, would be a totalitarian state, with genocidal concentration camps, the de-industrialization of subjugated countries, and a vast police and military system. As the century draws to an end now, we are gaining a better sense of what the structure of barbarism might be, and I would like to briefly examine it.

Barbarism is partly with us now, and the form it is taking is, quite clearly, the destruction of the natural world. This destruction is caused by the market and competitive imperatives of global growth, particularly by commodification. We are witnessing the industrialization of the world, a global economy, whose effects are magnified by an ever-more-sophisticated technology. It's clear that if capitalism continues to exist, it will render the planet inorganic, turning soil into sand and oceans into sewage, undermining the basis for organic life. It may very well replace the biosphere as we know it today with a largely synthetic environment.

What will that synthetic environment look like, a century or perhaps fifty years from now? It is by no means inconceivable that people will have to live in specially created "ecospheres." Buckminster Fuller, a technocrat who was somehow mistaken for an ecological thinker, once suggested that we should put a dome over Manhattan in order to keep out polluted air. The world may become so industrialized that the natural world will essentially be reduced to little more than parks. Wilderness is already essentially gone, as I've noted. And vast areas of the world that once were farmed by peasants are steadily being urbanized. Within only a few decades, Indonesia, Malaysia, Sri Lanka, and other countries have made Southeast Asia into a significantly industrialized region. Few people, a mere generation ago, could have foreseen such a dramatic rate of industrial and urban growth. What lies before us in the coming century is beyond the grasp of our imagination.

Another major feature of the coming barbarism is the change that is taking place in consciousness. We risk the loss of our knowledge of history – of what the past was like and the lessons it has to teach future generations. We are faced with the loss of tremendously important social and political theories that have been evolving for the past two hundred years, that are precisely concerned with how to prevent this barbarism from developing. We are already seeing a loss of the socialist *idea* – not simply specific socialist parties – and especially the socialist dimension of anarchism. The growing popularity of lifestyle anarchism – with its mysticism, irrationalism, primitivism and technophobia – at the expense of social anarchism is part of this process of dememorization, this loss of socialist consciousness. The identification of communism with Stalinism is another part of the process. Socialism is being cast aside, dismissed as obsolete, and with it revolutionary anarchism. Tremendously important libertarian traditions are being lost, and so is our knowledge of past revolutions.

At the same time, what remains of radical leftism is accommodating itself to the capitalist system. "Leftists" today are inviting us essentially to fight for the integration of minorities and women into the capitalist system. People who profess to be socialists and anarchists are trying to make capitalism more agreeable and to give it a human face. We are being called upon to defend the right of women and people of color to become generals, as though they should celebrate the fact that they can become military instruments of American imperialism.

More fundamentally, we are losing all sense of the fact that capitalism is an irrational society, that it is not only unique in human history but that it is only a few centuries old. Today people dress all of reality in bourgeois terms, as though capitalism has always existed since the very emergence of humanity and is destined to be eternal. This mentality has blurred all the contradictions that really exist in the present society and at the same time is producing people who in growing numbers are accommodating themselves to the present social order.

Business concepts are even implanted in the mind in such a way that people cast all aspects of experience in capitalist terms. Increasingly people think about various aspects of their lives the way they think about the market, as if living itself were a business enterprise. They "invest" in their marriages and in their children. When they contemplate making some kind of change, they weigh its "cost-effectiveness." "What's the bottom line?" – I hear that question continually, and it makes me shudder. Is life simply a balance sheet? And then one hears, "What's in it for me?" which what most people think whenever something new is proposed. Then language becomes bizarrely electronic, when "input," "output," and "feedback" replace dialogue. Whenever I can, I try to persuade people not to speak in these terms – "invest," "bottom line," "input," "cost-effective," and so forth. The words that people use tend to shape the way they think about reality, and this bourgeois vocabulary places them squarely within the framework of the prevailing social order.

The counterrevolution, the barbarism of which I am speaking, may well produce not only a synthetic society and a complete breakdown in social life but a consciousness in which people accept the notion that history is at an end, that capitalism, corporate enterprises, and the nation-state are eternal, and that there is nothing anyone can do to basically alter capitalism. The public interest groups around Ralph Nader are very militant, but they act as if what they want is for the corporations to be nice. That is equivalent to asking a lion to desist from eating meat!

Corporations never evolved to be nice, they evolved to be destructive and vicious. Still other "leftists" are asking us to accept something called market socialism. I take it that a market socialist is a "socialist" who accepts the existence of the market, which is to say a socialist who has not examined the logic of the market sufficiently to realize that its tendency is to colonize all areas of experience.

The notion that capitalism is eternal compels us to stop thinking about the real social relations that constitute capitalism, just as technophobia and mysticism deflects our thinking from the growth of the market, wage labor, capital, and commodities. If we are told that the main social problems we face are technology and population growth, for example, instead of the social system that misuses technology or that leads to mindless population growth, then we will emphasize the predicate instead of the subject of the sentence. Instead of talking about capitalism as an intrinsically inhumane system, this kind of consciousness focuses on humanizing capitalism, and the predicate begins to subvert the significance and centrality of the subject.

Finally this mentality lulls us into forgetting what the past was like, how we are rooted in it, and what it has to teach us. Today we're suffering from an enormous decline in radical social consciousness. The great ideals of human emancipation are fading from public awareness, leaving us with no knowledge of the lessons we should learn from the past if we are to fundamentally change the present society.

I've been told by anarchists that the "isms" are all now "wasms." Really! People who make such statements are themselves actually adhering to an "ism", even if they fail to give it a specific name. Their new "ism" may be postmodernism or relativism or pluralism, or it may be Taoism, with its homilies about "letting everything be," and I cannot help but wonder how they propose to exclude corporations from that injunction. But these are still "isms" – they are still ideologies.

Anarchism, Marxism, and the Future of the Left

But you asked what we can do in these times of a tremendous loss of consciousness. Amid this barbarism, with its declining consciousness, it becomes extremely important to lay the bases for a Left, based on left-libertarian principles. We have to recover the Left's *independent* libertarian tradition, as reflected not only in anarchist writings but in many socialist works as well, including those by Marx. We have to recover that tradition, to transcend both the New Left and the independent Old Left while we retain certain basic precepts: radical democracy; communism and the need to overthrow capitalism; and the creation of a sane and rational social, cultural, and technological development.

When I speak of a Left, then, I am talking about a knowledgeable, coherent, and highly purposeful *revolutionary* Left. I am not talking about something that is simply left of center or that is either supporting or opposing a specific governmental measure. I am speaking of a Left that defines its own agenda instead of letting capitalism define its agenda – a Left that views all of capitalist society as irremediably diseased and seeks to replace it fundamentally. I do not care what you want to call this Left – social anarchism, or libertarian socialism, or libertarian communism. But minimally it has to be a form of *socialism,* to use the word in its most revolutionary sense, in the same sense that Kropotkin called anarchism a radical form of socialism.

Finally, let me add an important personal note. We have to create a Left precisely because we want to retain our human integrity. If we don't oppose capitalist society with a leftist movement and theory that are based on reason, history, civilization, and progress, that maintain the great traditions of the past, elaborate them, discard what is lifeless in them, that maintain coherence, rationality, and hope, *then we will be destroyed as individuals*. We will become trivialized, reduced to passive consumers, or we will become autonomous in a privatistic sense. To reduce radicalism merely or even primarily to matters of lifestyle is to withdraw from the real problems of society. People who wish to merely throw bricks are engaged in a juvenile riot; they are not creating a social movement. We should hold up the principle of freedom, of social freedom, not the principle of personal retreat into a "temporary autonomous zone."

Which is not to say that we must live a conventional lifestyle, nor that we should divest ourselves of desire and imagination. But we have to free ourselves from the belief that imagination and desire alone will produce a Left. We have to give meaning to our lives over the long run, and that meaning involves rationality, the fulfillment of what is most basic in our potentialities, our ability to think, and *to think beyond the given,* to think in opposition to the status quo and the existing state of affairs.

What do you mean by communalism?

What the Left should be fighting for, I believe, is democracy in the real sense of the word, that is, social self-management by the people in the form of a direct democracy – that is a fundamentally different notion of politics. It should be politics in the Greek sense of "management of the *polis,*" not what we have today, *statecraft,* a state with its top-down system of rule, bureaucracy, and force, that all but excludes the people from the management of public affairs.

By communalism, I do not mean communitarianism, in which people establish food cooperatives, communal living arrangements, community health clinics, and the like. Communalism, rather, is an attempt to *empower* the community – municipalities, towns, and neighborhoods. It is basically the same political system that I call libertarian municipalism, another term I often use, but *communalism* is simply an older word that comes from the vocabulary of revolutionary libertarian socialism. To the best of my knowledge, it emerged out of the Paris Commune of 1871, although the content of the idea is older than the name. What communalism and libertarian municipalism have in common is that they both refer to a program to create direct-democratic, face-to-face assemblies, in which people meet to make policy decisions about their community.

The citizens' assemblies that make up this democracy would be very similar to the traditional New England town meetings, with the exception that large cities would be scaled to human dimensions as soon as possible. At present, citizens' assemblies would be very numerous in metropolitan areas such as New York, Paris, London, and the huge megacities of the third world. They would be based on neighborhoods, wards, even blocks.

In these assemblies, people would become actively involved in making decisions about their communities. They would no longer be passive constituents, as people are today; they would become a new kind of citizen. Citizenship would come to mean again what it once did in the past: politically involved individuals collectively managing their own communities in face-to-face assemblies.

To address the problems that go beyond the boundaries of a single ward or neighborhood, the various citizens' assemblies in a town or city would send delegates to a city council, which in turn would send delegates to a confederal council. These various delegates would carry mandates for voting according to the wishes of their home assemblies. They would try to work out the affairs of the entire city or region, and then bring their proposals back to the people for approval. Through this kind of give and take with local assemblies and city councils, the confederal councils would finally arrive at decisions that are supported by the majority of the people.

Each confederal council in turn would send a delegate to a confederation of a still wider region. By no means do I refer to a bioregion – which, despite different ecological attributes, might well be united by cultural similarities. In the confederal council, too, the same process of decision making would take place, accepting or rejecting proposals by bringing them back to their city councils and ultimately from there to the local assemblies.

Basically, then, all regional interrelationships would be structured around local assemblies, confederated or unified through city and confederal councils, in a Confederation of Confederations. In contrast to the state, which is based on top-down rule, these confederations would manage society from the bottom up. This system of self-managed political life would be more like a network than a statelike pyramid.

As I'm always at pains to emphasize, it's important to draw a distinction between policy-making and administration. Policy decisions, such as a decision on where a road should be constructed or how a plot of land should be used, would be made by the citizen assemblies. The technical execution or administration of these policies would be carried out

by the appropriate specialists. The most important functions of the confederal councils would be administrative. In fact, these city and confederal councils would have to ultimately refer all policy-making decision to
the assemblies and only with their approval undertake their administration. These policy decisions would be made by a *majority* of the people
themselves in their face-to-face assemblies. The city and confederal
councils would merely execute these decisions, or at most adjust differences between them.

This direct democracy would exist in growing tension with the
nation-state – not coexist with it. I regard this tension as vital.
Democratized communities would try to take power away from the state,
and then ultimately clash with it – and hopefully replace the state
machine with a system of confederations based on popular assemblies.

What would economic life be like in such a society?

Obviously the economy wouldn't be nationalized, as socialists traditionally sought to do and as was done in Russia. The nationalization of the
economy presupposes the existence of a nation-state and serves to rein-
force the state's power with economic power. Nor would we have privately
owned property, as capitalists traditionally want. What we would try to
achieve instead is a *municipalized* economy, one in which the citizens'
assembly in each community would control economic life and, through
city councils and confederations, decide on economic policy for an entire
region. Confederal councils would help work out how best to coordinate
the production and distribution of economic life that extends beyond the
confines of a given community and, with the consent of the overall
majority of the population in a confederal network, see to it that goods
are produced and distributed according to the needs of the citizens in the
confederation.

I regard municipalization – communalism – as the basic politics of
social ecology. The old syndicalist idea of workers' control of industry
often led workers in a particular enterprise to act as collective capitalists,
which led them to think more in terms of their well-being than the interests of the community as a whole. Their enterprise, in effect, became

another capitalist enterprise. Workers' control often reproduced all the problems created by the marketplace: economic competition and a disregard of the public's needs.

What we require is citizens' control of the facilities, the land, and the other resources that exist in a particular community or a region. Accordingly, a printer, let us say, would be expected to cease to think in terms of his or her special interests as a printer and instead think as a *citizen*, in terms of the community's interests. It is fair to hope that people would come to their municipal assembly without being burdened by their occupational status. They would resolve their problems as citizens on behalf of the community as a whole, not in terms of their own enterprises. Production and distribution would be administered merely as practical matters, based on an ethics of "from each according to ability, and to each according to need," the ethic integral to communism. The community would formulate the distribution of goods according to what is available and what individuals and families require. All of these issues could be decided quite reasonably and appropriately, especially after a period of revolutionary change.

You speak of "citizens" as though there were no classes today that separate people and their interests. Does your view of libertarian municipalism exclude the reality of classes, their conflicts in the economy, and their basically divergent interests?

Categorically not. For one thing, the existence of classes is not a matter of theory but a historical and contemporary *reality*. Marx, by his own admission, did not "discover" classes and the class struggle; he tried to give them meaning and programmatic importance. However unconscious class conflict may be today, it definitely still exists. And it is our responsibility to bring class differences to the surface and to foster class consciousness among the proletariat and consciousness of oppression among all oppressed classes.

Libertarian municipalism makes the *added* contribution – by no means original – that class conflicts also have a civic or territorial dimension. Working people, certainly the ones I knew in northern New Jersey, do not simply think of themselves as toilers. They also think of themselves as fathers and mothers, sons and daughters, brothers and sisters, who live in a distinct urban environment. They are concerned not only with their wages, hours, and working conditions but with the schools, parks, sanitation, crime, environmental conditions, and the like in their communities. They wish to uphold not only their rights as union members but their rights as residents of specific communities. And they prefer to think of themselves not as "proletarians" and "instruments of historical development" but as human beings – as citizens who have certain rights and duties apart from their rights and duties in factories and trade unions.

In short, they occupy a distinctly civic space – even if it is little more than a street corner or a park. Historically, the existence of such spaces made it possible for radicals to create revolutionary Paris in the nineteenth century, Red Petrograd in the early twentieth, and Red-and-Black Barcelona in the 1930s. Years ago in New York City certain districts were distinctly "red," which meant that most of the people there voted for the Socialist Party or the Communist Party or both. They made civic spaces into arenas for rallies, and at lecture halls and cultural centers they listened to speeches, had debates, played and listened to music, sang in choral groups, and the like. These civic spaces were as precious to them as their trade unions and political organizations.

In the 1930s working people in Manhattan spontaneously gathered in parks and squares by the thousands – most strikingly, Union Square just above the Village and in Tompkins Park in the Lower East Side – to discuss all kinds of radical ideas and current issues. A huge city like New York could be mapped according to its political life, based largely on shared class orientations.

My point is that the oppressed are not exclusively class beings, important as this is, but also neighborhood beings, and that class consciousness always has a civic dimension, a geographic and residential as well as an industrial locus it requires for its existence. Regrettably, few if any anarchists or Marxists have paid much attention to this dimension or tried to develop a municipalist approach to give it reality. But libertarian municipalism, far from ignoring the economic conditions for the existence of classes, tries to shed light on the geographic and spatial basis for the existence of a class-oriented politics.

What I am trying to emphasize is that libertarian municipalism and the associated concept of citizenship find their concrete expression in a politics based on neighborhood and town assemblies, in which the interests of proletarians and other oppressed strata can be expressed and mutated into a general social interest – that is, a libertarian communist interest. This would nourish class consciousness and class struggle not only in the economic realm but, very significantly, in the communal or civic realm. Conflicting class interests would be expressed *in the popular assemblies themselves* and would ultimately produce a revolutionary situation in which a general interest would be oriented toward the abolition of classes and the transformation of proletarians and members of other oppressed groups into citizens actively engaged in creating a new society. With the abolition of classes, proletarians would cease to be mere class beings and would become citizens in the fullest and most humanistic sense.

I have no belief that such a transformation could ever come about in a reformist manner or that property will remain private. But these issues, of course, are not ones that your question raises.

Note

1. Eugene Genovese, "The Question," *Dissent*, vol. 41, no. 3 (Summer 1994), pp. 371-76.

The Unity of Ideals and Practice

Recently I have begun to encounter, especially among young people, individuals who call themselves "leftists" who have little or no awareness of the most basic features of the Left's longstanding analysis of capitalism, or of the history of the revolutionary movements that have stood in fundamental opposition to bourgeois society. It distresses me that the ideological contours that have long defined capitalism and the Left are being forgotten today, as well as the most critical insights of libertarian socialism and revolutionary anarchism. Given this spreading social amnesia, I find that before I can summarize my political and social ideals, I must briefly outline the trajectory of capitalist society and the responsibility of the revolutionary Left, since my own ideas are integrally embedded in the tradition of that Left.

Certain basic concepts are fundamental to traditional leftists, especially to social anarchists, and when I encounter people who call themselves social anarchists, I must assume that, if their politics is to have any meaning, they still uphold these concepts. I must assume that social anarchists, like other leftists, understand that capitalism is a competitive market system in which rivalry compels bourgeois enterprises to continually grow and expand. I must assume they understand that this process of growth is *absolutely inexorable,* driven by the "competitive market forces" of production and consumption – as the bourgeoisie itself acknowledges. Nor can these "forces" be eliminated as long as capitalism exists, any more than a class-dominated economy could ever put an end to the exploitation of labor. Social anarchists, I must assume, understand that if capitalism continues to exist, it will yield catastrophic results for society and the ecological integrity of the natural world. So inherent are these features to capitalism that to expect the capitalist system not to have them is to expect it to be something other than capitalist.

Further, I must assume that social anarchists, like other leftists, believe that if humanity is ever to attain a free and rational society, capitalism must be completely destroyed. Social anarchists are distinctive among leftists, however, in maintaining that the social order that must replace it must be a collectivist, indeed a libertarian communist society, in which production and distribution are organized according to the maxim "From each according to ability, to each according to need" (to the extent, to be sure, that such needs can be satisfied given the existing resources of the society). Social anarchists agree, I must assume, that such a libertarian communist society cannot be achieved without the prior abolition not only of capitalism but of the state, with its professional bureaucracy, its monopoly over the means of violence, and its inherent commitment to the interests of the bourgeoisie.

Social anarchists agree, I must further assume, that the state must be replaced by a democratic political realm, one that comprises "communes" or municipalities of some kind that are in confederations with one another. Anarchosyndicalists believe that it is essentially workplace committees and libertarian unions that will structure these confederations. Anarchocommunists advance a variety of other forms, and my own will be summarized later. But when I meet a social anarchist, I assume that he or she shares these minimal, underlying common principles: the basic analysis of capitalism and its trajectory that I have described, as well as the imperative to replace competitive market-oriented social relations with libertarian institutions.

Didactic as my presentation may seem, I contend that to abandon any of these principles is to abandon the defining features of social anarchism, or of any revolutionary libertarian Left. To be sure, it is not easy to advance such ideas today. Former leftists who have themselves surrendered some of these principles in order to accommodate themselves to the existing society incessantly sneer at revolutionary leftists who still maintain them, accusing them of being "dogmatic," dismissing the coherence they prize as "totalitarian," and impugning their resolute social commitment as "sectarian." Moreover, in a time when social and political ideas are being blurred beyond recognition, principled leftists are advised repeatedly to relinquish their militancy – and presumably succumb to the mindless incoherence and pluralism that is commonly hallowed in the name of "diversity." Most of all, they are subjected to pressures to renounce the Left and blend in with the accommodation that is prevalent today, as so many of their former comrades have done.

Despite these personal and cultural pressures, social anarchists, I believe, must not allow their views and activities to be fragmented and thrown into the postmodern scrap heap of unrepentantly contradictory ideologies, any more than they should embrace the bourgeoisie in a love festival of class collaboration. In such times it is all the more imperative that a socially oriented, revolutionary libertarian Left firmly maintain its own integrity and ideals. If those ideals are to be maintained, there are lines that social anarchists cannot cross and still remain social anarchists.

This assertion, let me emphasize, is not an expression of intolerance. It is an appeal to preserve specificity, clarity, and self-definition against an overwhelming cultural decadence that blurs serious distinctions in the intimidating name of a specious "diversity," "harmony," and "compromise," as a result of which the clarification of important political differences becomes impossible to achieve.

Nor am I trying to cast the issues that social anarchists face or the practice they should follow in needlessly harsh "either-or" terms. When a corporation or state takes action to worsen working conditions, reduce wages, or deny poor and vulnerable people the elementary amenities of life, social anarchists should raise their voices in protest and join in actions to prevent such measures from being executed. In short, they should fight exploitation and injustice on every front and become part of a variety of struggles for eliminating economic, social, and ecological abuses wherever they occur, at home or abroad. Social anarchists are no less humane in response to human suffering and no less outraged by social afflictions than the best-intentioned reformists.

But their actions should not be limited merely to advancing remedial measures – which the bourgeoisie can usually adopt if it chooses to, with little loss to itself. Indeed, bourgeois society is sometimes more than willing to ameliorate social afflictions within its own framework, all the better to conceal broader social problems or to neutralize the danger of wider social unrest.

Anarchism, Marxism, and the Future of the Left

There is a major difference, in my view, between the way social
democrats, liberals, and other well-meaning people engage in everyday
struggles and the way social anarchists and other revolutionary leftists
do. Social anarchists do not divorce their ideals from their practice. They
bring to these struggles a dimension that is usually lacking among
reformists: they work to spread popular awareness of the roots of the
social affliction – patiently educating, mobilizing, and building a movement that shows the *connections* between the abuses that exist in modern
society and the broader social order from which they stem. They are profoundly concerned with showing people *the sources of their afflictions and
how to consciously act to remove them completely by seeking to fundamentally change society.* Disseminating this understanding, which in the past
went under the name of class consciousness (an expression that is still
very relevant today) or, more broadly, social consciousness, is one of the
major functions of a revolutionary organization or movement. Unless
social anarchists take the occasion of a protest to point to the broader
social issues involved, unless they place their opposition in this context
and use it to advance the transition to a rational social order like libertarian communism, their opposition is adventitious, piecemeal, and essentially reformist.

In the course of demonstrating how specific social abuses can be
traced to capitalism as such, social anarchist practice, in my view, must
increasingly make apparent that, if those abuses are to be fully remedied,
it is society as a whole that must be changed. Whether a given reform is
attained or not, the *issue* that generates the need for it must be expanded,
cast in ever broader social terms, and linked with less obvious but related
social abuses until a *unified view* emerges from apparently disconnected
parts and challenges the validity of the existing social order.

On the other hand, to ask that social abuses be addressed merely by
reforms and that they be resolved by the state is to deepen the mystification, to abet the legitimation, and to gloss the ideological patina so indispensable for the existence of the entire system. From 1848 to 1997, this
reformist practice, whatever ideals it claims for itself, has been the most
pronounced flaw of movements for change. Indeed, struggles conducted
within the framework of the existing system – while they may yield many
palliative reforms – ultimately perpetuate the mystification that capital-

ism "can deliver the goods" (as Marcuse put it) and that the state can rise above the conflict of contending interests to serve the public good.

II

In the United States, as in other Western countries today, there is no lack of social-democratic organizations and environmental groups that concern themselves with social and environmental problems – even if it means little more than lobbying powerful officials. Despite their tendency to compromise on key issues, these groups are visible and vocal. Inasmuch as they work within the framework of the state, they sometimes find places where the system bends to the needs of the poor and the vulnerable. The widely celebrated "realism" of these groups, their lesser-evil politics, and their attempts to work amelioratively within the system sometimes lead to palliatives that seem to improve the lives of those who need help.

But the state rarely bends to popular demands for changes that are inimicable to the *basic* interests of the bourgeoisie. Despite the opposition of many labor unions and environmentalists as well as large sectors of the population, for example, the North American Free Trade Agreement (NAFTA) was passed by the Congress and signed by Clinton. Capital – big Capital – wanted NAFTA, and that was that! Doubtless there are states and states. Historically, there have been slave-owning states, feudal states, monarchical states, republican states, and totalitarian states. It would be naive to suppose that they are all alike just because they are states. Yet even the most rhetorically "free" and constitutionally constrained republics in the so-called First World – which we euphemistically call "democracies" – are *class* institutions. They are structured by their traditions, constitutions, laws, bureaucratic and judicial institutions, police, and armies to assure that the property, profit-making, competition, capital accumulation, and the economic authority of the bourgeoisie and other privileged strata are protected. This relationship is *fundamental* to the modern state.

The question of the state has been an issue of profound importance for anticapitalist revolutionaries, including social anarchists, throughout the history of socialism. Marxists are at least consistent when they engage in parliamentarism, since Marx left us with no doubt that he thought the state was necessary, even after a proletarian revolution, in order to establish socialism, and in 1872 he even declared that it was possible to use the bourgeois parliamentary system to legislate socialism into existence in Britain, America, and possibly the Netherlands – to which Engels later added France.

When the people do not retain political power for themselves, that power is claimed by the state – conversely, whatever power the state does not have must be claimed by the masses. Modern political parties are either states in power or, when out of power, states waiting to take power. In order to function as statist organizations, the very exigencies of state power oblige them to replicate the state to one degree or another. They *must,* if they are to gain power, constitute themselves as top-down extensions of the state, just as capitalist enterprises must be organized to make profit at the public's expense, their claims to be performing a beneficent "public service" to the contrary notwithstanding. Indeed, the more parties and enterprises and even states cover themselves with a libertarian patina, the more insidiously they besmirch the very public trust they profess to hold most sacred.

The early claims of the German Greens to be a "nonparty party" reflected a tension that could not continue to exist indefinitely once the Greens were elected to the Bundestag. Whatever may have been the best intentions of their spokespersons, participation in the state of necessity reinforced every party-oriented tendency in their organization at the expense of their "nonparty" claims. Today, far from being a challenge to the social order in Germany, the Greens are one of its props. This is the product not of any ill will on the part of individual Greens but rather of the inexorable imperatives of working *within* the state rather than against it. Invariably, it is the state that shapes the activities and structures of those who propose to use it against itself, not the reverse.

Social anarchists, in contrast to Marxists, regard the state *as such* as a great institutional impediment to the achievement of libertarian socialism or communism. In bourgeois republics, the practical demand of social anarchists to desist from participating in national elections reflects their commitment to *delegitimate* the state, to divest it of its mystique as an indispensable agency for "public order" and the administration of social life. What is at issue in social anarchist abstention from these parliamentary rituals is their attempt to expose the authoritarian basis of the state, to dissolve its legitimacy as a "natural" source of order, and to challenge its claims to be a supraclass agency and to be the only *competent* institutional source of power – as distinguished from the *incompetence* of the masses in managing public affairs.

This responsibility of social anarchism to demystify capitalism, the nation-state, and their interconnection – indeed to challenge their legitimacy as a priori "natural" phenomena – is not simply a matter of theoretical elucidation. To be relevant to people generally, it must be embodied in a practice that is publicly visible, one that can mutate the need for reforms of the existing system (which may be allowed) into the need for a revolutionary transformation of society (which the system must resist).

III

My own version of social anarchism, as many readers already know, involves the creation of a direct face-to-face democracy in which people directly participate in the management of their community's affairs. In contrast to systems of "representative democracy" (the phrase is a contradiction in terms, I should emphasize), a libertarian democracy would be structured around popular assemblies, which would be formed at the municipal level and replace existing municipal governments. These popular assemblies would be open arenas for popular decision-making for all adults in a given community to attend (or not attend, according to their wishes). Here the people themselves would make decisions about how their communities' affairs should be run. The assemblies would be transparent and open to complete public scrutiny.

I have given this communalist system of civic self-management the name libertarian municipalism. As a political philosophy of direct democracy, libertarian municipalism stands in marked contrast to the state, parliamentarism, and the principle of representation. It reserves the word *politics* for the self-administration of a community by its citizens in face-to-face assemblies, which in cities with relatively large populations would coordinate the administrative work of the city councils, composed of mandated and recallable assembly deputies. At the risk of repeating ideas familiar to readers, let me emphasize that this kind of politics stands in direct *contrast* to and indeed in sharp *tension* with *statecraft*, the top-down system of professional representation that is ultimately based on the state's monopoly of violence.

Basic to libertarian municipalism is the view that the town and city – which historically antedate the emergence of the state – represent the most basic arena of human consociation beyond the social realm of family, friends, and co-workers. The town or city neighborhood – the municipality – is the authentic realm of politics, in the direct-democratic sense from which the word is etymologically derived: the Athenian *polis* of the fifth century B.C.E. (I must once again emphasize that I do not regard Athens as a "model" or "paradigm," still less as an "ideal" of a libertarian municipalist city, many of my critics' claims to the contrary notwithstanding. I am as acutely aware of the shortcomings and oppressive features of ancient Athenian society and politics as my critics, but I believe that those shortcomings should not prevent us from exploring the working *institutions* of a municipal direct democracy, which arose for a time in the self-managed Athenian *polis*.) The democratic *institutions* that Athens, in contrast to most cities in history, developed – especially the assembly, or *ekklesia* – and some of the its standards of citizenship, provide us with materials invaluable for forming a practical idea of a libertarian municipality.

There is a tendency within anarchism to reject democracy in any form as the imposition of the will of a majority on a minority. As distinguished from the socialistic tendency in anarchism that emphasizes social freedom, this essentially liberalistic tendency emphasizes instead personal autonomy. In my view, if any approach to decision making is authoritarian, it is not majority rule but the requirement, as many of these individualistic anarchists propose, of attaining consensus in a large formal setting. The right of a single individual to obstruct the wishes of the majority is a form of personal tyranny that would render any society dysfunctional.

Nor is libertarian municipalism a political philosophy based on a localism that presupposes that a municipality can exist autonomously, on its own. Quite to the contrary, in modern society all communities must rely on each other, and regions on other regions, to meet their needs. Social anarchism, I believe, offers a plausible alternative to the claims made by the state – namely *confederation,* whereby interdependencies can be fostered in a libertarian manner. Libertarian municipalities would send deputies, mandated and recallable, to a confederal council to execute the policies established by individual assemblies. The decisions these councils would make would be purely *administrative;* indeed, they would be expressly prohibited from making *policy* decisions, which would remain the exclusive province of the popular assemblies. Confederation is a system not of representation but of coordination. It is predicated, so far as policy-making is concerned, on decision-making by the overall majority of the citizens in the communities of the confederation.

As a form of anarchist communalism, libertarian municipalism calls for the municipalization of the economy: popular municipal assemblies themselves would take control of the productive forces within their precincts. The municipalization of the economy is to be distinguished from nationalization (which merely reinforces statism and leads quite easily to totalitarian systems of management) and from a syndicalist approach that would place the economy in the hands of worker-controlled collectives (which often foster collective capitalist enterprises). In a municipalized economy the citizenry in their respective assemblies would make economic decisions, guided not by occupational interests, which might easily bias such decisions in favor of particular enterprises, but by the interests of the community as a whole.

It seems to me that if we were to deny that humanity can create a direct-democratic society like the one outlined by libertarian municipalism, we would have to sacrifice our commitment not only to social anarchism but to any kind of humanistic and rational society. Syndicalism, to be sure, offers an alternative – a society organized around workers' control of economic production. If I felt that this alternative could be achieved in a consistently libertarian fashion, I might welcome it as a possible road to a social anarchist society. What troubles me is that syndicalism has been beleaguered by vocational particularism; nor is there reason to believe that syndicalist unions can avoid the hierarchical structures that are endemic to a society structured around factories.

As vital as the role of working people is in transforming society, the era has passed when the proletariat enjoyed the *hegemonic* role assigned to it by Marxists as well as syndicalists. Social anarchists, in my view, have to take a wider view of the social conditions and of the people who are likely to be involved in any libertarian transformation of society. In any case, working people are people as well as workers: They live in communities, experience problems of pollution, education, the logistics of city life, and the like. They are not creatures of the workplace – they are also civic or municipal beings, with all the concerns that such people have outside the workplace.

Indeed, as any close study of past revolutions reveals, every popular uprising has had not only an economic and social dimension but a profoundly important municipal dimension as well. It would be impossible, in fact, to understand how workers, peasants, and even radical sections of the middle-class could have been mobilized into revolutionary crowds without considering the neighborhoods and communities that brought them into contiguity and formed the basis for a political culture in their places of residence.

Critics of libertarian municipalism sometimes object that today's cities are far too large to accommodate self-government by popular assemblies. Even if one were to divide up a city like New York or Paris or Mexico City into neighborhoods and set up neighborhood assemblies, this criticism goes, the assemblies would still be too large for decision-making to be viable. But such proposals often presuppose that the entire population – infants, the infirm, the debilitated elderly, children, the insane – will participate in local assembly or will want to attend.[1] In 1793 Paris, a city with a population of more than 700,000 people, was divided into forty-eight sections, producing an assembly democracy in one of the most remarkable communalist revolutions in history. Nor was this sectional democracy forgotten in the revolutions in Paris of 1848 and 1871, by which time the city's population had swollen to about two million.

Moreover, this kind of criticism assumes that all parts of a large city will develop politically at the same pace; that everyone, even in the most favorable logistical circumstances, will want to attend every assembly meeting; and finally, that the modern city will always remain as it is unto eternity. The politics advanced by libertarian municipalism involves a *process* – a protracted one, to be sure – in which important changes will be made unevenly. Some neighborhoods and towns can be expected to advance more rapidly than others in political consciousness. Allowances must be made for institutional variations – possibly temporary, possibly permanent – that are not foreseeable today. At the present time we are at a point where only the initiation of an anarchist or communalist politics is possible; it will have to find its own momentum over a span of years, during which time urban life is likely to undergo considerable institutional and ultimately physical decentralization.

IV

Whatever mystique surrounds the role of the state in maintaining "public order" and adjusting social dislocations – including the growing abuses produced by modern capitalism – the commitment of state institutions is to the advancement of corporate (read: class) interests. The modern state remains the indispensable means by which corporations can expand and assert their power.

At a time when much is made of the "globalization" of capitalism, it is tempting for leftists to focus primarily on corporate power and, instead of opposing the state, to look to it as a means to restrain rapacious global corporations. To do so is to overlook a basic fact about the state: that it serves the interests of wealth and property. That corporations are authoritarian institutions does not justify strengthening the state to oppose them. Corporations have always been authoritarian. Some two centuries ago, during the Industrial Revolution, individual factory owners made decisions – often as arrogantly as a modern CEO – that profoundly affected the lives of hundreds of people. Having been on union negotiating committees myself and observed the predatory behavior of managers and capitalists, it surprises me that leftists today can be surprised by the authoritarian relations that exist in factories and corporations.

Inasmuch as capitalist enterprises constitute the most basic elements in the capitalist scheme, it is naive to assume that the statist institutions that exist to serve them can be deployed to significantly control them, still less challenge them. The drift of present-day leftists into statist politics with the intention of restricting the power of capital is vitiated by a basic contradiction: the very state machine that they suppose *can* control the bourgeois forces of production and expansion is precisely the machine that capital has in great part created to extend its control over social life.

We can no more countervail and confront the state by entering into it than we can countervail and confront the corporations by entering into them. A counterpower has to be established against both the state and capitalism. It must draw on a variety of forces, some of them quite traditional but readapted to present exigencies, to oppose the entire system of what can properly be called state capitalism.

This counterpower can be created only out the great masses of people who feel neglected and denied economically and politically, and alienated and oppressed by statist institutions. At this level of social sensibility, the classical lines of proletariat and petty bourgeoisie are waning in importance. The industrial worker who, like the professional, may at any time be phased out of his or her occupation by a new technological advance; the retailer whose existence is being threatened by huge corporate chains; the educator who is being supplanted by electronic means of instruction – such instances are almost unending in number – are literally faced with the loss of a place in the existing society.

From this increasingly socially undefined mass, united by residence and facing the problems of a deteriorating community infrastructure, pollution, insufficient child care, overwork, proliferating malls, and the destruction of city centers, the problems of capitalism are being pooled into a fund that is no longer definable exclusively along traditional class lines. At the same time, at least in the United States, inequalities of income and wealth are wider than they have ever been in history. Most ordinary people understand that there are those who "have" and those who "have not"; those who are obscenely wealthy, and those whose income, educational opportunities, access to health care, and social mobility are dwindling at a terrifying pace.

Without in any way ignoring the elementary insults that the present society inflicts on the poor and underprivileged, libertarian municipalism raises the issue of a popular reclamation of power by the community from the state and the corporations. Most leftists are so committed to exercising their infinitesimal influence through statist institutions that social anarchists are uniquely positioned to redefine a practical politics that is consistent with their highest ideals. They alone can demand the development of *community* power – real, institutionalized, and concrete power – in opposition to the state. They alone can try to create confederal organizations at the local and regional levels that have political tangibility and that constitute a sphere for a public debate on all the issues that concern community members.

The "Commune," or in more contemporary language, the municipality, has always been the building block of a social anarchist vision of a libertarian society. Not only has the municipality antedated the state historically; it has often been the antithesis of the state in struggles between towns and feudal lords, absolutist monarchies, and centralistic institutions created by elitist revolutionaries such as the Jacobins and their heirs, the Bolsheviks. The tension between the municipality and the state is a longstanding historical one, and although it is more recent, the tension between the confederation and the modern nation-state is no less compelling.

What I am suggesting is that a new libertarian politics has to be formulated and put into practice that calls for a restoration of political power to people in their municipalities, in opposition to the state. The practice of my version of social anarchism involves not only radical participation in protests, as I have described it, but the building of a movement that aims to create this kind of face-to-face democracy. Social anarchists, I submit, should raise the demand for the empowerment of citizens in towns and cities in the form of directly democratic assemblies, rewrite their city charters (where they have them) to legally empower these assemblies with the authority to make far-reaching decisions about their immediate concerns, and – yes! – even run candidates for local town and city councils with a view toward creating and coordinating citizens' assemblies with the structural authority to regulate the municipality's affairs.

I do not expect for a single moment that these activities will be recognized by existing civic institutions, many of which have functions that are distinctly statist or that rely on state support. Nor do I believe that social anarchists who initiate such assemblies will be more than a minority among the citizens who participate in them. But a sphere of *potential* political power, discussion, and education will have been created in which, over time and with much effort, a counterpower could develop in opposition to the state and, with enough support in the economic realm, the corporations. This dual power, once it gained the support of a large number of people, could ultimately constitute a force to confront the state and the capitalist system and replace them with a libertarian communist society.

The practice that I am suggesting is consistent with the social anarchist ideal of the "Commune of communes." Indeed, I find it difficult to conceive of any other public practice that potentially challenges the state machinery and capitalist system in a libertarian fashion. After many decades in labor unions and direct-action organizations such as the civil rights movement, the Clamshell Alliance (a mass antinuclear organization), and the New Left, and as a participant in the formation of the American Greens (*before* they decided to engage in national politics), I share the social anarchist conviction that parliamentary politics is inherently corruptive.

To confine antistatism to the realm of ideals without seeing its immediate relevance to practice risks making a mockery of both ideals and practice. Choosing a reformist parliamentarism and a statist form of "political" activity, including participation in parties, amounts to saying the capitalism and the state are here to stay, and that we are essentially compelled to submit ourselves to authoritarian institutions – allowing for a modicum of room to maneuver within limitations that are tolerable to the modern bourgeois social order.

A practice that is in accordance with social anarchist ideals is the only way of making our ideals relevant to people who are unfamiliar with them. Ideals easily turn into daydreams – or worse – when they stand in flat contradiction to the realities of one's practice. By separating ideals from practice, crusading movements with erstwhile high ideals, like Christianity and even various socialisms, have historically wrought enormous social harm. Without a practice that can embody our ideals, those ideals easily become mere creatures of the imagination and can be adopted or cast off at will – or, worse, be used to add spice to commonplace political behavior that has nothing in common with social anarchism.

March 25, 1997

Note

1. I am not suggesting that someone who wants to participate in an assembly should be excluded simply because he or she is infirm or elderly. But to welcome the participation of the pathologically insane or the visibly juvenile would be absurd. We need to exercise a modicum of common sense: Reasoned discussion is necessary to practice citizenship, and neither children nor the insane are capable of exercising it.

Building a Movement

Interviewer: Doug Morris

The Chinese say that if you are going to walk a thousand miles, you have to take the first step. Many people look at a libertarian communist society, or even basic improvements in society, as the thousand-mile walk. What would you suggest as the first step?

The Chinese were not alone in presenting a "first step" aphorism. But let me offer my suggestions. I strongly believe that the existing social order will finally generate revolutionary impulses, basically because of the damage it must inflict on people's lives. When this begins to happen, groups must be in place – explicitly *revolutionary* groups – that can educate, mobilize, and help the majority of people work for basic social change. More than enough reformist organizations are in existence today, trying to remedy the various insults that this society inflicts, the specific issues ranging from toxic wastes to antiracism that arise daily. What we emphatically need are organizations that are trying to develop a far-reaching consciousness of the interrelations among seemingly disparate problems and their common roots in the society as a whole, and to engage in a practice that can bring people to effectuate fundamental changes. I cannot stress strongly enough the need to form such revolutionary leftist organizations.

As I've already indicated, society today is in the midst of an ideological counterrevolution. I would not compare it to the McCarthy events in the early 1950s, when people were being physically persecuted for their leftist beliefs. Nor would I call it fascism, in which people were sent to concentration camps. The ideological counterrevolution that is occurring now is rather a counterrevolution based on amnesia, a loss of continuity with a revolutionary past, and a general dumbing down of the entire population. I find the retreat in the general level of knowledge and education today to be astounding – the so-called information age is an extraordinarily uninformed period. An immense number of young Americans, for example, can't even locate the state in which they live on a map, or point to major world capitals. They are remarkably ignorant even about general political theory and history, let alone revolutionary leftist ideas and the history and the meaning of socialism, anarchism, communism, and communalism.

Our first step in reviving the Left, I believe, will be to reclaim the knowledge that past generations possessed and master it for ourselves. That will require a major educational process that certainly cannot be found in ordinary schools and campuses. Revolutionaries who are committed to this vital task must first develop their own consciousness. I'm not speaking about engaging in politics yet – that's a separate question. Today a revolutionary Left can have only a very limited social impact; hence it must use this valuable time to recover and rebuild radical consciousness. We can do so by forming groups that intensively study not only present-day problems but also the ideas and movements – as well as the lessons they offer – that constitute the revolutionary tradition.

At the same time such study groups would want to go into philosophy and ethics, as well as history and social thinking. They would want to learn the lessons of the past, as well as those of the present. In my opinion the lessons of the past would lead them logically to social ecology as an overall outlook and to libertarian municipalism as a political theory and practice. They would want to understand the logic of these views, formulate them coherently, express them in contemporary terms, and – let me emphasize – put their conclusions in programmatic form that can reach large numbers of people.

Anarchism, Marxism, and the Future of the Left

Could you discuss your approach to forming study groups?

My approach is hardly original – I make no pretense of being inventive in this area. Study groups have been part of the revolutionary tradition since the eighteenth century. A study group emerges when a number of individuals decide that they have a shared interest in a particular body of ideas. Normally a study group consists of a small number of serious people who choose a particular book or series of books that they particularly respect. If they are Marxists, they might pick *Capital,* a work I would recommend for *any* revolutionary group, or if they are social anarchists, they might pick Kropotkin's *Factories, Fields, Workshops,* or his history of the French Revolution. They might explore a utopian socialist novel. Whatever it is, they would read it together, perhaps guided by someone who is more knowledgeable about radical ideas than most of them, and discuss it fully at their meetings. Or they could read a different work aloud at their meetings, and discuss it and analyze it carefully. The book would basically be a guide for learning new ideas and developing their thinking. After they finished one work, they would continue with others, hopefully choosing subsequent readings in as systematic a manner as possible.

A study group that continues in this way can constitute itself into a sort of intellectual community, in which the members draw up an agenda of the subjects they want to discuss each week. In the process of reading, studying, and discussing together – as a result of the give-and-take of discussion and the absorption of the knowledge that books have to offer – they can gradually develop into a collection of study groups based on shared interests, even knit together by a coordinating group. A study group we had in Burlington several years ago multiplied into several subgroups, in which some studied revolutionary history, others dialectical philosophy, and still others radical political theory, but their members also met in joint meetings.

Such groups do not have to be fixated on study alone. Once study has given the members a common basis in shared political ideas, the group may take on a political life. In fact, it would be my hope that such groups would become political. I believe that a study group should not be a mere academic exercise but the nucleus for building a movement.

One of the first steps in becoming political would be for the study group to publish a newsletter or another small periodical, a mechanism by which members would develop their *writing* abilities and formulate their ideas as clearly as possible. Such a periodical would not be intended for wide circulation – in fact, we should disabuse ourselves of the mystique of having to publish a periodical that will reach thousands of people. Today, if we attempt to reach too many people, we will probably fail, and the intellectual level of our periodical will tend to decline. The periodical should be a medium for generalizing about social issues rather than a mere information bulletin or a one-issue publication.

Above all, the group would want to make its political ideas as coherent as possible. Coherence is very important, in my view, because if we are to build a large political movement – one that will be an organized one – the ideas on which it is based should clarify the interconnections between, and sources of, various public issues. That doesn't mean the study group should become dogmatic in an unthinking, rigid sense – ideas should always be subject to modification when changes are necessary. But the ideas should be focused on the goal of creating a rational, ecological, libertarian society.

Unless the group is focused, it will stray in many different, often contradictory directions, with disastrous results. The story of the 1960s – its rise, its promise, and its decay – shows how important it is to have a coherent outlook. The nervous, often mindless twists and turns that the New Left suffered from after 1968 are dramatic evidence that the movement simply used itself up in a strange combination of uncertainty and fanaticism, and of urgency and futility.

If the group absorbs enough of the revolutionary tradition and formulates its own ideas coherently, many of its members may well become committed revolutionaries. Many ideological changes, to be sure, are likely to occur in the group members unconsciously. Indeed, one of the most important roles that a revolutionary organization can play is to bring to the surface revolutionary desires and impulses that were previously unconscious, hopefully turning people who feel an inchoate alienation into revolutionaries who *consciously* reject the present social order.

Let me emphasize that during periods of deep reaction such as we have today, well-organized study groups of committed people have been the mainstay for preserving serious opposition to the social order. Study groups actually date back to the eighteenth-century French Enlightenment, a time when the French monarchy sat like a dead weight on French society. In the decades before the French Revolution of 1789, the Encyclopedists, or *philosophes* as they were called, would meet in what could be called study groups on Sunday afternoons. Men such as Diderot, D'Alembert, Holbach, and others would meet regularly, dine together, fervently discuss ideas, and read their manuscripts aloud or pass them around – writings that are now classics in the history of philosophy and politics. They even wrote novels and read them to each other. Such brilliant study groups, or "circles," were rare, to be sure, but they existed at all levels of French society.

These groups provided the indispensable intellectual ferment that fed into the French Revolution. Many of their writings appeared as pamphlets or were reworked into simple form so that ordinary people could read them. In the early days of the Revolution, the king's guards read radical pamphlets at the very gates of the palace. Arthur Young, an Englishman who traveled through France at that time, reported that in Paris, even the coachmen were so preoccupied with reading that the reins that directed the horses became slack, and the coachmen had to be reminded to guide the horses.

The social ecology study groups I would suggest for our own day would hopefully meet together and link up with each other and exchange publications. It is not extravagant to think that they could form a network on a local, regional, and if possible national scale, perhaps even internationally, and repeatedly hold joint conferences, share ideas, and work out common problems. It is out of such endeavors, historically, that movements were formed, and they can be formed the same way today.

When one presents the idea of forming a study group to many people, they often respond very pessimistically that you just can't get people together in groups anymore. People work jobs during the day, and they have responsibilities at night. They're worried about feeding their families, living from one day to the next. They say they don't have time to participate in organizations to change society. What would you tell them?

I shall be quite frank. Clearly there are times – especially in periods of deep reaction – when the difficulties facing the kind of groups and networks I'm describing are very profound. But I am becoming more impatient with people who claim that they are "too busy" to cultivate or develop themselves morally and intellectually. Many people have become terribly trivialized and are concerned with their own personal interests at the expense of public affairs. It is for this reason that I have written so fervently against the lifestyle anarchists and spiritualistic Marxists who are depoliticizing the Left today.

People who contend that they lack the time to form a study group often spend hours looking at inane television programs, attend sports events, and form long lines waiting to play golf. It's not that they can't get together in groups – they can and do form other kinds of groups, with other intentions. I question, basically, the sincerity of this objection.

In stadiums people get together by the tens of thousands.

Indeed. My point is that such people probably aren't interested in forming a study group, and for my part, I would not try to induce them to do so. There are always a small number of people, especially in times like the present, who *do* want to study, indeed who are starving to learn. These are the people I'm really interested in – people who have active minds and want to study social issues. Every week Janet, my companion and collaborator, and I receive letters from people who say, "We've got to stay in touch with you, we wish we were living in Burlington so we could work with you."

Unfortunately, many people do have to work long hours or engage in arduous toil. They only have time to eat and sleep and can barely enjoy the simple amenities of life. All I can suggest to them is that they examine their lives and ask themselves what values they cherish. What are they living for? Life must have some meaning beyond mere survival. In my view they should make every effort to rise above the level of mere survival.

How do study groups go on to form a revolutionary left?

I believe that once they develop their ideas, our study group members should begin to immerse themselves in the communities in which they live. They should begin to engage in the communalist or libertarian municipalist politics that I've suggested and described elsewhere. They should try to reach people on the local level. I'm not suggesting that they become mere localists, either ideologically or practically. What I mean is that they should try to create a libertarian municipalist movement on a grassroots basis.

They should try, as I've suggested, to form a *movement* to educate people about the creation of a direct face-to-face democracy, especially in collaboration with people who are interested in social change but have yet to clarify their ideas as to what direction they are going to take. They should try to create a radical political *culture* by holding lecture series and public forums by writing and publishing community newsletters, and by organizing events and demonstrations around various community issues.

Most importantly, they should try to help people take control of their own localities, the places where they work, and the neighborhoods, towns, or villages in which they live. They should help people create neighborhood assemblies, town assemblies, ward assemblies, or village assemblies, where ordinary people can get together and discuss their common problems. They should even establish ward assemblies where people get together once every month, or once every two months. Attendance may be small at first, but in times of social unrest people will participate in them in ever greater numbers.

I should warn you that forming citizens' assemblies is not, in itself, necessarily revolutionary. If I went to a ward assembly meeting this week in Burlington – we have them here – I might well encounter developers, real estate agents, stockbrokers, and bankers. These people have been known to come to popular assemblies in order to promote their own agenda. Thus the creation of an assembly is at best an *initial* step toward forming a radical political arena. By debating issues with the reactionaries in the community, the study group members can show community members that an alternative viewpoint exists and clarify the differences between them.

It is incumbent upon our study group or political group to raise political consciousness. This might develop in at least three stages. The group should first present a minimum program, a program structured around practical, immediate demands that would improve the quality of life in a community. Such a program might well consist of desirable, even elementary reforms. Our group could publicize such a program by running candidates for local office in municipal elections. One of the most important demands in their program could be the very demand for popular assemblies or citizens' assemblies, in order to *empower* the people in the community.

The second stage would, I suspect, emerge as we engaged in public education, hopefully gaining more and more popular support for our ideas. We would then advance a transitional program, in which we would expand our demands so that they are more far-reaching than elementary reforms. Then, if the community becomes even more radicalized, we would expand our transitional program until we are in a position to advance our maximum demands: namely, demands for the full restructuring of political power and advancing our first steps toward municipal control over the economy.

Simultaneous with this local activity, we would engage in interlocal work. That is to say, where our communities, even neighborhoods, have been able to form citizens' assemblies, we would try to establish a common confederal council in the hope, over time, of even establishing regional and ultimately national confederations. The citizens' assemblies of various communities, working through their city councils, would send deputies to confederal councils, and form regional confederations that would function as coordinating and administrative bodies.

Finally, if these interlinked groups and confederations become a major force in society, they would contest the State for power over society. The public power that they have accrued to themselves would necessarily have to be acquired at the expense of the power of the nation-state. Hopefully the nation-state's power would be sufficiently diminished that people would withdraw their support from it, and it would collapse like a house of cards. But if not, the confederations would have to defy the nation-state – that is, claim their sovereignty in a revolutionary manner.

How do you propose to form viable popular assemblies in large cities, when possibly thousands of assemblies would be needed for everyone to attend?

You know, in Paris in 1793, if someone had given this purely arithmetic argument against the call for power to the city's forty-eight popular assemblies or sections – because a few thousand sections would be needed to include the *whole* population of 700,000 – they would justly have been called reactionary by the revolutionary *enragés*.

First of all, in a libertarian communist society, the city would be physically as well as institutionally decentralized, making possible the full participation of every able citizen in assemblies. Based on all past experience, including the Athenian assembly in Periclean times, however, it is unlikely that the full body of citizens would attend and participate in every assembly meeting. During even the stormiest periods of the French Revolution of 1793, when political interest among ordinary Parisians was at its peak, the sectional assemblies never saw the full attendance of all neighborhood residents at their meetings. Not even the admission of women to the radical sections made an appreciable difference; although politically concerned women were free to attend and participate in those sections and did so, the total number of participants was still not always very large.

Libertarian municipalism, while certainly not counting on the absence of a portion of the citizenry from the assembly, can realistically assume that attendance at assemblies, today and in the foreseeable future, will be no different numerically than was the case during the height of the Athenian democracy and the French Revolution. Once again the establishment of popular assemblies would likely involve primarily the most politically concerned individuals, possibly only a fraction of the population as a whole.

Many individuals may not want to attend the assemblies, a right which they should be free to have. A libertarian municipality, however, would open its assemblies' doors to the participation of all competent adult citizens. Those who decide to enter the assembly doors, sit down, listen to discussions, and participate in them are, ethically as well as politically, qualified to participate in the decision-making process.

By the same token, those who do not wish to participate in an assembly should not be forced to do so. Those who choose not to enter the doors (allowing for difficulties produced by adverse circumstances) certainly have a right to abjure the exercise of their citizenship, but by their own volition they have also disqualified themselves from decision-making. Nor do they have the ethical right to refuse to abide by the assembly's decisions, since they could have influenced those decisions by simply attending the assembly.

Citizens should make policy decisions not casually but after a thorough and rational discussion. Decisions that are not the product of rational discussion are often worthless and even undesirable. For similar reasons, "electronic" democracy is not desirable. Someone who votes by pushing a green or red button on a computer or other electronic device is not functioning as a citizen but is participating in a mere plebiscite, in which little if any of the reasoning and discursive process of developing a policy are involved. This kind of "lazy" democracy, which has been the subject of considerable discussion, is a farce and should be rejected.

How do we convince people that we need to make fundamental changes in society, to radicalize society?

It's very seldom that a revolutionary organization can "convince" people that they should make fundamental changes in society. The need to make such changes, not to speak of the conviction that they should make them, is overwhelmingly the work of historical forces, such as serious economic crises, social instability, ecological breakdown, and the like. But it is one of the tasks of a revolutionary organization to offer them hope, the sense that the world could be better if they acted as social beings. People must sense that they need not be forever beleaguered by the demands of modern capitalism, that insufferable conditions need not exist, that a better world is possible if they act. No radical movement can replace the workings of history, so to speak, but it can provide an avenue for people to have better lives if they change society.

The failure of many ecologists and lifestylers to offer realistic alternatives to the status quo – their turn toward mysticism, technophobia, misanthropy, Malthusian notions, and even primitivism – is very lamentable because they deprive people of hope and deny them that motivating force to change the world. No ordinary person wants to hear that they are responsible for the problems of the world because they have too many children, or consume too much, or own a car or a computer. Such reproaches understandably alienate people who might otherwise be eager for major social changes.

A serious revolutionary movement can provide hope to discontented people who feel oppressed by bourgeois society but do not clearly know why by making the problems created by capitalism explicable to them and providing them with a clear direction that they can understand and pursue. The movement places itself at their disposal as an instrument for achieving a new society, bringing its wealth of experience, insights, and coherence to their service. The two – the social forces that stir people up and the movement that makes their problems comprehensible – must come together before change can occur. Until people are stirred into action, the movement, small as it may be, must prepare itself for a time when such a juncture is possible. It should become very knowledgeable and responsible, and it should work slowly but persistently to win over new people who will be able to function as revolutionaries in a time of social unrest.

Murray Bookchin

Do you think it's reasonable for the U.S. Greens to be running a presidential candidate, Ralph Nader, rather than concentrating their efforts on local politics?

Allow me to give you my own background in the Greens, since people are now busily rewriting their history. I was involved with the German Greens when they began to organize as far back as the late 1970s and early 1980s. I knew most of the Green leaders in Germany, including Joschka Fischer and Dany Cohn-Bendit, at a time when they were still anarchists. I also knew outstanding founders of the Greens, such as Jutta Ditfurth and Manfred Zieran, who wrote the program of the German Greens – the first Green program to appear in either Germany or the United States.

In the United States, I was working with the Institute for Social Ecology, which I co-founded in 1974 – and some people from the Institute were at the founding meeting of the U.S. Greens movement, in Minneapolis. I was the keynote speaker at the first Greens gathering in Amherst, Massachusetts, in 1987, which was where I presented my critique of deep ecology.

Both in Germany and in the United States, before the Greens became large organizations, one of the main points I emphasized was the importance of using a libertarian municipalist approach to politics. I vigorously opposed the German Greens for going into the Bundestag, the German parliament, publicly arguing against their entry. I warned that if the Greens entered the Bundestag, they would become corrupted. I argued that they were not creating a solid basis in local communities, that they were not creating viable organic entities among people in Germany, and that they were leaping into the Bundestag very quickly, without any basis in local communities. I argued that they should avoid the Bundestag altogether.

Today German Greens sit in the Bundestag. Joschka Fischer, the former anarchist, was minister of the environment in Hesse (in coalition governments with the Social Democrats) and is now the leading figure in the party. "We need to build a modern consensus between government and business," he recently said, advocating a policy of "offer[ing] workers stock options instead of ever higher salaries." This head of a formerly pacifist party now supports a strong American military presence in Europe and NATO: "Only the Americans can provide the 'big stick' to enforce peace in Europe."[1] Dany Cohn-Bendit, for his part, is now a deputy in the European parliament. Where the Greens had originally refused to make alliances with any other party in Germany, they were later prepared to form a governing coalitions not only with the alleged socialist party of Germany, the Social Democrats, but with the Christian Democratic Union, the CDU, of Helmut Kohl, which is the large conservative party in Germany.

A similar development occurred, at least in principle, in the United States, but on a much smaller scale. The U.S. Greens originally committed themselves to functioning on a local level, although not by using a libertarian municipalist approach. But the Greens later decided that they were going to run for *any* office, local, state, or national, that was open. The result has been that that movement has degenerated into a basically liberal organization that, while "progressive," is trying to find a place for itself within the present system.

The U.S. Greens have essentially surrendered their original commitment to operate on a strictly local basis, and many Green groups are now prepared even to work with the Democratic Party. For the most part they are reformists and no longer have any stirring vision of creating a Green society. The result is that "Green" has become a fashionable word that is no longer idealistic. In fact, even corporations use the word "green" today to merchandise their presumably environmentally sound goods and practices.

In 1996 the U.S. Greens decided to run Ralph Nader as a presidential candidate. Nader, by his own admission, is not a Green – he said so publicly. Nor did he belong to the party, or even accept its program. He simply allowed the U.S. Greens use his name as their candidate for president. His campaign was absurdly passive, and its mixed messages mainly succeeded in confusing people. I regard the Greens as naive at best and opportunistic at worst. There are many sincere people in the Greens' ranks, I'm sure, but they are still politically very naive.

Murray Bookchin

Many people find it difficult to remain revolutionary for long periods of time. But you are continuing into your seventy-eighth year. What does it take to remain a revolutionary for the long term?

In the past, under conditions infinitely worse than the present ones, revolutionaries have retained their commitment to their social ideas to the end of their lives. Historically it is nothing unusual, but what has changed are the times. The post-World War II generation, I find, tends to demand immediate gratification, and to demand it so intensely that they very often become ideologically unstable.

These days I have to admit to feeling something like a ghost from an age gone by. What compels me to fight this society is, of course, outrage over injustice, a love of freedom, and a feeling of responsibility for perpetuating and enlarging the human spirit – its beauty, creativity, and latent capacity to improve the world. I do not care to come to terms with an irrational society that corrodes all that is valuable in humanity, that eats away at all that is beautiful and noble in the human experience.

Capitalism devours us. At the molecular level of everyday life, it changes us for the worse, and it compels people to make extremely unsavory rationalizations for why they believe things that they know – or at least they once knew – are false and for doing things that are trivializing and dehumanizing.

When we struggle against capitalism, we are really struggling against our own dehumanization, and once we become fully cognizant of that, then the danger of surrender to the system reinforces our resistance. As revolutionaries, we are fighting not only for a better society but for our very humanity. I can't emphasize strongly enough how important it is to preserve a coherent outlook, to bring our ideas together, to understand the connections between the phenomena around us. Having this theoretical understanding reinforces our resistance, first because it gives meaning to our opposition to the prevailing society, and second because it gives us the hope that we will be able to change that society. Preserving that hope – even if we do not live to see our ideals realized – can keep us striving to achieve a good society.

Coherence, resistance, and hope give us a sense of what the future *could* be. By means of speculative thought, we can work out from real potentialities in human beings, the rational unfolding of their actualization. To think dialectically is to think in terms of self-development and self-actualization, and of social development and social actualization.

We can formulate an ethics in which people complement rather than dominate each other. If we as individuals believe in freedom, in self-consciousness, and in cooperation, then other people can too – indeed, the very recognition of the possibility is evidence that complementarity lies within the realm of human potentiality. Everyone can have this understanding, provided that he or she is educated and informed and looks candidly at reality instead of through a television screen.

Now, what are the conditions that could make the potentialities for freedom unfold? Reasoning out that problem can provide the moral basis for a critique of society. After all, unless we have a standard of what constitutes a rational world, we cannot explain why this world is irrational. To contend that this world lacks justice or freedom, we require a standard by which to define justice and freedom. What is rational is "what ought to be," and we can arrive at that "ought" through a process of dialectical reasoning.

Dialectical reasoning informs all my thinking, that is, reasoning from human potentialities and recognizing that thought can look beyond the existing reality and see the possibilities for a society that meets the challenges raised by rational insight. If our capacity to rationally project ourselves succumbs to "what is," then we become "realists" in the worst possible sense. We allow our thinking to bog us down in the pragmatics of what exists today.

A movement that agrees to work within the system confines itself to choosing between only the alternatives that are presented *by* the system. It forces the movement to choose the lesser evil rather than the greater good. Admittedly there are situations when such choices do have to be made. But when a movement is willing to enter and remain inside the system, these choices become habitual. Over the course of time lesser-evil politics invariably leads step by step to the worst possible evil.

German history provides a striking historical example. In 1919 the reformist or Majority Social Democrats essentially took over the government by crushing the extreme left, an effort that involved the murder of Rosa Luxemburg and Karl Liebknecht, who were the founders of the

German Communist Party. Then the Social Democrats, wanting to keep the conservative party out of power, began to support the liberal and center parties. But eventually the Social Democrats, to keep Hitler out of power, had to support the conservative party. Thus they threw their support to the conservatives – who then appointed Hitler as chancellor, and the SPD was completely crushed. This account of lesser-evil politics still appalls me, even after sixty-five years.

Avoiding lesser-evil politics is another reason it is important for us to remain revolutionaries and form a revolutionary movement. This series of German events is part of the revolutionary education that study group members must acquire. Without knowing the lessons of German social democracy and many other parties, young revolutionaries will simply repeat the errors that were made in the past. Unless we learn such lessons thoroughly, we will sink back into a mysticism and personalism, in which exclamations about desire, imagination, and art delude us and dissolve the message we offer to a bewildered world. Above all, we should make a revolutionary decision to acquire knowledge, gain theoretical understanding, and commit ourselves to principle.

At my age, I'm not at all concerned about whether I will see the revolution I have fought for all my life. Not even the youngest revolutionaries among us may live to see a revolution in their own time. But we should still fight for it, even if only to retain our integrity as human beings. People today have to give up the fast-food radicalism of the 1960s, the kind that wants a revolution and a good society tomorrow. "If I can't get it tomorrow," they seem to say, "I'll do what Jerry Rubin did and become a stockbroker." People who want instant revolutions lack the human substance – the patience, the constancy, the ability to do hard and mundane work – that is essential to the formation of a real Left.

There's something narcissistic – and narcissism is one of the plagues of our era – about demanding "our" revolution now or not at all, about feeling no commitment to future generations who will replace our own, of having no belief in social progress, of reducing social change to sybaritic lifestyles and the fulfillment of personal desires. If that had been the state of mind of past generations of revolutionaries, there would never have been a revolutionary movement at any time. My grandmother's generation of socialist revolutionaries in Russia never thought that they would see a Russian revolution in their lifetimes, yet many of them went to Siberia in the course of fighting for it – and many of them died there long before 1917.

We may not get our revolution tomorrow, and maybe not even during our lifetimes. Yet by working for it, we will be doing only what great revolutionaries whose names are unknown to us have done for at least two hundred years: fighting for a rational society and human freedom.

To all of these ideas, let me add the great maxim that Marx put so well in his eleventh thesis on Feuerbach: "The philosophers have only *interpreted* the world, in various ways; the point, however, is to *change* it." We have to *act* to change the world. Rich opportunities still lie before us, as well as grave dangers, and whether human beings will finally live in a cooperative society depends in great measure on what we do today. Either we will have a truly collectivist society based on citizens' assemblies, the municipalization of property, and municipal confederations – a society where people really manage society; or we will have some form of totalitarianism and ecological collapse. This choice faces us now as we move into the twenty-first century, and if we fail to live up to the challenge it poses, our planet will truly be divested of the rationality and consciousness that gives it meaning.

Note

1. William Drozdiak, "Germany's Greens Grow Up," *Washington Post*, August 2, 1997.

A Note on Sources

The interviews by Doug Morris were conducted in Burlington, Vermont, over the course of several years: on October 10, 1993; October 24, 1993; December 2, 1993; July 5, 1994; August 31, 1994; and December 11, 1996. Morris videotaped the interviews and has made them available to the public through Turning the Tide, P.O. Box 850, Wilton, NH 03086. The Morris interviews have been extensively edited and revised for publication here.

The two interviews by Janet Biehl were conducted on December 17, 1997 ("A Marxist Revolutionary Youth") and January 3-4, 1998 ("Reflections on Marx and Marxism").

"Communalism: The Democratic Dimension of Anarchism" was originally published in *Green Perspectives,* no. 31 (October 1994).

"The Unity of Ideals and Practice" was originally published in German translation in *Schwarzer Faden,* no. 61 (1997). It has been revised slightly for publication here.

Major Works by Murray Bookchin

On social ecology:

Post-Scarcity Anarchism (originally published 1971; reprinted by
Montreal: Black Rose Books, 1977).

The Ecology of Freedom: The Emergence and Dissolution of Hierarchy
(originally published 1982; reprinted with new introduction by
Montreal: Black Rose Books, 1991).

The Modern Crisis (Philadelphia: New Society; and Montreal:
Black Rose Books, 1986).

Remaking Society: Pathways to a Green Future (Boston: South End
Press; and Montreal: Black Rose Books, 1991).

The Murray Bookchin Reader, edited by Janet Biehl (London:
Cassell, 1997).

On dialectical philosophy:

The Philosophy of Social Ecology: Essays in Dialectical Naturalism,
second revised edition (Montreal: Black Rose Books, 1995).

On libertarian municipalism:

From Urbanization to Cities (originally published 1987; reprinted by Montreal: Black Rose Books, 1992 [Canada only], and London: Cassell, 1995).

Also recommended: Janet Biehl, *The Politics of Social Ecology: Libertarian Municipalism* (Montreal: Black Rose Books, 1997).

On revolutionary history:

The Third Revolution: Popular Movements in the Revolutionary Era, 3 vols. (London: Cassell, 1996-99).

The Spanish Anarchists: The Heroic Years, 1868-1936 (originally published 1977; reprinted by San Francisco and Edinburgh: A.K. Press, 1998).

Cultural criticism:

Re-Enchanting Humanity: A Defense of the Human Spirit Against Anti-Humanism, Misanthropy, Mysticism and Primitivism (London: Cassell, 1995).

On lifestyle anarchism:

Social Anarchism or Lifestyle Anarchism: An Unbridgeable Chasm (San Francisco and Edinburgh: A.K. Press, 1995).